Rescuing Capitalism from Corporatism

Greed and the American Corporate Culture

by
John David Rose

If stockholders own a corporation and CEOs are employed to manage it, why do the hired hands come out so far ahead and the owners so far behind?

authorHOUSE™

1663 LIBERTY DRIVE, SUITE 200
BLOOMINGTON, INDIANA 47403
(800) 839-8640
WWW.AUTHORHOUSE.COM

First published by AuthorHouse 01/11/05

ISBN: 1-4184-9554-9 (sc)

Library of Congress Control Number: 2004097025

Printed in the United States of America
Bloomington, Indiana

This book is printed on acid-free paper.

Table of Contents

ACKNOWLEDGEMENTS

Almost fifteen years ago in the New York Public Library I happened upon *Economic Power* and the *Free Society* by A. A. Berle, Jr., a booklet I had last seen as a Junior High student some fifty years earlier in the public library of Idaho Falls, Idaho.

Written in the 1930s, Berle's main assertion was that our nation's founders believed corporations were dangerous creatures that needed to be carefully controlled. His argument seemed especially appropriate to current circumstances. Curious, I began a search for the proof of Berle's un-annotated allegations. The result was a bundle of ideas and a stack of documents and clippings begging to be organized.

When news of Enron et al began to fill the media, I felt impelled to share what I'd learned. This book is the result.

The serendipity of this work's initiation was matched over and over during its research and writing. Material seemingly appeared by magic when needed. The ability to reach a world of sources through the Internet has proven invaluable. Thus the foundation of this work is the research, work and thought of hundreds of others far more learned and informed than I. My task was to provide a framework for the multitude of voices speaking to the subject of corporate power and shape what I hope is a coherent and impelling argument for change.

I owe the incentive to see this work through to my friend Porter Thompson. His encouragement and thoughtful editing contributed greatly to its readability. My economist brother, Donald Rose,PhD., through dimming eyesight, directed me to valuable resources, and clarified basic economic concepts. Retired corporate attorney Pat Amer kept my polemic rants in check and steered me away from obvious gaffs. My musician step-daughter, Ann Gerschefski, did the painstaking work of correcting my grammatical and punctuation errors. Finally, my wife provided encouragement by not complaining too much over stacks of newspaper clippings and computer downloads covering the floor of our spare bedroom, and graciously granting time on the word-processing computer.

The work is dedicated to my oldest brother "Rod", Rogers K. Rose, now deceased. He reluctantly took over the presidency of a small Idaho corporation upon the death of our father, its president. With minimal formal education and business experience, but blessed with a wagon load of horse sense and rock solid ethics, he weathered 40 years of storms of competition, government regulations, labor unions, a changing marketplace and stockholder squabbles to keep it going and growing.

In wrestling with the weighty topics of corporatism and capitalism, I would often engage in an imaginary debate with Rod. "We" would explore each issue until I felt that the explanation would satisfy him and his Idaho Falls Rotary Club peers as fair, reasonable and workable, even when at first blush, a little bit hard to swallow.

I hope I have not disappointed him.

JDR, 10/16/03

INTRODUCTION

Between the start of the millennium in 2000 and the end of 2002, investors, retirees, big and small business people, and working folks as well as the very rich, lost some $7 trillion in the value of their holdings in American corporations.

The bulk of the losses wasn't caused by "market" conditions, nor by the 9/11/2001 terrorism attack, nor by a depressed world economy. Theft, pure and simple, caused the loss. Fraud, deceptive accounting, and seductive and deceitful lending schemes backed by the nation's most respected financial institutions. Stockholders watched their portfolios shrink by 30% and more. Employees saw their 401k retirement funds evaporate even as hundreds of thousands found themselves out on the street without jobs.

At the same time, while boards of directors nodded in benediction like bobble-head dolls, CEOs complicit in the frauds, the instigators of the deceptions, stuffed their personal bank accounts with hundreds of millions of dollars in compensation for their "brilliant" managerial performances.

Money losses, however, are only the most visible and countable parts of the corporate crime iceberg. Below the surface of TV sound bites and business page news briefs are stories far more disturbing and malodorous.

> Secret meetings of chemical industry executives who have been told by their medical and safety staff that chemicals used in their plants are stripping the flesh from workers' bones. Company doctors are sworn to secrecy. No warnings are given. Protective measures are not taken.
> Auto insurance customers face bankruptcy because a "good neighbor" insurance company uses fraudulent "peer reviews" to deny payment of their medical bills.
> Cities, counties, and states looking for economic and job growth are whipsawed by corporations bargaining for tax breaks, free utilities, and subsidies. Then, after collecting on the deals, the corporations often move their plants elsewhere.

These are but a few of the sad but true stories rising out of one flawed decision by the Supreme Court of the mid-1800s and the fraudulent recording of another *(Santa Clara County vs. The Union Pacific Railroad)*. Influenced by corporate wealth and power, these two events triggered the descent of the United States from Democracy to Corpocracy.

A wonderful German mechanic I once turned to in desperation (after making a ham-fisted amateur mechanic's mess of an expensive Porche engine) smiled reassuringly: "Anything man makes, man can repair."

The application is obvious. God did not create the corporation, man did. We made it, we broke it and once we put aside the mythology and misconceptions surrounding this creation, we can fix it.

This is the story of how we started out as the land of capitalist free enterprise, where everyone might own a piece of America, and reached a point where corporations own us and America.

What follows is the author's attempt to remove the blinders of corporate mythology that keep us enslaved to these creatures of our own making. To enlist the help of entrepreneurs, investors and students of business in rescuing capitalism from those who are abusing it. To loose the powerful engine of free enterprise from the grasp of corporate monsters now holding it captive.

One more thing before we begin: exactly what is "capitalism," and why is it worth rescuing? From Grolier's Encyclopedia:

> Capitalism is an economic system in which the means of production are privately owned. Business organizations produce goods for a market guided by the forces of supply and demand.… Underlying capitalism is the presumption that private enterprise is the most efficient way to organize economic activity.…
>
> The marketplace is the center of the capitalist system. It determines what will be produced, who will produce it, and how the rewards of the economic process will be distributed. [a]

If we believe that capitalism is the fairest way to distribute a finite amount of wealth and goods across an infinite demand, then it's worth saving.

JDR
October 13, 2003

---

[a] ©1998 Grolier Interactive Inc. All Rights Reserved.

CHAPTER ONE
CORPORATE AMERICA
<u>IS</u> AMERICA

It was the start of the work-week, Monday, October 5, 1992, during a record-breaking heat wave in Northern California. Oklahoma-born Texas oilman T. Boone Pickens had been turning up the heat on his audience.

"Chief executives, who themselves own few shares of their companies, have no more feeling for the average stockholder than they do for baboons in Africa," Pickens scolded. "Far too many executives have become more concerned with the 'four P's' — pay, perks, power and prestige — rather than making profits for shareholders." [1]

T. Boone Pickens styled himself the champion of the common shareholder. Even as he pillaged giants of the oil industry in generally unsuccessful but highly profitable takeover attacks — using blocks of stock and the threat of a hostile takeover bid to blackmail companies to buy him out at elevated prices — he delivered scathing denunciations of "good ol' boys in the boardroom." [2]

Finally he leaned over the Commonwealth Club of California podium and assured Northern California's rich and powerful that, despite what he had just said, he was really one of them and on their side.

For some members of the Commonwealth Club's prestigious Business Council, Pickens' arrows had hit too close to home. Thus they were relieved to hear Pickens end his reprimand with a ringing reaffirmation that "Corporate America <u>is</u> America." [3]

There was, if not a sigh, a collective settling back. The room full of business executives needed reassurance after hearing their kind roughly castigated by the multi-millionaire corporate raider.

Pickens' concluding declaration was an unintended irony. For even as he railed against unresponsive corporate officers and boards, Pickens declared his allegiance to a business structure specifically employed to take control away from a corporations' shareholders and board and place it in the CEOs' hands.

Most business people, most Americans for that matter, would agree with Pickens about the place corporations hold in the nation's life. Our obsessive love of bigness in general and Big Business has become *Corporatism*, an unquestioning allegiance to the goodness and rightness of corporate power over our national and global life.

Norman Lear, television producer ("All in the Family," "Sanford and Son," "Maude," "One Day at a Time," etc.) and founder of People for the American Way, made a similar point in a speech to the National Press Club.

> Walter Lippman once spoke of the institutions of the church, the family, education and civil authority as that old ancestral order which was largely responsible for purveying values to the society. As those institutions and their impact have waned, it is my belief that inadvertently, American business has come to fill the vacuum. It, business, is now the fountainhead of values in our society. [4]

Our 30th president, Calvin Coolidge, is best remembered for telling Congress that "the business of America is business." In 1953, "Engine Charlie" Wilson, then President of General Motors, told Congress, "What's good for General Motors is good for the country."

Recently, however, a growing number of Americans, including corporate leaders, have come to question the power wielded by America's corporate giants over society and government.

Charles R. Fulweiler, Ph.D., president of a popular computer software company, described the relationship of corporations to the American public: "It is a never-ending source of amazement to me that we are cheated, lied to, murdered and, in general, treated like mindless supplicants...." [5]

Even the prestigious pro-business *Fortune* magazine, in an article delving into a series of corporate scandals in late 2002, titled their report "Enough Is Enough. White-Collar Criminals: They lie they cheat they steal and they've been getting away with it for too long." [6]

The growing numbers of Americans who publicly question the rise of corporate power [a] represent a variety of political philosophies. What they have in common is a strong belief in individual enterprise and competition – qualities the corporate world outwardly lauds but actively discourages.

---

[a] "72% of Americans say business has too much power over too many aspects of American life," noted within "Too Much Corporate Power," Business Week, September 11, 2000.

One aspect of modern life which has gone far to stifle men
is the rapid growth of tremendous corporations.
William O. Douglas, Justice
U.S. Supreme Court (1939-1975)

The invasion into American life of what I have chosen to call corporatism is, however, not a modern phenomenon. It began in the earliest of the original thirteen colonies and grew as the influence of agriculture waned and industrialization waxed. In the mid-1900's, stimulated by the growth of advertising/news media and consumerism, the power of corporations in commerce, politics, and daily lives accelerated.

During the past fifty years, industry in corporate form has moved from the periphery to the very center of social and economic existence. "Indeed, it is not inaccurate to say that we live in a corporate society," wrote William T. Gossett, former Vice President of Ford Motor Company, in 1957.

Much of this has occurred with little public notice. Philosopher, historian, law professor, and author Charles A. Beard (*An Economic Interpretation of the Constitution*, 1913, and numerous others [b]) addressed this lack of public involvement in a notebook-sized, 93-page tract published in 1936 by the National Home Library Foundation as the nation was recovering from the Great Depression:

> In every age, in every society, there is a group of persons,
> more or less closely united, who have a realistic view of
> affairs and policies. Their knowledge is wide. Their wits
> are sharpened by experience. They know what they want.
> They are acquainted with ways and means calculated to
> attain their objectives. Usually at the other pole there is an
> opposing group, likewise with realistic views, knowledge
> and policy. They too have positive ideas on ways and
> means of realizing their aims when the times are ripe.

---

[b] Charles A. Beard, 1874-1948. Dr. of Philosophy, Columbia 1904, virtual
"founder" of Columbia school of politics 1907, and professor, 1907-1917,
President of the American Political Science Association in 1926, President
of the American Historical Association in 1933. First book, a study of
the Industrial Revolution, initially published 1901, 10 reprints. Textbook
American Government and Politics first published in 1910, ten reprints.
Numerous other books and writings. Considered the most influential
scholar of constitutional/economic issues of the mid-1900's.

3

Between these groups is the great mass of people almost wholly absorbed in the routine of living. Food, clothing, shelter and amusements occupy most of their labor and thought. Their knowledge of society is narrow. Their ideas about the world and its works are hazy. They read little. Their experience is limited. As long as the routine runs fairly well, they have little curiosity about 'what makes the wheels go around.' Only in time of some domestic or foreign crisis are they deeply stirred about anything outside the daily grind and its diversions. In such times they are likely to be swept one way or another by signs, symbols, myths, and slogans. [7]

The result, says Richard Grossman, co-director of the Program on Corporations and co-author of *Taking Care of Business: Citizenship and the Charter of Incorporation,* is that:

Giant corporations govern. Corporations are in fact making the fundamental decisions that shape our society. They determine essentially what work we do, which technologies get developed, which production methods are used. [Yet] in the Constitution of the United States they are delegated no authority to make our laws and define our culture. Corporations have no constitutions, no bills of rights. So when corporations govern, democracy flies out the door. [8]

The sudden meltdown of utility-trading giant Enron over the span of a few months, commencing in the autumn of 2001, focused media and public attention upon corporate governance and raised troubling questions. Exactly who was in charge and calling the shots? Where did responsibility lie for the firm's sudden bankruptcy? And why were the company's mid-level management, banks, debtors, and investors, especially highly sophisticated investment and research firms, taken so by surprise?

"The Biggest Casualty of Enron's Collapse: Confidence," was the headline of a *New York Times* "Week in Review" section. The accompanying story laid out the problem:

For two generations, a rigorous system of private disclosure and public oversight has given American investors confidence that they will not be fleeced when they buy stocks.

Enron is not the first big company to be felled by bad accounting. But the fact that a company as large and well known as Enron could essentially be vaporized in a matter of months has shaken even the most cynical investors on Wall Street.

So when Paul A. Voelker, Jr., the former chairman of the Federal Reserve, said last week, 'Accounting and auditing in this country is in a state of crisis,' he was not just speaking to men in green eyeshades, but to the millions of Americans who hope to pay for their retirement or their children's education by investing in stocks. [9]

Although Enron's mismanagement caused the company's failure, what was most shocking to investors was that the auditing firm Arthur Andersen LLP, one of the largest accounting and auditing firms in the world, had approved Enron's off-balance-sheet tactics and highly dubious, insider-owned financial vehicles. Even more damaging was Arthur Andersen's complicity in hiding the company's true financial picture from its shareholders and lenders.

The Enron debacle stimulated a rash of accusations over accounting practices of respected, old-line firms. David Tice wrote in *On Wall Street*: "Investors should realize, however, that accounting games are played by scores of companies, not only a handful of high profile disasters." [10]

Tice, author of the monthly "Big Bear" column, went on to describe other misleading company financials from such blue chip firms as IBM and Coca-Cola.

Within a month of Enron's disintegration, investors were shaken again by the collapse of Global Crossing Ltd., a highly touted telecom that had spent billions of dollars of investors' money and borrowed funds to lay undersea fiber-optic cables connecting the continents. Again, dubious accounting and financial practices were held to be the primary contributor to the firm's failure as well as investment analysts' and banks' inability to predict impending financial problems.

5

What spurred the public's ire over what was primarily a Wall Street matter were the enormous sums taken out of Enron and Global Crossing by executive officers, while employees saw their jobs and retirement savings disappear.

"As Global Crossing Crashed, Executives Got Loan Relief, Pension Payouts," headlined *The Wall Street Journal's* "Marketplace" of February 21, 2002.

> Renee Hinton says it was hard enough when she was laid off last August from Global Crossing Ltd. after 14 years with the company and its predecessor. But when the former fiber-optic darling declared bankruptcy last month, it dragged the systems manager into bankruptcy, too.
>
> Like thousands of other laid-off employees, Ms. Hinton was required to take her severance package in spread-out payments rather than a lump sum. With the company's bankruptcy filing, those payments stopped. Medical benefits were also terminated. Many of the workers' 401(k) retirement plans, loaded with Global Crossing shares, became nearly worthless as the stock price plunged.
>
> But for many Global Crossing executives, the outcome has been quite different. Global Crossing's new chief executive, John Legere, received a $3.5 million signing bonus when he took the job in October – even though he already was employed as CEO of Asia Global Crossing.
>
> At about the same time, Global Crossing forgave a $10 million loan to Mr. Legere and eased the terms of an $8 million loan to Thomas Casey, Global's departing chief executive.
>
> The company also moved up its late pay date by a week so that executives and others still employed at Global could get paid before the company declared bankruptcy January 28. Severance payments to the already laid-off workers weren't paid. [11]

A table accompanying the story noted that Global Crossing's CEO and two former CEOs received a total of $33.4 million in bonuses and forgiven loans immediately preceding the bankruptcy filing. Enron's executives fared even better.

At the same time that employees were locked into much of the Enron stock in their 401(k) plans, executives sold shares valued at about $128 million on top of $486 million in sales in 2000 ... Mr. Lay [CEO] alone sold shares valued at $29.8 million during that period.

According to company filings, Enron will pay Mr. Lay a pension estimated at $475,042 for life. In addition ... it agreed to pay a total of $1.25 million in insurance premiums through 2001 on a $12 million life insurance policy. [12]

Commenting on *Wall Street Journal* writer Paul Krugman's February 12, 2002 column "Business Versus Bizness," an account of "executive excesses," a reader noted in a letter to the Editor:

Too many of us now worship at the altar of business success. Success leads some managers and entrepreneurs to believe that their talents and skills, their very persons, put them above everyone else. Sometimes it's as if they've become gods, accountable and beholden to no one, their sense of entitlement unbounded. Can pharaohs be wrong? Who would tell them that they were? Would they listen? Not in my experience. [13]

Congress, of course, mounted multiple committees and subcommittees to investigate the financial and ethical lapses of Enron and Andersen. But none of the committees or Congressional questioners addressed the fundamental issue: if investors own a corporation and the CEO and its executives are simply "managers" hired to run it, *why did the hired hands come out so far ahead, and the owners come out so far behind?*

That conundrum and many other puzzling aspects of what is called corporate "governance" are explored in the following chapters.

[1] Compilation of quotations from various sources, including *Harvard Business Review*," May/June 1986 and The Ultimate Success Quotations Library, 1997.

[2] ibid

[3] Speech to Commonwealth Club of California, October 5, 1992.

[4] National Press Club luncheon, December 9, 1993.

[5] "Message From The CEO," February 16, 2002; Casady & Green, Inc. Internet Web site.

[6] *Fortune magazine*, March 18, 2002; by Clifton Leaf.

[7] *Jefferson, Corporations and the Constitution* by Dr. Charles A. Beard, published by National Home Library Foundation, Sherman F. Mittell, editor, Washington, D.C., 1936.

[8] Richard Grossman Interviewed by David Barsamian, Provincetown, MA, August 23, 1998.

[9] *The New York Times*, "Week in Review, Oversight," by Alex Berenson, February 10, 2002.

[10] "Financial statements should retain their 15 minutes of fame," in "Big Bear" column written by David Tice, *On Wall Street* magazine, January 2002.

[11] *The Wall Street Journal*, "Marketplace," February 21, 2002, by Wall Street Journal staff reporters Rebecca Blumenstein, Deborah Solomon and Kathy Chen.

[12] "Enron Pensions Had More Room at the Top," by Ellen E. Schultz and Theo Francis, Staff Reporters of *The Wall Street Journal*, January 23, 2002.

[13] "In America, Where Business Is King," letter to the Editor by Donald S. Warner, Bronx, NY, February 17, 2002.

CHAPTER TWO
OUR FOUNDERS' VIEW

Corporations Are Dangerous

Most Americans, especially champions of business deregulation and the free market, but also many members of Congress and state legislatures, would be shocked to learn that the Founding Fathers firmly believed that corporations were dangerous organizations which, if left unchecked, threatened the very freedom of the nation. Even 100 years after the American Revolution, farmers, men of commerce, and financiers feared corporations. "Chartered [corporate] privileges are a burthen, under which the people of Britain, and other European nations, groan in misery," wrote Liberty Party candidate for Vice President Thomas Earle in 1840. [1]

Immigration to the American Colonies was not just a flight toward land and opportunity. It was also a flight from the excesses of the Industrial Revolution. As described by business historian Miriam Beard, at the opening of the 18th Century, middle class and poorer families of England were subject to the lawless cruelty and barbarism of early industrialization unleashed by a government enamoured of laissez faire.

> The horrors of early industrialism have been told often enough, and reports of investigating committees and travelers have depicted the conditions among which infants labored in the cotton mills. According to these reports, poor-law authorities delivered pauper children, in batches of 50 and 100, to factory-owners, making no accounting for their welfare or even survival …. Sir Robert Peel had a thousand children in his plants. Children were the chosen operatives of the cotton-industry … [and] worked as many as 18 hours a day, put in irons or whipped, kept prisoners.(p.127) [2]

With the human and environmental degradation of England's industrialized, laissez faire economy still fresh in memory, it is little wonder that the constitutions adopted by the original 13 states included strongly worded restrictions on businesses, especially those that had the potential for market, economic, and political power.

The merchant and landed gentry among the founders had good reason to view the corporate form of business with suspicion. They were forced to deal with the oppressive power that Crown-granted chartered corporations wielded in England and then in the colonies. Beard described what entrepreneurs in the young colonies faced in the late 1700s and early 1800s:

> America, in the formula of Pitt, was not to be allowed to make a nail or a yard of cloth for sale abroad. She was to be compelled to remain a perpetual purchaser of British products. This was not merely a policy formed by the Crown; indeed it was often forced through by lobbying business interests against the better judgement of the gentlemen on the government's Board of Trade.(p.43) [3]

But even as colonial merchants and tradesmen argued against allowing English excesses to be repeated in the New World, they also recognized that the corporate structure was essential for development. The corporate form attracted capital by providing investors with a legal shield against personal responsibility for the firm's debts or failure. The colonies needed to attract capital to develop the transportation infrastructure and industrial capacity that would free them from dependence upon England and the Continent.

The legal basis of incorporation was imported to the Colonies. What few corporations existed before the Revolution operated under English law. Most were organized to perform a social function: a town corporation, a church, a university, a professional guild. Implicit in the writing and granting of private corporate charters was that they would serve public functions before private interests.

While the pursuit of capital and profitable enterprise was acknowledged as a normal and desirable human activity in the Colonies, its status in the community was balanced by egalitarian concerns rising from many philosophical sources. Oscar and Mary Flug Handlin, in their *Commonwealth – A Study of the Role of Government in the American Economy write:*

> Many elements had coalesced into a common body of ideas on the nature of the state. The federal theology of the first settlers supplied the concept of a society formed

by a covenant voluntarily entered into; the Baptists and the influence of the Great Awakening destroyed the notion of a community of the elect; and from Locke and his contemporaries came the theory of natural rights. Civil government was a covenant among men to further their common interests and welfare by means of a social compact in which the participants surrendered certain privileges for the better attainment of others. But as a typical Pittsfield petition of 1776 pointed out, "every man by Nature has the seeds of Tyranny deeply implanted within."(p.7) [4]

The initiators and writers of colonial constitutions were men of wealth and position. Their goal in the New World was to create a favorable climate for their land holdings and commercial interests. But they also recognized the necessity for equilibrium between commerce and commoner. From *Commonwealth*:

The merchants came to the realization that the state could not operate on their behalf alone, that they could not simply write their own interests into interpretation of the common interest. Nor could any group gain for itself advantages the price of which the whole community would pay. A vigilant society would weigh special privileges in the scales of the common welfare.(p.50) [5]

Struggle For Control

A corporate charter creates a legal entity "permitting to a few ... what was forbidden to all others." [6] Legislatures struggled to maintain public control of corporate entities against the pressure of investors to loosen the reins. As Harbrecht and McCallin wrote in *The Corporation and the State in Anglo-American Law and Politics*, "Americans were quite conscious of the political consequences of the growth of corporations and were inclined to grant legislatures extensive control over them." [7]

John David Rose

Distinguished jurist James Wilson,[a] contributor to the Pennsylvania and the Federal Constitutional Conventions and one of only six of the nation's founders to sign both the Declaration of Independence and the U.S. Constitution, defined the status of corporations in the young nation's pecking order. As described in *Annals of America*, Conspectus II, Chapter 16, "The Corporation," "Colonial Corporations 1609-1789":

> Not only were these early corporations limited in the scope of their operations; also implicit in their charters was the notion that they must serve a public function. James Wilson declared in 1790 that business corporations though 'moral persons,' were 'not in a state of natural liberty, because their actions are cognizable by the superior power of the state. Another jurist held that acts of incorporation ought never to be passed except "in consideration of services to be rendered to the public. Corporations could make a profit, but this should not be the main end in view.(p.173)[8]

As the federal constitution was debated, drafted, and revised in the first Constitutional Convention, most delegations revealed their concern over corporate power by imposing severe restrictions on its formation and operation.

All four of Massachusetts' delegates to the Constitutional Convention, Elbridge Gerry, Nathaniel Gorham, Rufus King and Caleb Strong, came from merchant families. Three were active in commerce and shipping at the time they served. Yet even with this background, the Massachusetts delegation strongly backed an amendment "that Congress erect no company of merchants with exclusive advantages of commerce." An identical provision was attached to ratification by New Hampshire. [9]

---

[a] Often overlooked in modern listings of "Founding Fathers," James Wilson played a central role in debates surrounding the ratification of the Constitution and served in the Continental Congress and the U.S. Supreme Court. As described by Mark David Hall, author of *The Political and Legal Philosophy of James Wilson, 1742-1798*, "Wilson is one of the most interesting founders. ... He approached issues in a systematic and philosophical manner. Further-more, as a law professor and Supreme Court justice, he produced some of the period's most profound commentary on the Constitution and American law."

Concern was not limited to monopolies, or "merchants with exclusive advantages of commerce," such as the Crown-chartered Hudson Bay Company or Massachusetts Bay Company. From an 1830's law journal:

> Experience and the wisdom of modern times have demonstrated the necessity of regulating the rights and liabilities of corporations ... by the same principles of law that govern individuals.... Much yet remains to be done to secure to the public all the benefits that these bodies are calculated to give, and protect individuals from the evils which they have the power to inflict. [10]

Limits Placed on Corporate Life and Liberty

In 1821, the State of New York amended its state constitution to provide that no corporation could be created or renewed without the consent of two-thirds of the legislature. Most states limited or withheld the right of corporations to own land. Many required that a government official representing the public interest sit on a corporate board and be given veto power over corporate decisions. The prevailing attitude was that "the government that had made the corporation retained the power to alter or unmake it." [11] The Pennsylvania Legislature declared in 1834: "A corporation in law is just what the incorporation act makes it. It is the creature of the law and may be molded to any shape or for the purpose the Legislature may deem most conducive for the common good." [12]

The California Constitution of 1879 affirmed the subordination of corporate interests to those of individuals and the public:

> Article XII, Section 8: ... the exercise of the police power of the state shall never be so abridged or construed as to permit corporations to conduct their business in such manner as to infringe the rights of individuals or the general well-being of the state.

Corporate charters of the time were generally required to include a clause giving the state legislature power to alter, modify, or repeal the charter at the state's pleasure. [13]

In the early 1800s, most states granted charters limiting the corporation to one carefully defined line of business. An iron foundry, for example, could not own coal or iron mines. Conglomerates and vertically integrated enterprises were prohibited. The purpose was to prevent the domination of essential services and industries by a small group of wealthy investors.

The founders knew from experience how monarchs controlled and profited from charters granted to family and close political associates. English farmers, for example, were free to raise herds of cows and peddle the milk, but cowhides could only be sold to a firm possessing a royal charter. In turn, shoemakers and other fabricators were forced to buy hides through royally chartered brokers if they wanted to sell their finished goods through legal channels.

In addition, states generally required charters to include language that guaranteed public control over corporate entities, including rules limiting the power of large shareholders. "Scaled" voting was frequently employed to put large and small investors on an equal footing when choosing directors and setting basic corporate direction. Shareholders had the right to remove directors. Capitalization was often limited, as was the amount of debt allowed. Some states required corporations to turn over their books to the legislature upon request.

One of the most important restraints on corporate power was limiting the length of a corporation's life. For example, the Massachusetts colonial legislature "imposed well-defined conditions" when granting charters for bridges. These conditions were:

> completion in a limited period and construction in accordance with specified plans, the slightest change in which needed the consent of the General Court. All the corporations except those chartered in 1794 received a limited life term after which their spans were to revert to the Commonwealth which also retained the right to lower tolls after a number of years, usually forty.(pgs. 107-8)[14]

Corporate charters granted by the various states generally ran from 20 to 50 years, but never "in perpetuity." Maryland gave manufacturing a 40-year life span, Pennsylvania but 20. Mining companies chartered in Maryland could live for 50 years. The corporation was dissolved at the end of its allotted span of years and its assets distributed to the shareholders.[15]

State legislatures dominated by merchants and farmers and influenced by religious conservatives maintained that time-limited corporate charters were necessary to maintain parity between "unnatural" corporate entities and human-owned enterprises. The life span of sole proprietorships and partnerships is inevitably tied to the span of years enjoyed by the owners, whereas man-made "paper creations" could potentially live forever.

This concern was especially focused on a corporation's ability to acquire and control the ultimate source of power and wealth: land. As summarized by the Supreme Court of Georgia in the late 19th Century:

> All experience has shown that large accumulations of property in hands likely to keep it intact for a long period are dangerous to the public weal. Having perpetual succession, any kind of corporation has peculiar facilities for such accumulations.... Freed, as such bodies are, from the sure bounds – the grave – to the schemes of individuals they are able to add field to field, and power to power, until they become entirely too strong for the society which is made up of those whose plans are limited to a single life. [16]

The political reality is that wealth and political power go hand-in-hand. The longer the life, the greater the ability to accumulate wealth; the more wealth the greater ability to influence government. Without limits on corporate lives, the founders foresaw a nation soon controlled by a corporate aristocracy.

On the other hand, no matter how wealthy and powerful an individual proprietorship or partnership might become, death has the final say. Individual wealth and power diminishes as it is dispersed over time to heirs.

To preclude a "legal" entity's capacity to accumulate wealth and power without limits, state constitutions beginning with the original 13 but extending as late as the thirtieth and thirty-first states (Wisconsin, California), limited corporate charters to a specific period of time, most often 20 to 30 years . [17]

In addition, many states imposed on corporations some, if not all, of the following limitations:

- A corporation could not own land. It could lease or rent only.
- A corporation could be in one line of business only; vertical integration was not allowed, nor were mergers.
- The corporate charter would come to an end in a specified period of time, generally 20 to 30 years. Whatever assets the corporation had would be sold, creditors paid, and the balance distributed to share-holders.

- A majority (up to two thirds) of the state legislature would have to agree to issuance of the corporate charter. The legislature could apply its own set of requirements, regulations, and restrictions to the venture.
- Frequently, the charter would call for a state government official to sit on the board of directors. This official generally was given veto power over any board decision or action.

By the mid-1800s, reacting to excesses and the growing power of corporate-structured enterprises, some state governments added even more restraints:

- Incorporation did not relieve corporate management stockholders/owners of responsibility or liability for corporate acts.
- Corporate officers, directors, or agents could be held criminally liable for violating the law.
- Directors of the corporation were required to come from among stockholders.
- Corporations were prohibited from owning stock in other corporations.
- Corporations were prohibited from making any political contributions, direct or indirect.
- State legislature set the rates that corporations could charge for their products or services.
- Corporate records and documents were open to the legislature or the state attorney general.

The prohibitions were not without teeth. In People v. North River Sugar Refining Company, a quo warranto ("by what authority") action was brought to revoke the corporation's charter based on the corporation's conviction of a violation of anti-trust laws.[18] In a unanimous decision the New York State Court of Appeals revoked the Corporation's charter while acknowledging many of the issues involved with involuntary dissolution of a corporation – the innocent investors, employees, and trading community whose interests would be hurt by the action. [b]

The decision clearly stated the court's view of the relative standing in law of human and corporate interests (underlined):

---

[b] From the Syllabus: "It seems that, <u>as corporate grants are always assumed to have been made for the public benefit,</u> any conduct which destroys their functions, maims and cripples their separate activity, and takes away free and independent action, affects unfavorably the public interests." (Emphasis added).

The judgement sought against the defendant is one of corporate death. The state which created, asks us to destroy, and the penalty invoked represents the extreme rigor of the law. <u>The life of a corporation is, indeed, less than that of the humblest citizen</u>, and yet it envelopes great accumulations of property, moves and carries in large volume the business and enterprise of the people, and may not be destroyed without clear and abundant reason.... Corporations may, and often do, exceed their authority only where private rights are affected. When these are adjusted, all mischief ends and all harm is averted. But where the transgression has a wider scope, and threatens the welfare of the people, they may summon the offender to answer for the abuse of its franchise and the violation of its corporate duty.... The abstract idea of a corporation, the legal entity, the impalpable and intangible creation of human thought, is itself a fiction, and has been appropriately described as a figure of speech.... The state permits in many ways an aggregation of capital, but, mindful of the possible dangers to the people, overbalancing the benefits, keeps upon it a restraining hand, and maintains over it a prudent supervision, where such aggregation depends upon its permission and grows out of its corporate grants.... The defendant corporation has violated its charter, and failed in the performance of its corporate duties, and that in respects so material and important as to justify a judgement of dissolution. [19]

Race To The Bottom

The struggle to restrain corporate power was doomed from the beginning as states began to compete for development, economic growth, and jobs. Capital flowed to states with the most easily obtained and most lenient corporate charters. As is the case today, states and communities would vie with one another with tax incentives, rebates, and infrastructure development to attract or keep a major economic unit. Easing of restrictions in one state forced others to do the same. Inevitably the least restrictive regulatory climate prevailed.

Railing against the charter by Congress of the Bank of the United States, President Jackson, in his final address to the country declared:

"The planter, the farmer, the mechanic and the laborer ... are in constant danger of losing their fair influence in the government, and with difficulty maintain their just rights against the incessant efforts daily to encroach upon them. The mischief springs from ... the multitude of corporations with exclusive privileges which they have succeeded in obtaining in the different states and which are employed altogether for their benefit; and unless you become more watchful ...you will find, in the end, that the most important powers of government have been given or bartered away, and the control over your dearest interests has passed into the hands of these corporations.(pgs.307-8) [20]

With state legislatures allied closely to merchant and farm interests, industrialists made little headway in lessening controls imposed by state governments. so they turned to the courts for relief from state-imposed fetters.

Most often cited is the 1827 decision by Chief Justice John Marshall in what is referred to as "The Dartmouth College Case." The case revolved around a state's ability to amend or alter a corporate charter. Marshall's dissent in United States Bank v. Dandridge, a dispute surrounding the ability of a corporation and its agents to issue and accept binding contracts, added fuel to the effort to relieve corporate enterprise from state control. [21]

Marshall took the matter far beyond the question at hand to address state regulation of corporations. As described in *The Corporation And The State..."* by Harbrecht and McCallin:

Chief Justice Marshall's doctrine on corporations as set forth in the [Dartmouth] case amounted to a theory of corporations new to the law. He defined a corporation as:

'...an artificial being, invisible, intangible, and existing only in contemplation of the law. Being the mere creature of the law, it possesses only those properties which the charter of its creation confers upon it, either expressly, or as incidental to its very existence. Among the most important are immortality, and, if the expression may be allowed, individuality; properties, by which a perpetual succession of many persons is considered the same, and may act as a single individual. They enable a corporation to manage its own affairs, and to hold property without the perplexing intricacies, the hazardous and endless necessity of perpetual conveyances for the purpose of transmitting it from hand to hand. It is chiefly for the purpose of clothing bodies of men, in succession, with these qualities and capacities, that corporations were invented, and are in use. By these means, a perpetual succession of individuals are capable of acting for the promotion of the particular object, like one immortal being.... A corporation was a person, a citizen, with the rights of all citizens.'(p.68) [22]

Marshall clearly understood that he was turning a "legal fiction" into a "a citizen, with the rights of all citizens." Moreover, this new citizen was more than the equal of its human counterparts. It was super-human, or in Marshall's own word, "immortal." Harbrecht and McCallin:

Mr. Marshall ... proceeded then to strike down certain other elements which had always been emphasized in definition of a private corporation:

"...But this being does not share in the civil government of the country, unless that be the purpose for which it was created. Its immortality no more confers on it political power, or a political character, than immortality would confer such power or character on a natural person. It is no more a State instrument, than a natural person exercising the same powers would be ... Because the government had given it the power to take and hold property in a particular form, and for particular purposes, has the government a consequent right substantially to change that form, or to vary the purposes to which the property is to be supplied? This principle has never been asserted or recognized, and is supported by no authority."(p.69) [23]

The decision overturned and invalidated state laws limiting corporations to one activity. It ended prohibitions against a corporation's ability to own, buy, and sell land. And states could no longer require representation of the public interest on the Board of Directors, inspect corporate records, or discipline a corporation by threatening to revoke its charter. In short, all rights of states to regulate the corporate creatures they create through their charters of incorporation had been abolished.

Before his appointment to the court, Marshall had been a leading proponent of Federalism. This led to what has been billed as an "Epic Struggle" between Marshall and states' rights defender Thomas Jefferson to define the limits of federal power. Again, from Harbrecht and McCallin:

> We can say that the effect of Marshall's doctrine ...was to bring into American jurisprudence a new category of corporation. Henceforth, there were to be two kinds of corporations, each with a public interest: the public corporation and the private corporation. Robbins [c] calls the transmutation of the private charity of the English Common law, free from judicial intrusions, into the private corporation of American constitutional law, insulated from too much legislative control, "...a masterpiece of judicial politics." In 1819 the day was yet to come when individuals private or public would have to be protected from corporations.(p. 72) [24]

Marshall's decision marked the end of a 50-year battle by the nation's founders to keep a strong leash on corporate enterprise and the beginning of the transfer of rights to corporations heretofore reserved to human citizens by the Constitution.

As described by Thom Hartmann, author of *Unequal Protection: The Rise of Corporate Dominance and the Theft of Human Rights,* following the Civil War, the 14th Amendment to the U.S. Constitution was ratified by the states as one of the laws that were to provide former slaves with the full protection of the Constitution.[25] The Amendment's first article declares:

> "All persons born or naturalized in the United States, and subject to the jurisdiction thereof, are citizens of the United States and of the state wherein they reside. No state shall make or enforce any law which shall abridge the privileges or immunities of citizens of the United States; nor shall any state deprive any person of life, liberty or property, without due process of law; nor deny to any person within its jurisdiction the equal protection of the laws."

---

[c] James J. Robbins," The Private Corporation: Its Constitutional Genesis," *Georgetown Law Journal*, 1939, at p 170, cited by Harbrecht & McCallin.

With Justice Marshall having already declared that "a corporation was a person, a citizen, with the rights of all citizens" in the Dartmouth College case, the unintended consequence of the 14th Amendment was to encourage corporations to seek protection under the law as human "persons" rather than artificial entities – legal fictions.

Writes Hartmann:

> Using this argument for their base, the railroads repeatedly sued various states, counties and towns claiming that they shouldn't have to pay local taxes because different railroad properties were taxed in different ways in different places and this constituted the creation of different "classes of persons" and was, thus illegal discrimination under the 14th Amendment....
>
> For 20 years corporate personhood was debated. Across America, politicians were elected repeatedly on platforms that included the regulation of corporations, particularly the railroads. But the legal fight continued – and in 1886 the railroad hit paydirt.
>
> The Supreme Court ruled on an obscure taxation issue in the *Santa Clara County vs. The Union Pacific Railroad* case, but the Recorder of the court – a man named J.C. Bancroft Davis, himself formerly the president of a small railroad – wrote into his personal commentary of the case (known as the Headnote) that the Chief Justice had said that all the Justices agreed that corporation are persons.
>
> And in so doing, the clerical recorder – not the Supreme Court – inserted a statement that would change history and give corporations enormous powers that were not granted by Congress, not granted by the voters, and especially not by the Supreme Court. [26]

The irony, as Hartmann points out, is that headnotes have no legal standing, and that the Chief Justice had written a note to Davis that the court had not ruled on constitutional issues of personhood. (The original note can be seen on the "ThomHartmann.com" Web site).

Whether granting corporations the full rights of human persons was a fluke or a deliberate act of deception no longer matters. Based on Davis' headnote, courts through the years have given corporate persons the same

21

standing as humans, including freedom of speech. ("Will General Motors please address the court?") "Legal fictions," corporations, are now fully vested citizens blessed by law with the one attribute no human citizen possesses: immortality. No matter how heinous their crimes or egregious their acts against humanity, they can be put to "death" for only one fault, financial failure.

Did Justice Marshall or Recorder Davis understand what they were unleashing? Could they possibly have understood how the corporate form of business organization would come to dominate the social and political life of our nation?

[1] *Taking Care of Business: Citizenship and the Charter of Incorporation*, by Richard Grossman and Frank T. Adams, © 1993, Charter Ink, Cambridge, MA, pg. 6.

[2] *A History of Business, Vol. II — From the Monopolists to the Organization Man*, by Miriam Beard, Copyright by the University of Michigan 1938, 1963m Ch XXIII.

[3] ibid., Chapter XIX.

[4] *Commonwealth — A Study of the Role of Government in the American Economy: Massachusetts 1774 - 1861*, by Oscar Handlin and Mary Flug Handlin, (Revised Edition), © 1947, 1969 by the President and Fellows of Harvard College, The Belknap Press of Harvard University Press, Cambridge Massachusetts and London, England, Chapter 1, "Foundations of Political Power."

[5] ibid. Chapter 2, "Consolidation of Political Power."

[6] ibid. Chapter 3, "To Encourage Industry and Economy."

[7] *The Corporation and the State in Anglo-American Law and Politics*, Paul P. Harbrecht, S.J., and Joseph A. McCallin, S.J., 1959; from a draft found in the Fund For the Republic Archives.

[8] *Annals of America, Conspectus II*, Chapter 16 "The Corporation," "Colonial Corporations 1609-1789."

[9] Op cit., *Taking Care of Business*. Grossman and Adams

[10] Anonymous, *American Jurist and Law Magazine*, October 1830, as published in The Annals of America.

[11] Op cit., *Commonwealth*, Handlin & Handlin, Chapter 6, "The Law of Private Rights in a Commonwealth."

[12] Carter Goodrich, ed., *The Government and the Economy*, 1783-1861, Indianapolis: Bobbs-Merrill, 1967, p. 44 (Report of the Packer Committee of the Pennsylvania Legislature).

[13] *American Jurist and Law Magazine*, American Periodical Series, 1800-1850, Oct. 1830, from Michigan University Microfilms, 1964

[14] Op cit., *Commonwealth*: Handlin & Handlin, chapter 5.

[15] Op cit., *Taking Care of Business*. Grossman and Adams, pg. 8

[16] RAILROAD CO. V. COLLINS, 40 GA 582

[17] Berle, A. A., Jr., *Economic Power and the Free Society*, Fund for the Republic, date unknown

[18] 24.N.E. 834, (NY 1890)

[19] PEOPLE V. NORTH RIVER SUGAR REFINING CORP., 121 N.Y. 582, 24 N.E. 834, 1890 N.Y. Lexis 1446 and also as edited by Richard Grossman and published in "Rachel's Environment & Health Weekly #609, July 30, 1998, by Environmental Research Foundation, Annapolis, MD.

[20] Op cit. *Annals of America*, Vol. VI.

[21] WHEAT 12, 64

John David Rose

[22] Op cit., *The Corporation and the State in Anglo-American Law and Politics*, Harbrecht, S.J., and McCallin, S.J.

[23] Ibid., p69

[24] Ibid., p72

[25] *Unequal Protection: The Rise of Corporate Domoinance and the Theft of Human Rights* , Thom Hartmann, Rodale Books, 2002

[26] *Corporations are People, Too: How Human Institutions Subordinated Humans,* by Thom Hartmann, TomPain.common sense; first published on ThomHartmann.com as excerpt from above cited Unequal Protection...., Rodale Books, 2002

CHAPTER THREE
"TOO MUCH CORPORATE POWER?"

From a court decision in 1827, we jump ahead to the year 2000. It is not only the end of a millennium. It caps what Senior Economist Michael R. Pakko of the Federal Reserve Bank of St. Louis described as a "stellar" time for the U.S. economy.[1] There had been an unprecedented period of economic productivity generated by managerial and technological innovations in wholesale and retail trade, securities, semiconductors, computer manufacturing, and telecommunications. High Tech had fueled a near doubling of productivity growth rates. Moreover, reversing a prior decade of trillion dollar deficits, outgoing President Clinton was able to report the largest federal budget surplus in U.S. history.

"An overwhelming 81% of adults are steadfast in their optimism about what the 21st century holds for them and their families," reported the Pew Research Center for the People & the Press. [2]

The year 2000 was also a presidential campaign year. An avowed friend to big business, Texas Governor George W. Bush, II, challenged Vice President Albert Gore from a Democratic administration which took credit for the strong economic performance of the nation.

In the midst of apparent contentment with the status quo, however, the September 11, 2000, cover of *Business Week* magazine posed this provocative question: "Too Much Corporate Power?"

Author Aaron Bernstein wrote, "Amid the good times, citizens feel uneasy about Big Business." He supported his assertion with *Business Week*/Harris Poll numbers reporting that "72% of Americans say business has TOO MUCH POWER over too many aspects of American life," and "74% say BIG COMPANIES have too much POLITICAL INFLUENCE."[3] (Bernstein's emphasis).

These concerns became an issue in the 1999 Republican Presidential primaries. The public interest organization Common Cause (among others) had waged a decades-long struggle to limit the financial power of large campaign contributors — corporations, labor unions, and special interest groups. Surprisingly, their cause was taken up by John McCain, Vietnam war hero, Republican Senator, and Presidential primary candidate. With campaign finance reform his key issue, McCain attracted significant numbers of moderate GOP, independent, and cross-over voters. It was not enough, however, to overcome the loss of critical assistance from his Senate colleagues and the GOP party organization.

Americans troubled by corporate influence found another champion in third party candidate Ralph Nader. Nader crystallized their concerns in his nomination acceptance speech before the Green Party Convention, bringing forth roars of agreement and approval from conventioneers.

> Big business has been colliding with American democracy and democracy has been losing. Over the past twenty years we have seen the unfortunate resurgence of big business influence, generating its unique brand of wreckage, propaganda and ultimatums on American labor, consumers, taxpayers and most generically, American voters. [4]

More than three million Americans voted for Nader and against corporate influence in politics despite warnings from Democrats that they were giving the pro-business Bush the edge in the Presidential race.

As the Republican National Convention was getting underway in early December 1999, a rising tide of protests against world-wide corporate influence filled the media. The World Trade Organization's meetings in Seattle, Washington, drew protesters from the United States and the rest of the developed world. Marchers battled Seattle police with a passion that recalled the Vietnam War protests of the 1960's.

"The Seattle protestors expressed their anger at institutions like the WTO for elevating the interests of large corporations over everyone else," wrote Sarah Anderson in her "Study on Corporate Power on 1st Anniversary of Seattle Protests."[5] The national media, however, spent little time explaining why the protesters were marching. Instead, their stories concentrated on the isolated instances of vandalism by more radical elements drawn to the cause.

Then in January 2002, the seventh largest corporation in America, Enron, collapsed into bankruptcy, foundering in a sea of accounting deception, off-the-books financing schemes, and self-dealing by its top executives. Fall-out went far beyond this one firm or industry. "You can't trust companies. Can't trust auditors. Can't trust analysts," *Fortune* magazine warned investors. [6] In another Enron-related article in the same edition, *Fortune* columnist Andy Sewer wrote:

There's something terribly rotten with American business right now, and its making a lot of us sick. All the new-economy lying and cheating that went on back in the '90s has come back to bite us in the you-know-what.

Obviously, the trigger event here was the Enron scandal ... but its collapse has forced us to shine a halogen light on the books of America's public companies, and what we're seeing sure ain't pretty.

The price we, the public, pay for all this is absolutely mind-boggling. Former SEC chief accountant Lynn Turner, who's now teaching at Colorado State University, estimates that over the past six years, the cost to investors — in terms of stock market losses — of financial restatements is well over $100 billion. And that doesn't include Enron, which is in a league of its own.... The cost of Enron's failure is roughly six times the $15 billion loss suffered from Hurricane Andrew. [7]

Collusion between corporations and politicians didn't begin with the Teapot Dome affair in 1922 [a], nor has it ended with the Enron scandal in 2002. Every decade has seen its share of corporate swindles. Investors and the public inevitably come out on the short end of the stick.

Just twenty years earlier, the 1980's brought a rash of expensive-to-investor and public failures, including the $2.5 billion Lincoln Savings & Loan failure in 1987. Also in the mid-1980's, Drexel Burnham Lambert's junk bond scandal took investors for $50 billion.

In the 1990's, investors watched Cendant Corporation stock take a nosedive over financial misrepresentations. Then in late 1997 came the Federal Reserve bail-out of Long Term Capital Management (LTCM), requiring federal intervention to prevent what was called at the time a potential international banking "meltdown."

Despite a crescendo of accounting fraud-induced business collapses, most observers played them down as simple business failures. "There are always going to be bad apples," said Washington lobbyist for the accounting profession Jay Velasquez, reported Jane Mayer in "The Accountants' War," in the New Yorker magazine. [8] "We live in a free-market system," said Barry Melancon, head of the American Institute of Certified Public Accountants. "Businesses fail. People are not infallible." [9]

---

[a] Teapot Dome near Casper, Wyoming, was a federally owned oil reserve leased, without competitive bidding, to private developers, resulting in Secretary of the Interior Albert B. Fall being convicted of receiving a bribe.

Another perspective was offered to Ms. Mayer in an interview with Arthur Levitt, Jr., chairman of the Securities and Exchange Commission in the prior administration. Levitt attributed the Enron debacle to moral failure. "This is about corporate greed. It is the result of two decades of erosion of business . If there was ever an example where money and lobbying damaged the public interest, this was clearly it." Mayer then noted: "In fact, the number of publicly traded companies forced to re-state their earnings went from three in 1981 to a hundred and fifty-eight [in 2001]." [10]

Levitt's opinion was supported by another respected voice. *The Wall Street Journal* reported that in the first three months of the year [2002] the SEC had opened "an unprecedented 49 new financial-reporting cases involving mostly large companies and not limited to the technology sector." [11]

"There is something very broad-based going on, and it's not anything that passing a couple of laws is going to change," said William T. Allen, director of the Center for Law and Business at New York University, quoted in *The New York Times*. [12]

Others, including Marianne Jennings, professor of legal and ethical studies at Arizona State University, also held that Enron-style financial schemes were not a single-instance aberration in business ethics. "I think a lot of CEOs are down on their knees right now, thankful that Enron got caught before they did," she told *The Christian Science Monitor.*" [13]

The result of these ethical lapses, said Daniel Altman, writing in the "Money & Business" section of *The New York Times* under the headline "The Taming of the Finance Officers," "Accounting issues have even shaken investor faith in blue-chip companies like General Electric, I.B.M. and Xerox."[14] Altman's comment reinforced the point of the lead story on the same page describing an extraordinary reaction by investors to a positive report from General Electric's chief financial officer, Keith S. Sherin. "He pointed to the company's strong balance sheet and the diversity of G.E.'s businesses and said they enabled the company to produce what he called consistently excellent earnings growth." But, reported Gretchen Morgenson of *The New York Times,* "Just moments after Mr. Sherin uttered those words, shareholders began dumping G.E. stock. By the end of the day shares of G.E. had lost 9 percent of their value." [15]

Just weeks prior to the above (March 2002), General Electric had come under fire from a totally unexpected source. As *The Wall Street Journal* reported:

> In an unusual public rebuke, Bill Gross, manager of the world's biggest bond fund, lashed out at General Electric, saying the company is carrying too much debt and isn't dealing honestly with investors. Mr. Gross also counts himself among the analysts who have started to wonder how GE has been able to consistently beat Wall Street's earnings expectations. He said John F. Welch, Jr., former chief executive of GE, and his successor, Jeffrey Immelt, haven't been "totally forthcoming in the explanation for why GE has been able to grow earnings by nearly 15% per year for the last several decades." [16]

As expert financial analysts as well as ordinary investors lost faith in the honesty of even the most respected corporations, anxiety over corporate power grew substantially despite, or perhaps as the result of, the election of a business-friendly administration in Washington. A May 2001 search for books on "corporate power" at one Internet book seller, Amazon.com, immediately brought forth ten titles including *Corporate Predators, The Hunt for MegaProfits and the Attack on Democracy,* by Russell Mokhiber et al, to *Corporations Are Gonna Get Your Mama: Globalization and the Downsizing of the American Dream,* edited by Kevin Danaher. Within weeks of its March 2002 publication, the newest exposé/screed on corporate America, *Stupid White Men and Other Sorry Excuses for the State of the Nation by Michael Moore,* author of *Downsize This,* jumped to Number One on *The New York Times* Non-Fiction bestseller list.

Growing use of the Internet is feeding the rising wave of anti-corporation sentiment. Sites such as "Baobab's Corporate Power Information," [17] "Corporate Watch by Mokhiber and Weissman,"[18] and "How The System Works (or doesn't)"[19] create opportunities for people with similar concerns to connect.

Even those in the upper echelons of the business world are beginning to question the power of corporations over everyday lives. In his "Message From Our CEO," Charles R. Fulweiler, Ph.D., CEO of the software firm Casady & Greene wrote:

> I do believe that the more powerful these gigantic corporations get, the more their managers are trained in chicane [sic]. I believe that we, the people, suffer immediate disenfranchisement and the alienation of the poor and homeless as both direct and indirect consequences of this creeping corruption. [20]

John David Rose

Robert A.G. Monks, [b] founder of LENS, a highly successful, Maine-based investment firm, writes knowledgeably and extensively on the issues of corporate governance, more precisely on the lack of shareholder, government, and public control over large corporations. He, along with writers Nell Minow and Kit Bingham, have become, in their words, "Corporate Gadflys," relating tales of shareholder resolutions and how they are thwarted by management.

However, in spite of the misgivings and alarms raised in and out of the business world, Main Street America seems relatively unconcerned. The majority of Americans accept with few complaints the power of Big Oil, the Industrial/Military Complex, Big Timber, Big Industry, Big Medicine, and Big Media over their lives. And why not, the defenders of big business ask? As senior editor of *The New Republic*, Gregg Easterbrook, wrote in *The New York Times Magazine"*:

> By almost every measure, life in the United States today is the best it has ever been; ever-rising living standards; rising life expectancy and falling rates of disease; low unemployment; declining rates of crime, pollution and poverty; low risk of war; unlimited supplies of just about everything; personal freedom never greater. This is America's Golden Age. [21]

Has the United States' economic and social progress since the 1940s occurred in spite of, or because of, the growing influence of big business over our nation's domestic and foreign policy? Either way, what's the problem?

---

[b] Monks' extensive writings on historic and current corporate practice were extremely useful in the early stages of research for this book.

"Miss Dugan, will you send someone in here who can distinguish right from wrong?"

[1] "The U.S. Trade Deficit and the 'New Economy,'" Federal Reserve Bank of St. Louis, Review, September/October 1999.

[2] "Optimism Reigns, Technology Plays Key Role," Pew Research Center for the People & the Press, October 24, 1999.

[3] "Too Much Corporate Power?", *Business Week*, September 11, 2000.

[4] Nomination Acceptance Speech, 6/25/2000.

[5] Sarah Anderson, "Study on Corporate Power on 1st Anniversary of Seattle Protests, The Institute for Policies Studies, Web site, March 2001.

[6] "Don't Get Burned," by Shawn Tully, *Fortune* magazine, February 18, 2002.

[7] "Dirty Rotten Numbers," by Andy Sewer, *Fortune* magazine, February 18, 2002.

[8] "The Accountants' War," by Jane Mayer, *The New Yorker*, April 22 & 29, 2002.

[9] Ibid.

[10] Ibid

[11] "SEC Broadens Accounting-Practices Inquiry," by Susan Pulliam, *The Wall Street Journal*, April 3, 2002.

[12] "How Will Washington Read the Signs," by David Leonhardt, *The New York Times*, Money & Business section, February 10, 2002.

[13] Enron lapses and corporate ethics by Kris Axtman and Ron Scherer, *Christian Science Monitor*, February 4, 2002.

[14] "The Taming of the Finance Officers," by Daniel Altman, *The New York Times*, April 14, 2002.

[15] "Wait a Second: What Devils Lurk In the Details?" by Gretchen Morgenson, *New York Times*, April 14, 2002.

[16] "Fund Manager Gross Lashes Out At GE Over Disclosure, Debt Load," by Gregory Zuckerman and Rachel Emma Silverman, Staff Reporters, *The Wall Street Journal*, March 31, 2002.

[17] http://baobabcomputing.com/corporatepower/

[18] http://www.corpwatch.org/

[19] hhtp://www.enviroweb.org/issues/system/

[20] "Message From Our CEO" by Charles R. Fulweiler, Ph.D., linked to the internet newsletter of Casady & Greene, dated February 26, 2001.

[21] "A Hazard of Good Fortunes," by Gregg Easterbrook, *New York Times Magazine*, March 11, 2001, Section 6.

CHAPTER FOUR
THE PROBLEM

"Corporations cannot commit treason, nor be outlawed,
or excommunicated, for they have no souls."
Sir Edward Coke, 1612.

We have developed magnificent but insensate instruments of commerce
and industry capable of achieving world-changing scope, size, and wealth.
The problem is that the humans in control are the same fallible products
of nature and nurture that crawled out of caves, capable of both sublime
virtue and horrific deceit, saintly selflessness and callous greed washed in
an endlessly gushing spring of self-justification and self-deception.

"As far as the stars are from earth, and as different as
fire is from water, so much do self-interest and integrity
differ." Lucan: Pharsalia VIII.lxv.

Criminal Price Fixing – General Electric
Fortune Magazine began the 2001 edition of its annual feature
"America's Most Admired Companies" singing the praises of the company
that topped the list for the fourth year in a row.

Tireless innovation. Robust financials. The ability to lure
and keep the smartest people. According to more than
4,000 business people *Fortune* surveyed late last year,
no company in the nation demonstrates such enviable
qualities better than General Electric. [1]

Yet, if GE had been given the same treatment as a human perpetrator
for repeated criminal convictions, federal authorities would have long ago
locked it up and thrown away the key.

From 1911 to 1962, there were 39 antitrust actions against General
Electric. Included in that number is the 1949 anti-trust conviction for
monopolizing electric bulb manufacture, an action which created a $104
million rash of lawsuits which GE finally settled for $1.4 million.

By 1950, almost before the ink was dry on its '49 conviction, GE
executives were deeply involved with Westinghouse, Allen Bradley
Company, and 25 other electrical equipment competitors in a conspiracy

to fix prices, rig bids, and divide markets on electrical equipment sales valued at $1.75 billion a year (1949 dollars). The illegal practice continued for at least eight years, according to the U.S. Justice Department 20 count indictment of May, 1960.

As reported in *Newsweek*:

> The Justice Department, charging GE with 'a proclivity for persistent and frequent involvement in antitrust violations,' had asked Federal District Court in Philadelphia to issue an order forbidding the company ever again to break the law — under penalty of contempt of court, and possible jail terms. [2]

In passing sentence the judge declared, "This is a shocking indictment of a vast section of our economy, for what is really at stake here is the survival of ...the free-enterprise system." [3]

Despite the court's indignant words, the sentences handed down to seven company officers were less severe than those given to a shop-lifter: thirty days in prison and a $2,000 fine. This for a bid-rigging conspiracy that cost the U.S. taxpayers $50 million and electric utilities and their customers an estimated $461 million more. An additional 24 sentences were suspended.

GE Corporation paid fines totaling $437,500, Westinghouse $372,500. The total of all fines handed out to the 27 conspirators was $4,924,500, or less than .04 of 1% of the $14 billion in illegal profits obtained from their criminal activities. (All sums in 1960 dollars).

After the sentences were handed down, GE's Chairman told a packed meeting of the New York Society of Security Analysts, "We don't think anybody's been damaged." The company Treasurer, after reporting that GE had cash assets totaling more than $400 million, reassured the analysts that "we are in excellent financial condition to take care of anything that we see happen." [4] GE stock, which had fallen $7 during the trial regained more than $4 of the loss.

In *Fortune* magazine's 1961 essay "The Incredible Electrical Conspiracy," author Richard Austin Smith wrote:

> No thoughtful person could have left that courtroom untroubled by the problems of corporate power and corporate ethics. We live in a corporate society. Big Business determines institutionally our rate of capital formation, technological innovation and economic growth;

it establishes the kind of competition that is typical of our system and sets the moral tone of the market place. The streets of every city in the U.S. are crowded with small businesses that take their cue from great corporations, whether it trickles down from what some executive tells the crop of college graduates about free enterprise or how he himself chooses to compete. [5]

Defrauding Your Customer – State Farm

The phrase "insurance fraud" usually refers to dishonest policy owners and claim fakers. However, policy holders of State Farm, America's largest insurance company, discovered in the mid-1990's that the insurance company was defrauding them.

A State Farm policy holder, Lucretia Duffy of Fairbanks, Alaska, was hit broadside by a truck. Duffy's doctor concluded that her injuries were the result of the crash and began a series of treatments that used up the better part of $10,000.

The State Farm office, however, considered her injuries "questionable" and sent her medical records to a company specializing in "comprehensive medical review."

The CMR returned a negative report on Duffy. It said her injuries were far less serious than represented and were only worth compensation of $780. Unable to pay her medical bills, her clinic stopped treating her and she lost her business.[6]

The problem was that the medical reviews (often called "Peer Reviews") ordered by State Farm were usually phony. They were prepared by outside contractors directed by the insurance company to limit losses. Medical records were rarely, if ever, reviewed by a licensed physician. Language "disallowing" claims was boiler-plate often pulled together by students, not licensed physicians. Even the signatures of doctors supposedly reviewing cases were often faked.

In a similar instance, Mindy Sitton of Seattle, Washington, was sitting in a rush-hour jammed Interstate Highway 5, the major North-South artery of the state, when she was struck heavily from the rear. Rescue teams had to use the "Jaws of Life" to tear open the crushed vehicle and extract her. As her medical bills began to climb, her insurance company, State Farm, sent her file out for "review." Based on what she was told was an independent physician's judgement, State Farm paid less than a couple of hundred dollars of the total $5,500 of Mindy's medical bills.[7] Ms. Sitton was another victim of insurance fraud conducted by State Farm.

In a "Dateline" program aired June 23, 2000, the NBC Television Network reported to viewers that State Farm had deliberately cheated 22 million of its policy holders out of over a billion dollars.

Researchers at "Dateline" studied a substantial quantity of these so-called "peer reviews." Every single one recommended substantial payment reductions. Not one suggested that the charges were justified and should be paid in full.

Because the reviews came months, sometimes a year or more, after policyholders had been billed by medical service providers, the policyholders were left holding the bag. The more affluent had already paid; the less affluent had been dunned for payment, suffered damage to their credit ratings, and in some cases, follow-up medical care had been denied.

This, "Dateline" made clear, was not a one-time "mistake" but a deliberate fraud committed by State Farm against its own policyholders over a decade-long period.

When State Farm spokesman Jack North was interviewed and shown evidence of the fraud by the "Dateline" reporter he airily dismissed it with, "That just isn't the way we do business."

The courts found otherwise.

In 1999 alone, State Farm paid more than $1.5 billion to policyholders in court-ordered judgments arising from lawsuits for fraud and misrepresentation brought by policyholders and, revealingly, its own agents.

In Campbell v. State Farm (Utah, Civil Case No. 890905231, 8/03/98), Third Judicial District Court Judge William B. Bohling wrote the decision extensively quoted below. Its value to this discussion is the judge's clear description of the position consumers and small businesses are in when they attempt to contest the actions of a large corporation.

His decision read, in part:

> The record clearly supports the conclusion that State Farm's undisclosed policy of using its claims handling process as a profit center to systematically deny benefits owed to consumers is deliberately crafted to prey on 'the weakest of the herd', the elderly, the poor, and other consumers who are least knowledgeable about their rights and thus most vulnerable to trickery or deceit or who have little money and hence have no real alternative but to accept an inadequate offer to settle a claim at much less than fair value.

The record also contains ample evidence, that throughout at least the past two decades, State Farm has resorted to a variety of wrongful means to attempt to evade detection of and liability for, its unlawful profit scheme. Using these tactics State Farm has managed to construct a nearly impenetrable wall of defense against punishment for its wrong-doing, so effective that it is able to pressure its adjusters to deny consumers insurance benefits with impunity, knowing: 1) that few of its victims will even realize they have been wronged. 2) that fewer still will be able to sue 3) that only a small fraction of those who do sue will be able to weather the years of litigation needed to reach trial 4) that any victims who actually reach trial will have great difficulty establishing the basis for punitive damages when met with claims that only an 'honest mistake' was made, supported by a body of evidence that has been systematically sanitized, padded, purged, concealed, destroyed or rehearsed....

Finally, the evidence in this case supports the conclusion that State Farm has a regular practice of working to wear down and outlast plaintiffs and opposing attorneys in lawsuits seeking to punish it for bad faith claim handling, by using a variety of tactics to intimidate claimants, witnesses and attorneys who oppose it....

The effect of State Farm's policies is to put insurance companies that play by the rules at a competitive disadvantage, allowing State Farm to increase its market share or its profits (whichever it is putting the emphasis on) or a combination of both, by having an advantage that honest companies don't have: the shortchanging of policyholders on claim amounts that should be paid. As the Campbells demonstrated with expert testimony, this inevitably creates pressure on the honest companies to resort to the same sort of misconduct in an attempt to stay even with State Farm, extending the damage to consumers throughout the auto insurance marketplace as a whole.[8]

As the Judge noted, State Farms fraud affected far more than its own customers. The entire insurance industry, including executives of competing firms, felt the pressure to produce the kind of financial results the dishonest company was able to produce.

Judge Bohling awarded the Campbells $2.6 million in compensatory damages, plus $145 million in punitive damages, sarcastically noting that the amount, representing about 1/4 of 1% of the company's wealth, was probably not enough to prevent State Farm from continuing to defraud policy holders. State Farm's regional executive confirmed the judge's supposition. Upon questioning, the executive stated that he would probably not bring the punitive damage award to State Farm headquarters' attention because the $147.7 million award was so "insignificant" it would not be reflected in the company's financial statements. [9,a]

Homicide – Union Carbide

Sometime in the night of December 2, 1984, poisonous methyl isocyanate gas burst from an underground storage tank behind the gates of Union Carbide's pesticide plant in Bhopal, India. Like the Biblical plague of The Passover, the deadly gas flowed silently down the near empty streets and through the poorly-fitting doorways of the slum homes jammed up against the plant's gates before moving into better neighborhoods and Bhopal's commercial district.

Unlike the plague of Moses, there was no Passover for those in the path of this lethal mist. The nearest victims died painful, gut-wrenching deaths within hours. The lesser-touched awakened coughing and choking, unable to contain their bladders and bowels, with burning, sightless eyes. Eight thousand people died within days.

Eighteen years after the disaster, the death toll directly attributed to the gas leak had risen to 20,000 with 10 to 15 people continuing to die each month from exposure-related causes. At least 150,000 people were left with permanent, crippling health problems. Forty percent of the area's pregnant women exposed to the gas aborted their fetuses. Stillbirths in the affected area continue at three times the historical rate. Twenty percent, or 1 million, of the exposed population of 5 million, continue to suffer from lung fibrosis, impaired vision, bronchial asthma, TB, recurrent fever, painful and irregular menstrual cycles, neurological disorders, and more.[10] Researchers have found chromosomal aberrations in the exposed population indicating a strong likelihood of congenital malformations for generations to come. [11]

---

[a] On April 7, 2003, the U.S. Supreme Court struck down the damage award as "excessive and violating the Due Process Clause of the 14th Amendment." Following the principles laid down by the court the punitive award would be no more than $10 million and very likely closer to $4 million.

It was the worst industrial disaster ever recorded.

Union Carbide Chairman Warren M. Anderson flew to Bhopal within days of the disaster to confer with India's foreign secretary and U.S. Embassy officials. There he was "detained" for six hours by Indian officials, charged with culpable homicide and negligence, before being released on an equivalent of $2,000 bail and asked to leave the country.

A flurry of lawyers also flew to India, among them Melvin Belli, who began gathering evidence for a $15 billion lawsuit that had already been filed in the United Sates.

Moving to put the best face on the disaster and reassure Americans working and living near its U.S. based plants, Union Carbide quickly released a barrage of press releases assigning fault. The leaking underground tank was described as a "double-walled, presurized [sic] tank" with a backup safety system. [12] Indian employees "responsible for helping stem the poisonous gas leak …ran away rather than try to control the high-pressure burst of fumes, senior police and company officials said today…. As a toxic cloud drifted toward a densely populated slum nearby, the workers left a supervisor to fend for himself." [13] A leading authority was asked to comment on the effects of the poison gas and reassured the media that "methyl isocyanate has been in use for more than 50 years with no major accidents in the United States." [14]

As "a posse of American lawyers is fanning out in Bhopal, signing up thousands of Indian plaintiffs," Union Carbide Chairman Anderson attempted to calm the storm with a contribution of $1 million to an emergency relief effort and a promise to compensate the victims fairly.[15] Nevertheless, class action damage suits rose to over $35 billion. Chairman Anderson reassured stockholders that the families of the dead and tens of thousands injured could be "fairly and equitably compensated without a material adverse effect on the financial condition of Union Carbide Corporation." [16]

In India, reports of safety and maintenance problems at the plant began to surface.

> A local journalist and a city administrator has seriously questioned, in recent years, the safety of the pesticide plant …but their efforts were largely belittled and ignored. Rajkumar Keswani, writing for Hindu papers, published parts of a then-secret Union Carbide Corp. survey … containing the results of a 1982 inspection made by three company engineers and citing specific safety problems at the plant. [17]

It was learned that to save $50.00 a day as part of a Union Carbide economy drive, the management of the plant had switched off the refrigeration unit which, if running, would have prevented or at least slowed the runaway reaction in the tank. Required fortnightly inspections of critical valves and pumps had not been made for two years; the workforce had been cut in half, and safety training of workers had been cut from six months to fifteen days.

Management of the plant learned of the gas leak at 11:00 P.M. The factory alarm for the employees was started by a desperate worker at 12:50 P.M. Management turned off the alarm within minutes, then delayed the sounding of the public siren for another hour "by which time all the gas that could leak had leaked." [18]

In May of 1982, 2 1/2 years before the deadly accident, a Union Carbide Safety Audit of the Bhopal plant found "a total of 61 hazards, 30 of them major and 11 of them in the dangerous Phosgene/Methyl Isocyanate units."[19] The report was sent to senior Union Carbide officials marked "Business Confidential." The company had also been forewarned of the potential for runaway reactions in MIC storage tanks by its own Safety and Health Inspectors in Institute, West Virginia. The report was not forwarded to the Bhopal plant.

The Indian Government then appropriated sole power to represent the Bhopal victims and, in place of the $35 billion awards sought by Belli and other American attorneys, filed suit against Union Carbide for $3 billion, then settled for a total sum of $470 million, or $350 per victim. Of the settlement, $200 million was covered by Union Carbide's insurance and $200 million had been set aside by the company to cover the liability. Union Carbide described the settlement as "fair and reasonable." [20] Its stock increased $2 a share.

Reported CorporateWatch India:

> Even today [2002], Union Carbide's toxic legacy continues to haunt the people of Bhopal. Thousands of tons of toxic wastes abandoned by Carbide at its factory site in Bhopal have leached their poisons into the groundwater feeding nearly 5000 families. Union Carbide has refused to clean up the contaminated site. Dow Chemicals, which acquired all of Carbide's assets, also has refused to accept the liabilities. [21]

In May 2003, the government of India requested extradition of Warren Anderson, ex-Chairman of Union Carbide, to face trial in Bhopal for "culpable homicide relating to the deaths of 20,000 people." In July 2003, eighteen members of Congress sent a letter to Dow Chairman William Stavropoulos demanding that his company assume liability for its Union Carbide subsidiary, provide medical rehabilitation, economic reparations for victims of the tragedy, provide alternate sources of water, and take other environmental repair actions. As of September 2003, the U.S. had made no response to the Indian government, nor has Dow Chemical to Congress.[22]

Investor Fraud – multiple culprits

The editorial and opinion pages of *The Wall Street Journal* consistently call for deregulation of business and reduced involvement of government in the marketplace.

To the attentive and regular reader of its news sections, however, the paper might be called "The Crime Street Journal," as characterized by Ralph Nader. Its readers depend on it for full and objective reporting: the good, the bad, and the ugly of business and financial news. Thus while its editorial pages promote deregulation and *laissez-faire,* its news sections report the enormous and varied forms of corporate and financial misconduct — larceny, fraud, theft, mugging, embezzlement, extortion, graft, piracy, gun-running, and treason.

The Enron Scandal, as it came to be known, filled the pages of the financial media long after the stories had been relegated to the back pages of daily newspapers and magazines. Reports of financial trickery were not limited to Enron, however. As the Securities and Exchange Commission and the investing world dug deeper, they discovered that many of the blue-chip companies of America had engaged in questionable accounting and financing practices. Where questions existed as to the legality or criminality of the schemes employed, it was obvious that investment analysts and individual investors had been deliberately misled.

In his investor newsletter, *Investment Outlook*, Bill Gross made the point that not only were investors being defrauded by deceptive financial reporting, but the United States Treasury was also being cheated.

> One could not find a more exemplary 'Honest Abe' in the financial world than Warren Buffett. His annual reports are legend and they contain not only words of bonafide investment wisdom, but self-recrimination when deemed necessary.

41

In stark contrast, however, has been the deceptive and in some cases, illegal information disseminated by some of our New Age corporate elite. *The Economist* in a February 23rd issue reported that the companies in the NASDAQ 100 for the first three quarters of 2001 reported combined <u>losses</u> to the SEC of nearly $82 billion, while at the same time reporting <u>profits</u> of $20 billion to their stockholders. *The Economist* explained the discrepancy by the companies' use of generally accepted accounting principles for regulators, and the distinctly more favorable New Age 'pro forma' accounting for owners of their shares. Charles Ponzi would undoubtedly have approved.[23]

Out of a total of 17 items listed in the "What's New" column on the front page of *The Wall Street Journal* of April 12, 2002, eight were about corporate wrongdoing such as the following:

1 The SEC accused Xerox of having 'misled and betrayed investors' with a scheme to manipulate its earnings and enrich top executives. The agency said senior Xerox officials used improper accounting techniques to accelerate the recognition of over $3 billion in equipment revenue from 1997 through 2000.
2 Computer Associates is the focus of a probe into whether it improperly boosted its financial results to help produce $1 billion in stock awards for executives.
3 Options trading in Bristol-Myers soared April 3, just before the firm issued a profit warning that sent its stock reeling the next day.
4 The IRS estimates that up to $40 billion in revenue is being lost due to tax scams. Senators unveiled a plan to curb a tax dodge.

On the same front page, two adjoining columns were devoted to "Accountability," beginning with a chart listing six top executives currently "in the federal government's sights."

Paul Allaire	Xerox	Ex-Chairman
Told he could face civil charges		
Barry Romeril	Xerox	Ex-CFO
Told he could face civil charges		
Michael Conway	KPMG	Partner

Told he could face civil charges

Dean Bruntrock Waste Management   Founder, Ex-CEO
            Accused of civil fraud
Phillip Rooney Waste Management   Ex-CEO
            Accused of civil fraud
John Donehower Kimberly-Clark   CFO
            Accused of violating reporting rules

Expanding on the Bristol-Myers item, *Wall Street Journal* writer Peter McKay asked:

> Did someone profit from early hints that Bristol-Myers Squibb Co. shares would tumble last week? Options trading in Bristol-Myers' stock soared 40% above its daily average on April 3 – just before the drug company announced a steep earnings shortfall and the firing of its pharmaceutical-operations chief. [24]

An Enron-related story relegated to the back pages of the April 12th issue was of particular interest to Californians who had seen electric power bills jump several hundred to up to a thousand percent higher with deregulation. How could power produced and sold profitably in June at 10 cents a kilowatt hour cost 10 dollars a kilowatt hour in November? From *Wall Street Journal* Reporter Greg Hitt:

> Power trading back and forth among affiliates of Enron Corp. stoked the energy crisis that gripped California during the fall of 2,000.
>   Loretta Lynch, president of the California Public Utilities Commission, said Enron swapped the same power repeatedly among affiliates as part of a scheme to drive up the wholesale price of electricity and create turmoil in the West Coast energy market. [25]

The standard phrase appended to most settlements of corporate wrongdoing is some variation of, "The company neither admits nor denies guilt," as in the following:

> Xerox Corp. agreed to settle Securities and Exchange Commission accusations that it improperly recognized lease revenue over the last five years and said it will pay a $10 million fine. Xerox didn't admit or deny the SEC's accusations, which include claims of civil violations of the antifraud, reporting and other provisions of the securities laws. [26]

Only the stockholders of Xerox suffered from the fraud and settlement. The fine reduced dividends and may have depressed the stock's market value. The officers of the company that perpetrated the fraud will not be punished nor will they pay out of their personal funds any portion of the fine. If they shrewdly timed their exercise of stock options they may have personally profited from the illegal acts.

In the case of Enron, two years after the initial revelations of fraud appeared, the CEO, Ken Lay, had not faced criminal charges for what he and his firm did to California utility customers or to the company's investors. They may never come before the bar of justice, for courts have struggled to define corporate crime since corporations were first created.

Reacting to the Enron outrage, Fortune magazine revisited an article they had published in 1999 "about some accounting bad guys who seemed to have airtight cases against them. Guess how many went to jail?"

> Raise your hand if you think one or more Enron executives should go to jail. The yes votes on that one would surely put President Bush's approval ratings to shame. We might even get past 99.99% affirmative, with only the Lay, Skilling and Fastow [Enron executives] families voting no.
>
> But the fact is that putting bigtime executives in jail for perpetrating accounting frauds has proved very hard to do. Some 1 1/2 years ago Fortune … spotlighted the accounting scandals of the time. Of the big ones then generating tales of absolutely egregious behavior, none has produced jail sentences. [27]

Racketeering – Bankers Trust

In 1993, Proctor & Gamble was looking for a way to lower the rate at which it borrowed money. It was what *Business Week* described as "an active and sophisticated player in the financial markets … and it carefully managed its financing costs." When it entered into an agreement with

Bankers Trust for derivatives contracts, it became a victim of what P&G alleged was "a pattern of mail, wire, and securities fraud spanning a number of years and involving multiple victims." [28]

Business Week described evidence provided by a recording system that bank and investment firms routinely use to settle disputes involving transactions.

> It's Nov. 2, 1993, and two employees of Bankers Trust Co. are discussing a leveraged derivative deal the bank had recently sold to Proctor & Gamble Co. "They would never know. They would never be able to know how much money was taken out of that," says one employee, referring to the huge profits the bank stood to make on the transaction. "Never, no way, no way," replies her colleague. "That's the beauty of Bankers Trust." [29]

After reviewing 6500 hours of tapes and 300,000 pages of evidence, P&G asked the court to add RICO (racketeer-influenced and corrupt organization) charges to its lawsuit over a $102 million after-tax loss on derivatives sold by the bank. One piece of evidence cited was a training film in which a Bankers Trust spokesman told the trainees, "What Bankers Trust can do for Sony and IBM is get in the middle and rip them off – take a little money." [30]

"Fraud was so pervasive and institutionalized," charged P&G, "that Bankers Trust employees used the acronym 'ROF' – short for rip-off factor, to describe one method of fleecing clients." [31] One piece of evidence offered was an internal bank document describing a proposed derivative for another of the bank's clients. The memo gloated that the deal would make the bank $1.6 million thanks to a "'7 basis point rip-off factor.'"

"In a different instance," says P&G, "two Bankers employees are discussing a client's loss on a trade. One tells the other: 'Pad the number a little bit.' Then P&G quotes another bank employee: "Funny business, you know? Lure people into that calm and then just totally f--- 'em." [32]

Taped conversations between Bankers Trust employees laid bare an almost school-boy glee over their scam. Reports Business Week: "The second employee ...says P&G undertook an option trade as part of a derivatives contract, and Bankers Trust paid P&G only half what the option was worth. The employee allegedly remarks: 'This could be a massive huge future gravy train ... this is a wet dream.'" [33]

"Bankers concedes that some of the taped conversations 'were irresponsible and regrettable'" reported the magazine. But then Bankers notes in its defense, "Rather than putting its own house in order, and accepting its losses, P&G chose instead to bring this lawsuit." [34, b]

Treason – multiple perpetrators

Of all crimes committed against the social order, none except murder is considered as heinous as trading with the enemy in time of war and nothing more despicable than betrayal for money, as Judas betrayed Jesus. When human traitors are convicted of treason, as were Ethyl and Julius Rosenberg in their 1951 spy case, the sentence is death. Not so for corporations.

In one Trading With The Enemy case, the U.S. Department of Justice sought and won a guilty plea for violations of the 1986 Presidential embargo restricting trade with Libya. The penalty? The two convicted businessmen agreed to pay a $5,000 fine and were each sentenced to three years probation. [35]

In this day of globalization, treasonous trade is not unusual. From a CBS2 Investigation aired in February, 2002:

> In the late '90's computer manufacturers Gateway and Dell were caught selling restricted computer equipment to terrorist nations like Iran and Syria. Around the same time, a subsidiary of industrial giant IBM was caught exporting technology for the manufacture of nuclear weapons to a Russian lab. And, while it wasn't selling to a terrorist-sponsoring nation, two years ago pharmaceutical leader Bayer was busted for exporting materials used in the manufacture of biological and chemical weapons. [36]

"In virtually every case where a big company has gotten caught," said government watchdog Gary Milhollin quoted in the CBS2 report, "the company simply writes a check, and the check isn't very big, and they just look on it as the cost of doing business." [37]

---

[b] Business Week's reports of the P&G/Bankers Trust suit was itself the subject of court action for having allegedly disobeyed a court order sealing the documents relating to the RICO charges. See "Business Week VS. The Judge," Business Week, October 16, 1995.

Joining Libya on the government's current [2002] "enemy list" are Iran, Burma, Nigeria, and Cuba. Despite that, petroleum/gas giant Unocal co-owns a billion-dollar natural gas pipeline in Burma in partnership with the military dictatorship that the U.S. State Department says provided slave labor to build the pipeline. Mobil and Texaco have major investments in Nigeria; Caterpillar has a major dealership in Burma. Between 1992 and 1994, Boeing sold one tenth of its airline production to China. [38]

Libya is especially attractive to petroleum companies because "Libyan oil is cheap to extract, of high quality, and close to European markets," as described by the BBC in a February 1, 2002 broadcast. Despite President Reagan's description of Libyan leader Muammar al-Gaddafi as "this evil man" after U.S. intelligence linked Libya to a deadly disco bombing in Berlin, U.S. petroleum companies actively pursue working relationships with Libya, circumventing the D'Amato-Kennedy Act of the 104th Congress prohibiting trade with that nation.

Not treasonous, but disdainful of the nation's security are those enterprises that overcharge for defense goods, deliver faulty war materials, insert non-related costs into defense contract invoices, and defraud the military establishment.

From "A Year In Corporate Crime," *The Nation,* August 20, 2001:

> Surprise! Arms Merchants Cheat. When one of the bolts holding a 500-pound Maverick missile to the wing of a military plane breaks, and the missile is left dangling, attached by only the remaining bolt – and when that sort of accident begins to happen rather often – you'd think the Pentagon's sleuths would quickly find out what the hell was going on. But it took the military years to figure out that United Telecontrol Electronics was knowingly using defective bolts to hold the launchers in place. Phony computer-controlled measurements made it look like the parts had passed inspection. [39]

And:

> The Navy blames defective gearboxes on Navy F-18 fighters for seventy-one emergency landings and several in-flight fires, as well as the loss of an F-18 during the Gulf War. They came to that conclusion after inspecting 150 gearboxes and finding that all – 100 percent – were defective. Lucas Industries pleaded guilty to falsifying quality records.... [40]

From *The Wall Street Journal:*
> A federal judge awarded $11.5 million to a former General Electric Co. employee for exposing a defense-contract fraud at the company." [41]

The last item is particularly damning considering GE's extensive history of criminal wrongdoing. After reporting on the $69 million in fines and penalties paid by GE to settle civil and criminal charges, the story also noted that rather than expressing regret and chagrin over its fraud, the company challenged the law that tripped it up: "The award prompted GE, based in Fairfield, Conn., to renew its call for reform of the False Claims Act." [42]

On one 1988 page of Facts on File:

> **Northrup Corporation** fined $17 million for fraud; **Sundstrand** paid a settlement for defense-fraud of $115 million; **Norden Systems** involved in conspiracy and conversion of government property in a $100 million **Marine Corps** contract; two **Teledyne Electronics** executives' conviction for fraud was upheld; **Hughes Aircraft, Raytheon, Boeing, RCA Corp.,** Grumman Corp. and more pled guilty to fraud and were fined a total of another $8.67 million. [43]

The illegal acts noted above involved theft from the U.S. Treasury. Worse, they put lives at risk, and undermined the nation's military fitness.

Other crimes and misdemeanors

Morality and ethics in the Big Business world are probably no better or worse than those of an open-market bazaar. But Big Business crime is more destructive to society than street-corner chiseling because of the amount and breadth of damage done to competitors, the industries themselves, as well as individuals, communities, states, the nation, and the world.

Malefactors are often honored and respected brands and corporations. Again, from "A Year In Corporate Crime":

• Archer Daniels Midland (ADM), the world's largest grain processor. The company pleaded guilty to criminal price fixing and paid an anti-trust penalty seven times larger than the largest fine ever before levied, $100 million.

- Metropolitan Life, largest stock insurance company in America, fined $20 million for cheating its customers.
- Prudential Insurance, 2nd largest insurer, fined $35 million plus required to pay more than $1 billion in restitution to policy holders.
- Mutual of New York, paid $12.5 million to customers in a settlement characterized by *The Wall Street Journal* as "the latest in a series involving alleged deceptive sales practices at many of the nation's biggest insurers."
- SmithKline Beecham's clinical laboratory unit was close to a $300 million settlement over bilking Medicare for unneeded blood tests.
- Corning paid $6.8 million to settle allegations that its Bioran Medical Laboratory regularly billed Medicare for blood tests doctors hadn't requested. Eight months later Corning was forced to pay $119 million to settle charges of fraudulent billing of Medicare by its Damon Clinical Laboratory subsidiary. *The Wall Street Journal* noted that Corning had previously paid $39.8 million in 1993, and $8.6 million in 1995 to settle Medicare fraud charges. [44]

What must again be emphasized is that the fines and court judgments levied against corporate criminals are not paid by the officers who initiated, approved, or stood silent as these illegal acts were committed. Only the investors are stung, paying the price for criminal wrongdoing in lost dividends and reduced stock value. Culpable executives rarely suffer damage even to their reputations. In short, corporate crime is a "win-win" situation for the criminals, and a "lose-lose" situation for stockholders and taxpayers.

It's obvious, however, that the fault – the tendency or impetus toward illegal behavior — does not simply lie with "bad apples" in the corporate barrel. The crimes of General Electric, for example, spanned more than 50 years, six or seven chief executives and dozens if not hundreds of lesser officers. Yet in spite of fines levied against the organization, and jail time, dishonor, and embarrassment for officers, corporate crime continues as if it were genetically implanted in the corporate organism. Perhaps it is.

Criminal Negligence
A chilling history of the chemical industry's conspiracy to hide health dangers was presented by journalist, author, and public policy maven Bill Moyers in "Trade Secrets: A Moyers Report," initially aired on PBS television stations March 26, 2001.

When the chemical industry's own scientists discovered that certain compounds caused sterility, liver cancer, brain cancer, and disintegration of the bones in employees exposed to high concentrations of highly profitable chemicals, they hid the information, rather than reduce exposure and attempt to mitigate the damage. Further, they failed to inform the government agency charged with monitoring chemical safety of their findings.

Vinyl Chloride

Much of Moyers' material originated from a 1998 investigative series published by The Houston (Texas) Chronicle: "In strictest confidence: The Chemical Industries' Secrets," under the byline of Jim Morris. The series focused on health hazards created in the production of vinyl chloride and the chemical industry efforts to keep that information from its plant workers and public.

Morris's reports were based on material unearthed through the dogged enterprise of Houston attorney William Baggett, Jr., pursuing a client's suit for damages for cancer contracted, they believed, as a result of working in Conoco's Lake Charles, Louisiana, chemical plant.

Over a ten year-long process of discovery, Baggett acquired an estimated one million memos, reports, and minutes of chemical industry meetings documenting the industry's knowledge of vinyl chloride's destructiveness to human health and its attempts to bury that information. Wrote Morris: "Major chemical manufacturers closed ranks in the late 1950s to contain and counteract evidence of vinyl chloride's toxic effects." [45]

Dow Chemical Company's research labs informed management via a July 3rd, 1958, memo that prolonged exposure to a key ingredient in vinyl chloride, DBCP, could cause atrophy of the testicles. They recommended an exposure standard of no more than 1 part per million. According to Moyers' report, after learning of the medical problem, "Dow ... did not reduce exposure [of its workers] to DBCP...." [46]

Twenty years later, DBCP production process were little changed. Scientists at another producer, Occidental Petroleum, informed management that their plants were contaminating not only their own wells but all the water wells in the area. They warned: "THIS IS A TIME BOMB THAT WE MUST DE-FUSE." [47]

Late in 1971, twenty vinyl chloride-producing companies met to hear a report from a leading European scientist who theorized that vinyl chloride was absorbed by body fats and carried to the brain. Again, from Moyers: "...The companies took no action — and told no one." [48]

The Houston Chronicle reported:

> Thirty-one former executives of two Italian chemical companies are standing trial and may go to jail for ignoring warnings and allowing their employees to breathe horrific amounts of vinyl chloride and its relative, ethylene dichloride...." 'Cagionavano il delitto di strage,' the *indictment* reads. 'They caused the crime of massacre.'
>
> More than 150 former workers at the plant — owned first by Montedison, then Enichem — have died of cancer since 1973, and another 600 or so are thought to be suffering from work-related illness. [49]

The U.S. industry fought to keep the dangers of vinyl chloride production hidden despite clear evidence from their own scientists in the 1960's and '70's that it was carcinogenic and caused the bones in workers' fingers to dissolve (acroosteolysis). According to the Moyers' Report, the companies continued to produce and sell DBCP well into the 1980's.

Benzene

Benzene has been a known toxic since the late '50's, with a mounting body of evidence linking it to leukemia. The chemical industries own researchers warned of the dangers it posed. From a 1958, internal Esso Oil medical research division memo: "Most authorities agree the only level which can be considered absolutely safe for prolonged exposure is zero."[50]

When OSHA (Occupational Safety and Health Administration) ordered in 1977,that workplace exposure be limited to one part per million, the chemical industry went to court asserting that the new limits on benzene exposure "would represent an intolerable misallocation of economic resources." [51]

The companies named as conspirators in the Moyers' Report — B.F. Goodrich, Conoco, Dow, Ethyl Corp., Imperial Chemical Industries, Monsanto, and Union Carbide — are long established, respected members of the corporate community. Yet their official policy, arrived at jointly in "confidential" sessions, was to withhold health and safety information from the public and fight strenuously all federal and state attempts to regulate their dangerous practices.

Sadly, thousands of incidents similar to those related within this chapter take place every year. Rarely a week goes by that the media does not report on another respected business organization charged with or convicted of cheating consumers, stockholders, taxpayers, the government, or the country.

Are chemical corporate executives uncaring brutes, completely evil or merely irresponsible? Are the people who direct or approve these crimes flawed human beings, unable to live within society's moral norms? Or are they more or less willing agents of a power stronger than they can resist; captives of the corporation? How do they reconcile the human suffering they cause with their personal moral values?

Whatever the rationale, we must understand that the future of our nation, how we and our children's children will live, is determined by executives driven by the same moral code that stripped the flesh from chemical workers' bones, cheated insurance customers, caused the deaths of thousands in Bhopal, and defrauded Enron's stockholders and employees of billions.

Can capitalism survive this kind of behavior? Can we?

"Harper, we'd like you to become the company fall guy. The position comes with a generous severance package."

[1] "America's Most Admired Companies," *Fortune* Magazine, June 18, 2001.

[2] "Antitrust: What's Contempt?" Business and Finance, *Newsweek*, 1/8/62.

[3] "The Incredible Electrical Conspiracy," by Richard Austin Smith, *Fortune*, April 1961.

[4] "After the Great Conspiracy", Business, *Time*, 2/24/61.

[5] Op Cit, "The Incredible Electrical Conspiracy," by Richard Austin Smith

[6] "Like A Good Neighbor...?, Association of Trial Lawyers of America, posted July 5, 2000, to ATLA Consumer & Media Resources.

[7] "Class Action Lawsuit Claims State Farm Has A Secret Policy to Reject Claims of Its Policyholders," press release by Stritmatter Kessler Whelan Withey Coluccio, April 10, 2000.

[8] Third Judicial District, Salt Lake City, Utah, Civil Case No. 890905231, filed August 3, 1998; Curtis B. Campbell and Inez Preece Campbell, plaintiffs.

[9] Ibid..

[10] Drawn from: "Bhopal: The Struggle Continues," CorporateWatch India Web site, updated to March 2002; "A History of Massacre," PP#15, 16, bhopal. net.

[11] "Grief Turns to Anxiety in Bhopal," by William Claiborne, *Washington Post*, January 27, 1985.

[12] "Regulatory Void Cited in U.S. Gas Leaks," *Washington Post*, December 6, 1984.

[13] "Two Indian Plant Workers Fled During Gas Leak, Officials Say," *Washington Post*, December 6, 1984.

[14] "Toxic-Gas Disaster Possible Here," *Washington Post*, December 6, 1984.

[15] "Buck Stops at Carbide," *Washington Post*, December 13, 1984.

[16] "Duty to India Victims Cited," *Washington Post*, December 11, 1984.

[17] "Bhopal Journalist, Administrator Questioned Safety of Pesticide Plant," *Washington Post*, December 11, 1984.

[18] "History of A Massacre," PP#3, PP#6 bhopal.net/ucc25

[19] Ibid, PP#12, bhopal.net/ucc25

[20] Ibid, PPs 7, 8, 13, bhopal.net/ucc25 and "Bhopal's Legacy" by Sandhya Srinivasan, CorporateWatch India, December 6, 2001

[21] "Bhopal: The Struggle Continues," Issue Library: Bhopal, CorporateWatch India, updated 3/23/2002.

[22] From Bhopal.net site, 9/2/2003

[23] "Buffetting Corporate America," by Bill Gross, *Investment Outlook*, March 2002.

[24] "CBOE IS Probing Big Bristol 'Puts' Before Stock Drop", by Meter McKay, *The Wall Street Journal*, April 12, 2002.

[25] "Enron's 'Sham' Trading Fueled West's Power Crisis, Officials Say," by Greg Hitt, *The Wall Street Journal*, April 12, 2002, page A4

[26] "Xerox Agrees to Settle Charges of Improper Revenue Recognition, *The Wall Street Journal* Online, April 1, 2002.

[27] "Hard Time? Hardly," by Carol J. Loomis, *Fortune*, March 18, 2002

[28] "The Bankers Trust Tapes," *Business Week*, October 16, 1995.

[29] Ibid.

[30] Ibid.

[31] Ibid.

[32] Ibid.

[33] Ibid.

[34] Ibid

[35] "Guilty Pleas In Trading With Libya Prosecution," news release of October 12, 2001, from U.S. Department of Justice, United States Attorney, Southern District of Texas.

[36] "Trading With The Enemy; Are America's Best Known Companies Supporting Terrorist Nations?" CBS2, with John Slattery, New York, February 1, 2002.

[37] Ibid.

[38] "So You Want To Trade With a Dictator," by Ken Silverstein, *Mother Jones* magazine, June 1998.

[39] "A Year In Corporate Crime," by Robert Sherrill, *The Nation*, April 7, 1997, found at www.contentville.com/efull/archives/9703

[40] ibid

[41] "Whistle-Blower At GE to GET $11.5 Million," by Amal Kumar Naj, *The Wall Street Journal*, April 26, 1993.

[42] Ibid.

[43] Facts on File, Rand McNally & Company

[44] Op cit, "A Year in Corporate Crime," by Robert Sherrill, *The Nation*

[45] "Toxic Secrecy", of the series "in strictest confidence; The chemical industry's secrets," by Jim Morris, © 1998 *Houston Chronicle*

[46] Ibid.

[47] Ibid.

[48] Op cit. Transcript, "Trade Secrets" A Moyers Report."

[49] "High-Level Crime," of the series "in strictest confidence; The chemical industry's secrets," by Jim Morris, © 1998 *Houston Chronicle*

[50] Ibid.

[51] Ibid.

CHAPTER FIVE
CRIME AND PUNISHMENT

Can a corporation commit a crime?

> Only dim echoes linger today in the jurisprudence of the
> United States, England, and Canada of the once-intense
> debate about whether it is proper - ethically, juridically,
> and in terms of effectiveness — to punish a corporation
> criminally rather than, or in addition to, punishing
> individuals within it. [1]

So begins "Should We Prosecute Corporations and/or Individuals?", a
critique of the principles of corporate criminal liability by Gilbert Geis and
Joseph Dimento of the University of California at Irvine.

For years there has been a running debate whether a corporation could
commit a crime requiring criminal intent. How could a legal fiction, a
creature of words on paper, have "intent" to do anything? Crimes can
be committed only by the humans directing the organization into illegal
actions.

On the other hand, one might ask, how can a corporation without a
brain, breath, or larynx of its own have the right of "free speech" granted
by the highest court in the land?

"But now," writes B. Coleman in the *Southwestern Law Journal,* "it is
almost unquestioned that an agent's intent, knowledge, or willfulness may
be imputed to the corporation." [2]

Write Geis and Dimento:

> The rationale that has led to far-ranging corporate criminal
> liability was set out by a Canadian court, which noted that
> corporations are "more powerful and more materially
> endowed and equipped than are individuals and, if
> allowed to roam unchecked in the field of industry and
> commerce, they are potentially more dangerous and can
> inflict greater harm upon the public than can their weaker
> competitors." [3]

A similar view was expressed by the judge in *United States v. Hilton
Hotels Corp,* (1972), cited by Geis and Dimento.

The judge insisted that it was "reasonable to assume" that Congress had intended to "impose liability upon business entities for the acts of those to whom they chose to delegate their affairs...." Yet the same judge noted, "legal commentators have argued forcefully that it is inappropriate and ineffective to impose criminal liability upon a corporation, as distinguished from human agents who actually perform the illegal act." [4]

Authorities hold that it is public anger over corporate offenses that stimulates legislative action, note Geis and Dimento, creating laws that impose criminal liability to support government regulations. Yet, "the law has developed the concept of corporate criminal liability without rhyme or reason, proceeding by a hit or miss method, unsupported by economic or sociological data," writes G. Mueller in *The University of Pittsburgh Law Review 19.* [5]

While the law may hold that corporations can commit criminal acts, this view is strongly resisted by the business community itself. "Corporations Aren't Criminals" wrote Louisiana State University law professor and consultant to the Reagan Justice Department John S. Baker, Jr., in a *Wall Street Journal* "op-ed" piece.

The Justice Department can cite precedents and statutes that justify criminal prosecutions of business entities. Indeed, federal prosecutors have been indicting corporations for decades, usually under the auspices of the 1970 Racketeer Influenced and Corrupt Organizations Act. Two justifications are most often carted out. First, the complexity of modern corporations is said to justify criminal liability due to the difficulty of proving the responsibility of a particular individual. Second, it is argued, corporations ought not to benefit from the criminal acts of their agents.

What prosecutors seem to have forgotten, however, is that individuals – not organizations – commit crimes. Under the common law, a corporation could not be guilty of a crime because it could not possess mens rea, a guilty mind. Generally speaking, the moral basis of criminal law,[is] the requirement of personal moral fault. [6]

What Is Corporate Crime?

Just what is "corporate crime?" Steven Box, author of *Power, Crime and Mystification,* defines corporate crime as:

> Illegal acts of omission or commission of an individual or group of individuals in a legitimate formal organization, in accordance with the goals of that organization, which have a serious physical or economic impact on employees, consumers, ... the general public and other organizations.[7]

The key phrase differentiating corporate crime from street crime is "illegal acts of omission or commission." Most interesting is the concept of "acts of omission." Not doing something is rarely a crime in a social or civic sense. No harm occurs when a robbery is not committed, for example. Yet harm may be done if a chemical company fails to communicate to employees or the public the dangers inherent in the handling of its products, or if a company fails to fully disclose its financial condition in reports to the stockholders.

The second key phrase is "in accordance with the goals of that organization." Box contends that it is an organization's objectives that determine criminal intent.

When computer code written by a small software developer intentionally limits the application's ability to function with other software, no harm is done except, perhaps, to the developer itself. Potential users may not buy the product because of its lack of compatibility.

But the concept of anti-competitive activity changes dramatically when a company such as computer industry giant Microsoft commands an 80%+ share of the market. If in the creation of its "Windows" operating system it intentionally includes code making it difficult to use anything but other Microsoft products for other user functions — an internet browser, for example — an anti-competitive "crime" may be committed.

The court must determine if the product was intentionally designed to stymie or limit competition or only an unwitting result. If the court decides the exclusionary code was part of the dominant company's product development plan, the company is deemed to have created an illegal monopoly. But even if the competition-limiting exclusion was not intentional the court may require the company to "unbundle" or remove exclusionary parts of the program. The rationale is that users must have a choice. This is an approximation of key issues in the anti-trust cases brought against Microsoft in 1998 by the U.S. Justice Department's Anti-Trust division and a number of state Attorneys General.

Corporate crime goes beyond "street crime" to include ethics, morality, and a multitude of government regulations. People generally accept a certain level of dissembling, exaggeration, and hyperbole in people-to-people relations. But when a corporation deceives, it generally costs someone money.

From a *Wall Street Journal* report:

> Merrill Lynch & Co. agreed to pay a $100 million fine and change how it monitors its stock analysts, to settle the New York State Attorney General's inquiry into allegations that the nation's largest brokerage firm misled individual investors about the stock of its investment-banking clients. [8]

The State of New York levied the fine based on evidence that Merrill's stock analysts promoted certain stocks to small investors to strengthen its investment-banking relationships with the companies being analyzed. The analysts would issue a "buy" recommendation to Merrill Lynch's brokers despite the analysts' own doubts about the worth of the stock. Entered as evidence by the state were e-mails such as one from Merrill's star analyst, Henry Blodget, to a colleague, referring to an Internet stock to which the firm had given a "buy" recommendation as a "piece of shit."

Merrill duped small investors into buying stocks which its own analysts felt were overpriced and/or worthless in order to reap profits from its investment-banking unit. The firm accepted the fine as a "settlement" but denied any wrongdoing, the usual corporate stance in these cases.

Unlike fraud committed by a human person, business fraud is usually subject to regulatory rather than criminal law. As to the ethics of the firm's actions, consider first that there is no law preventing a brokerage firm from having investment-banking clients. Second, being an investment banker is far more profitable than being a stock broker.

The firm's objective is to attract and hold on to its highly profitable investment-banking clients. It extends credit to those clients using their stock as collateral. It has a powerful incentive to protect its loan by promoting the debtors' stock to investors. It's good business even though it creates a conflict of interest.

The dilemma facing Merrill Lynch's chief executive is which has the higher priority, the traditional activity on which the firm's reputation and power is based, or its investment banker activity? His responsibility to Merrill Lynch stockholders is to produce profits. Stockholders have no concern with the source of the profit, only the amount. Investment banking creates the greater share of profits but also the greater potential for loss.

On the other hand is the firm's duty to its investor customers. It promises to guide them intelligently and honestly into secure and possibly profitable stock holdings. Yet it may be impossible to accomplish both of these objectives and maintain the firm's integrity.

Another factor: what's the risk to the CEO should fraud be discovered and prosecuted? Except for embarrassment, the answer is little or none. "The history of punishment in corporate cases is not very good," according to Stephen Meagher, an ex-federal prosecutor quoted in The New York Times. "These are complex schemes, and it's sometimes difficult to unwind them from an investigative standpoint and ultimately explain them to a jury."

The article explained:

> Prosecutors have to prove that defendants intend to defraud, not just that people lost their life savings by believing what they said. Money missing from the cash register is a crime; money missing from an investment might not be.
>
> So corporate criminal cases often revolve around a concept called 'professional reliance' – meaning that everything the executive did was first approved by accountants and lawyers, so there could not be the intent to commit a crime. [9]

Finally, even if the prosecution is successful in proving both criminal act and intent, the punishment meted out is hardly crippling. Again, from *The New York Times* article:

> Officers with Archer Daniels Midland Company were caught red-handed on audio and videotape, rigging prices of agricultural products with competitors to steal millions from their own customers. A federal judge sentenced the two ringleaders to only two years in prison, in part citing their history of charitable contributions – arguably made with money they obtained illicitly. An outraged appeal court increased the sentence to the statutory maximum of three years each. Again, executives who effectively cheated every grocery store in the country received shorter sentences than if they had robbed just one. [10]

The disparity between punishment for white-collar and street crime, as many writers have pointed out, is enormous. So when a notorious case such as that of Enron et al comes to the public's attention, calls for stronger punishment escalate. "Pursuit of corporate crime can't end with Enron," was the title of a *USA Today* editorial page debate. "Otherwise, companies will have nothing to fear in breaking the law." [11]   Accompanying the editorial was a table entitled "White-collar wrist slaps" charting the sentence for robbery at an average of 108 months, and for fraud, the most common white-collar crime, 13.2 months. White-collar fraud might steal the life savings from thousands if not hundreds of thousands of people while robbery steals from only one.

> Fines tend to be easily absorbed by companies found guilty
> of wrongdoing. Just 10 companies paid fines of more than
> $50 million in the 1990s, according to *Corporate Crime
> Reporter* – a pittance for firms that measure revenue in
> the billions. [12]

Opposing *USA Today's* support for harsher penalties, Merrill Mathews, Jr., visiting scholar with the Dallas Institute for Policy Innovation, declared, "Risk-taking is not a crime. The country must be careful that 'reform' efforts don't make it so." His viewpoint was that "Occasionally, risk-takers fail. They make bad decisions or are caught short by changes in the economic climate. Some may even break the law either before or after the fall." [13]

Mathews apparently equates theft by fraud with normal but risky business activities, then suggested that Enron's officers had suffered sufficient punishment by having their failure and/or fraud exposed. "Ken Lay and the Enron executives have lost everything and have suffered national disgrace." [14]

In New York State's case against Merrill Lynch, the fine was levied against the firm, not the CEO or officers of the firm. The court determined that the corporation, not its managers, was at fault.

In fact, rarely do corporations or their officers suffer any consequence for illegal acts. Only the stockholders, total innocents with no complicity in the fraud, take a hit. In a letter to *The New York Times* Money & Business section, chairman of the House Financial Services Committee, Michael G. Oxley,(R-Ohio), observed:

Merrill Lynch's investors know that, in addition to the penalty, they have suffered market losses totaling about $10.3 billion (yes, billion) in recent weeks, largely due to the New York attorney general's foray into the company's activities. All of this comes directly from the hides of investors, who, by the way, will not receive one dollar of the settlement: it goes to the states. [15]

Even if the stockholders had known about the incestuous relationship between Merrill Lynch's analysts and its investment banking subsidiary, there was not a thing they could have done about it. Despite their purported ownership of a corporation, stockholders can exercise no control after a corporation has millions of shares of stock outstanding and tens of thousands of shareholders. Moreover, they have no effective voice in selecting the leadership, officers, and board members of a corporation, nor any influence in keeping them honest.

A study published in *The Academy of Management Journal* and conducted by Melissa S. Baucus and David A. Baucus of Utah State University compared the performance of 68 convicted corporate lawbreakers with those of 250 corporations with no major infractions of the law. They found that convicted firms consistently lagged behind their peers in sales growth and returns on both assets and sales. In cases of criminal fraud and/or product liability suits, the firms suffered noticeably at the bottom line.[16]

Consider the business climate in which the CEO of Merrill Lynch works and competes and what must be the focus of his power as CEO.

During the stock market boom [of the 1990's], nearly every public company, from the most admired to the most reviled, was gripped by an unhealthy obsession with earnings growth. [17i]

Like any other publicly owned corporation, Merrill Lynch was caught up in "The Earnings Cult," as New York Times Magazine author Harris Collingwood titled his analysis of the '90's market meltdown.

Continued earnings growth ensures their company's access to affordable sources of capital. It also enables executives to keep their jobs and collect stock options and other earnings-related incentives. [18]

Merrill Lynch's market value – the value of its stock — depends solely upon the sum of its earnings, not how it achieved them. "In recent years, earnings have so dominated the financial conversation that it's hard to remember that there are other ways to judge and compare corporate performance," Collingwood concluded. [19]

With 70% of the firm's profits derived from investment banking, it's easy to understand why the CEO of Merrill Lynch did everything possible to maximize that aspect of its business. Profit is the inescapable *sine qua non* of why he is being paid by the shareholders. Merrill Lynch's standing in the investment community and the CEO's own reputation among the highest achievers in the world of finance hang on that one criterion. Little wonder that he leaned on Merrill's stock analysts to hype the stock of their investment banking clients. To do less would have been, in a purely business sense, irresponsible.

On the other side of that equation is the investor relying upon Merrill Lynch to deliver honest, if not prescient, evaluations on the stock it recommends they buy. In public relations material the CEO acknowledges individual investors as the source of Merrill's position of leadership in the industry. But individual investors – the moms and pops saving for the kids' college education or their own retirement — are far below the threshold of his everyday concerns. Merrill's investor customers are faceless numbers. But he and his minions meet the heads of investment banking clients frequently and face to face. For all his elevated position, the CEO is only human. He is judged by his peers. He takes care of the people he knows, the ones in front of him, not the faceless customers he'll never meet.

One final consideration in the "right or wrong" equation: firms may earn higher margins of profit through ignoring regulations than by following them. This is particularly true in heavy industry, manufacturing, and chemical fields, but it extends to small business as well. Regulatory agencies are notoriously understaffed and deliberately kept that way until an epidemic of misdeeds, such as the 2002-3 broker-banker scandals catch Congress's attention. Thus, for most, being caught in infractions of regulations is an infrequent, if ever, occurrence and the cost of whatever fines are levied can generally be absorbed as a cost of doing business.

Except for the executives and corporations caught in high-profile cases, there's little risk to reputations. The business community is generally hostile to government regulation and sees no breach of ethics or etiquette in breaking them. The attitude is often "there but for the grace of God go I."

Firms charged and convicted of the more serious crimes of fraud, price-fixing, anti-trust, etc. may suffer some loss of clientele or confidence, as noted above in the Baucus & Baucus study. In law firms or the accounting professions the damage may be more severe. The very nature of their business is based on probity and maintaining professional standards.

Over the past 40 years, conservative business interests have mounted a heavily funded campaign to discredit government in general and government regulations in particular. Writes Sally Covington, Director of the Democracy and Philanthropy Project of the National Committee for Responsive Philanthropy:

> Spearheading the assault has been a core group of 12 conservative foundations: the Lynde and Harry Bradley Foundation, the Carthage Foundation, the Earhart Foundation, the Charles G. Koch, David H. Koch and Claud R. Lambe charitable foundations, the Phillip M. McKenna Foundation, the JM Foundation, the John M. Olin Foundation, The Henry Salvatori Foundation, the Sarah Scaife Foundation and the Smith Richardson Foundation. In 1994, they controlled more than $1.1 billion in assets; from 1992-94 they awarded $300 million in grants, and targeted $210 million to support a wide array of projects and institutions.
>
> Over the last two decades, the 12 have mounted an impressively coherent and concerted effort to shape public policy by undermining – and ultimately redirecting – what they regard as the institutional strongholds of modern American liberalism.... They channeled some $80 million to right-wing policy institutions actively promoting an anti-government, unregulated markets agenda.... The proliferation and continued heavy funding of policy institutions such as the American Enterprise Institute (AEI) and the Heritage Foundation... flood the media with hundreds of opinion editorials.... Their top staff appear as political pundits and policy experts on dozens of television and radio shows.... And their lobbyists work the legislative areas, distributing policy proposals, briefing papers, and position statements. [20]

John David Rose

The constant drum-beat of anti-regulation, anti-tax, anti-government propaganda has had a profound effect on Main Street. Today there's little acknowledgement among business people of the huge stake they have in supporting, maintaining and enforcing standards of business conduct. Without federal and state enforcement of business law, commerce would have to be conducted like the illegal drug trade – at gunpoint. Without government agencies regulating and enforcing trade, business cannot enforce contracts, collect loans, or have any confidence in the quantity and quality suppliers deliver to them.

Small businesses that supply large businesses already know how powerless they can be in attempting to resolve disputes or even collect in a timely manner. Their biggest customers are often the slowest payers, taking advantage of the "float" to smooth out cash flow without regard to the stress this places on the smaller firm. Big buyers hold all the cards, including a cadre of lawyers should the matter end up in court. Small vendors are placed in the same position as the individual working person, told either to accept the way the big business does business or work for someone else.

Life without government oversight becomes caveat emptor – buyer beware – for consumers. The toothpaste may discolor the teeth, poison the user, and the tube contain only six ounces instead of the labeled eight, but no recourse is available except "take your business elsewhere or to the courts." Big companies can pay more lawyers for a longer time than most consumers.

As important as government oversight is in making free enterprise possible, only when things go terribly wrong does the business community support government intervention ... for "the other guy."

After the Great Crash of '29, Congress limited banks to banking – holding customer deposits and making loans. Stock brokerage services, insurance, and business opportunities outside of the traditional banking field were not allowed because of the potential for conflicts of interest — conflicts similar to that of Merrill Lynch cited previously. The banking industry chafed under the restrictions, and eventually lobbied successfully to have many of them eased or removed. Their publicity "spin" promoted added public convenience despite the fact that there was obviously no lack of brokerage services available through regular stock trading firms. The end-result of freeing up the banks from the 1930's regulations was the infamous S&L scandal of the 1980s and a seemingly never-ending series of frauds on the public since.

What Keeps Most Businesses Honest?

The conservative ethos presumes an attitude of moderation and magnanimity (i.e., a willingness to restrain one's primitive appetites in the interest of civilization), but what corporation can afford to conduct its affairs on so admirable a premise?

Lewis H. Lapham, "Eskimo Economics,"
Harpers, December 1980

"Business ethics is an oxymoron" is the wry and oft-repeated cynical observation of business writers. But are government regulations and criminal law the only things that keep business people honest? What about ethics, morality, common decency?

The "founder" of economics, Adam Smith, suggested there might be some mitigation of mankind's single-minded pursuit of self-interest. The opening passage of his first book, *The Theory of Moral Sentiments,* a treatise on ethics, begins: "How selfish soever man may be supposed, there are evidently some principles in his nature which interest him in the fortune of others...."

Growing up in a "corporate" home — a small corporation, but listed on the American Stock Exchange — I saw firsthand how that might apply in business.

My father, the president of the company, was preparing for the arrival of those mysterious gods who must be appeased, "The Auditors," one of the more respected national accounting firms of that day, Ernst & Ernst. To this naïve youngster even the name seemed foreboding. Their "going over the books" to see if everyone had counted everything accurately and honestly seemed somehow insulting. That company's small administrative staff of men (mostly men in those days) who looked up from their desks or phones to smile and greet me, and the "girls," who would lean back from their typing or adding machine chores and smile: how could anyone think them capable of dishonesty?

At audit time the office would find places for a number of serious looking young men who, with desks piled high with ledgers and accounting books, kept fingers flying over adding machines and huddled with senior executives of the company. Smiles and greetings, if any, were fleeting and strained during audit season. But there would be smiles as before and relief at home when Dad announced that Ernst & Ernst had given the company a "clean" letter of approval for the annual report.

When my older brother graduated from college as an accountant and entered the business, he gave me a detailed explanation of the audit process. But it was Father's original explanation as to why an audit was necessary that stuck with me.

"It's for the owners, the stockholders."

"But I thought we owned the company."

"No, the stockholders own the company. We have stock in the company along with other people who work here. But there are other stockholders who don't work in the company but only invested in it ... put money into the company to get it started."

"Stockholders?"

"We send them a report every three months telling them what we're doing with their money. When we make a profit, we send them dividends — their share of the profit. And once a year we send them an annual report. The auditor's letter tells them that we've kept good records and that they received the appropriate amount of dividends."

"Do you know the stockholders?"

"Many of them," he replied. "But since we're traded on the stock exchange, people we don't know buy and sell the stock."

It was a stunning revelation. The company I'd always thought of as "ours" was owned by a lot of other people all over the country. I wasn't sure whether to be proud that our company was listed on the stock exchange, or humbled that my father, even with the title of "president," was only an employee like the others in the office.

From that time until the present, I also considered "The Auditors" as the "Untouchables," the FBI of the business world, hard-eyed sleuths in three-piece suits keeping shady operators honest and sloppy bookkeepers on track. My father might rant (and did) over government regulation and snooping, but there was never a question as to the need for the audit.

Then came the Enron energy trading company revelations of 2001, including the most market-shaking revelation of all: Enron's auditing firm, Arthur Andersen, had been in cahoots with their client to mislead shareholders and investors. Enron's annual reports to the stockholders were filled with deceptions and falsehoods. Millions of dollars of debt and millions of payments to company insiders had been hidden with accounting tricks, and the auditors never blew the whistle!

Arthur Andersen, the largest of America's Big Five accounting firms, had acted more like a partner than an auditor. Enron's Chief Accounting Officer summed up the relationship: "We expect them to be here and to be able to be responsive to our needs ... hopefully even being able to reach the conclusions we want."[21] An Andersen auditor working on the Enron account said: "Out here we don't call audit audit."[22] Jeffrey Skilling, Enron's president noted: "I think over time we and Arthur Andersen will probably mesh our systems and processes even more so that they are more seamless between the two organizations." [23]

Within months of the Enron/Andersen revelations came other stories of major auditing firms harmonizing too closely with their clients. "SEC's Xerox Case May Broaden to Ex-Executives and to KMPG," was the headline of the feature front-page report of *The Wall Street Journal* of April 10, 2002. Dozens of America's leading companies suddenly announced "restatements" of earnings to cover deals and debts not divulged in their annual reports. *Noted a Wall Street Journal*/NBC News poll published the following day:

> Public esteem for business leaders and executives dropped significantly following disclosures that Enron executives enriched themselves while concealing financial problems from investors, and that Enron's accountant, Arthur Andersen LLP, shredded documents pertaining to those matters. Moreover, that drop is matched by support for more government regulation. [24]

On the point of morality and ethics, the poll noted:

> Some 57% of respondents said the standards and values of corporate leaders and executives have dropped in the past 20 years... a stark reversal from four years ago, when Americans by a 53%-42% margin said business leaders' standards were the same or higher. [25]

Teeter and Hart, the pollsters conducting the survey, stated: "There is a sense that Enron is the tip of the iceberg."[26] They noted that one in four of those queried in the poll, as well as one in four who own stock, believe Enron's problems are representative of 'most' or 'many' U.S. companies.

Dishonesty in an industry is contagious, moving from the originator of fast and loose business practices outward to the entire industry. As *The Wall Street Journal* noted, several months after the Enron scandal became public, "Some critics say that Dynegy, long after Enron's collapse, is still using the aggressive accounting that was born during its heated rivalry with its crosstown rival." The Journal explained: "Dynegy and others gauged their success by comparing their performance with Enron, says Tom Matthews, a former Dynegy president. 'Enron led the game and everybody tried to keep up.'" [27]

The effect of business dishonesty, especially that of fraudulent financial reporting, moves beyond the originating industry out into the business community as a whole. In setting false standards of profitability, Enron's "success" became the standard by which investors and lenders judged totally unrelated businesses. Where profit ratios of 10 cents on the dollar were once considered generous, investors looked for those that might return triple, quadruple, or ten times that. Executive officers of even long-established companies were under pressure to raise profitability ratios to similar heights. The cost was high personally and to the companies themselves. Consider one small fall-out from WorldCom's $3 billion misrepresentation of its earnings:

> On December 6, 1999, AT&T replaced the chief of its huge business services division, Michael G. Keith, after barely nine months on the job.
>
> He was being held to WorldCom's margins and he was screaming to Armstrong that it couldn't be possible and so he got moved out.
>
> It is even possible that had it not been for AT&T's inevitable comparisons to WorldCom, [CEO and Chairman] Armstrong would not have felt compelled to set the company on the path to a three-way breakup. [28]

Estimates of investor losses resulting from restatements of earnings and misleading and fraudulent audits in the year of Enron's collapse were in the hundred billion-dollar range. Beyond the immediate losses, the loss of investor confidence caused an immediate and prolonged drop in the stock market, affecting millions of investors whose holdings were totally unrelated to Enron or the energy industry.

The cost of corporate dishonesty goes far beyond the pockets of shareholders in miscreant companies. It creates an economic tidal wave that slams the entire nation, from industrial sector to consuming public.

"What If Investors Won't Join the Party? Mistrust May Be Spoiling the Recovery," headlined *The New York Times* "Money & Business" section.

Even as economic output surges and corporate profits appear once more to be rising, one closely watched indicator of economic oomph remains depressed, the broad stock market indexes.... If stocks remain stuck in their underlying slump, consumers may rein in their spending, which would damage a fragile economic recovery. Even more ominous, if investors shun stocks for a prolonged period, companies will find it much more difficult to raise the capital they need to expand their operations and increase revenue and profits. [29]

Reservations about the integrity of American business spread overseas with damaging impact according to *The Wall Street Journal:*

The dollar's decline against the euro, the yen, and other major currencies signals a slackening of global investors' seven-year ardor for the American economy, which helped to propel this country's bull market of the late 1990s. A growing number of global money managers have begun to find other parts of the world more appealing, which threatens to reduce the more than $1 billion a day that foreigners have been sending to the U.S. in recent years.

A sustained fall in the dollar would have other consequences. The impact would probably be an uptick in inflation, by boosting import prices and making it easier for domestic manufacturers to raise their own prices.

Although the dollar has seen ups and downs before, the significance for markets could be far greater this time because the U.S. has become dependent to an unprecedented degree on foreign capital. [30]

Apparently we never learn our lesson. With the exception of the World War II and its aftermath years, 1940-1960, every decade has experienced a similar flare-up of fraud and misdeeds.

The 1920's saw not just the stock market crash of 1929 but the emergence of Ivar Kreuger, "The Swedish Match King," who took U.S. investors on a fraudulent ride based on his virtual monopoly of match production and sale in Europe.

The energy industry of the 1920s was in the grasp of Samuel Insull who built and then lost a utility empire through highly leveraged borrowing. An ex-president of the New York Stock Exchange, Richard Whitney, pleaded guilty in 1938 to embezzlement charges, having stolen from his own customers and the pension fund of stock exchange employees. In the mid-1960's came the price-fixing scandal involving General Electric and Westinghouse, described in Chapter 4.

Investors Overseas Services, a mutual fund syndicate founded by Bernard Cornfeld, later replaced by Robert Vesco, was looted by its founders. Ivan Boeskey and Michael Milken were the scoundrels of the 1980's with insider trading. Charles Keating, Jr., CEO of Lincoln Savings & Loan, took advantage of deregulation of the savings and loan industry at a cost to the U.S. Treasury of over $500 billion. Keating bilked investors of $200 billion and was convicted of securities fraud.

Options trader Nick Leeson bankrupted the 227-year-old Barings Bank of the U.K, by hiding $1.4 billion in trading debt. Martin Frankel, a Connecticut money manager, fled to Germany after bilking insurance companies of more than $200 million.

After each major scandal, congressional hearings are held, laws are discussed, fought over, and sometimes passed. Yet the cycle of business deception, revelation, finger pointing, contrition, and then forgetfulness continues decade after decade.

Mankind does not change. The sins bewailed in the Talmud and Bible are the sins of today. But where 2000 years ago one man's greed might damage a village, today it damages the world.

It Ain't Easy Being Green

In our numerous attempts to put an end to corporate fraud and scandal, lawmakers have usually focused on the "bad apples" in the business barrel with new regulations, enhanced enforcement of regulations on the books, or heavier penalties for wrong- doing. Generations of scandals and reformers have produced volumes of regulations that can force businesses, from the "mom & pop" to the largest conglomerate, into Hobson's choices, damned if they do and damned if they don't. Federal and state regulations are irregularly or spottily enforced, "more honored in the breach than the observance." The combination of a seemingly endless number of difficult-to-decipher-and-follow regulations, loose enforcement, and mixed signals from government agencies as to what is right and what is wrong has diminished respect for the laws and often obscures the foundation of their existence – "to do to others as you would have them do unto you."

In the final analysis, all laws, regulatory and criminal, are based upon the moral and ethical standards of the society that creates them. In the Anglo-Saxon-influenced world, the Ten Commandments could be considered the final word of what is right and wrong in business as in life. But for the officers and managers working within any business enterprise, applying even those straightforward standards is not easy.

Suppose you are the manufacturer of children's clothing and, both because it is mandated by safety regulations and also because you want your products to protect the children who wear them, everything you produce has been fireproofed using the approved, industry-standard Tris (2,3-dibromopropyl). Then Tris is found to cause cancer in laboratory animals. Federal regulations require you to recall all Tris-treated clothing you've sold. Your warehouses are now filled with the recalled, illegal-to-be-distributed goods.

You are then contacted by a firm that specializes in exporting "distressed" merchandise to foreign countries which do not have the same health and safety standards as the U.S. They can clear your warehouses of contaminated clothing and return at least some portion of your investment. Do you jump at the opportunity to put an end to the cost of storage, dispose of your contaminated goods and recover a portion of your loss? Or does your concern for the health of children who might end up wearing your contaminated clothing make you turn down the offer?

Confusing the issue is that "dumping" of distressed, out-of-date, unapproved, or otherwise unsalable goods is tacitly encouraged by the government. Trade laws do not apply the same standards to goods for export as goods for domestic consumption.

An investigative report published by *Mother Jones Magazine* in November, 1979, detailed the practice of dumping and some of the more egregious cases:

- 400 Iraqis died in 1972 and 5,000 were hospitalized after consuming the by-products of 8,000 tons of wheat and barley coated with organic mercury fungicide, whose use had been banned in the U.S.
- An undisclosed number of farmers and over 1,000 water buffaloes died suddenly in Egypt after being exposed to leptophos, a chemical pesticide which was never registered for domestic use by the Environmental Protection Agency (EPA) but was exported to at least 30 countries.
- Winstrol, a synthetic male hormone which was found to stunt the growth of American children is freely available in Brazil where it is recommended as an appetite stimulant for children. [31]

None of the export dumps noted by *Mother Jones Magazine* was illegal. In fact, as writer Mark Dowie noted, "To this day we allow our business leaders to sell, mostly to Third World nations, shiploads of defective medical devices, lethal drugs, known carcinogens, toxic pesticides, contaminated foods and other products found unfit for American consumption." [32] Further, he notes, the United States Export-Import Bank often finances large dumps while the Commerce, State, and Treasury departments which have statutory authority to stop dumping have not done so.

If dumping unsafe goods is not illegal, is it ethical? What's a CEO to do: reduce losses caused by unforeseen changes in government health and safety standards or, at great cost and without the legal necessity to do so, apply U.S. health and safety standards to foreign sales?

Corporate America is often sent very mixed signals. As another *Mother Jones Magazine* investigative report found:

> Even contractors that commit the obvious violations [of federal environmental and workplace safety laws] are never suspended or debarred. One federal study found that the government continues to award business to defense contractors that have committed fraud on prior contracts. [33]

Society generally, but especially the business community, practices "situational ethics." What may be law-breaking to an environmentalist is good woodland management to a lumber company. Still, there are some ethical standards considered basic to the conduct of business, standards of record keeping and accounting, for example. Where trust among working partners is expected in many activities, the essence of capitalism is that the books will be audited by an impartial third party with the professional experience and knowledge to sort through a business's activity and produce an honest account of its property, activities, profits, and losses to its managers, investors, and lenders.

Yet, as was learned in the fall-out from the Enron/Arthur Andersen scandal of 2002, even this most basic element of business morality was pushed aside in favor of the accounting firm's objective, the quintessential objective of all business, which is to make more money.

Can we fault those who press opportunities for profit beyond straight-arrow honesty and Rotary Club standards of fairness? They are business people. Making money is what they are about. It's the name of the game.

Since we cannot change the game or the humans within it, perhaps, then, we should focus less on the "bad apples" and more on the barrel, the structure that sustains, directs, and protects them from responsibility for their excesses: the corporation.

DILBERT reprinted by permission of United Feature Syndicate, Inc.

1. "Should We Prosecute Corporations and/or Individuals? by Gilbert Geis and Joseph Dimento in *Corporate Crime, Contemporary Debates*, University of Toronto Press, 1995.

2. "Is Corporate Criminal Liability Really Necessary," by B. Coleman, *Southwestern Law Journal* 29, quoted by Gilbert Geis and Joseph Dimento in *Corporate Crime, Contemporary Debates*.

3. Ibid.

4. Ibid.

5. "Mens Rea and the Corporation: A Study of the Model Penal Code Position on Corporate Criminal Liability," *University of Pittsburgh Law Review 19*, 1957, cited in Corporate Crime, Contemporary Debates, p 74.

6. "Corporations Aren't Criminals," by John S. Baker, Jr., *The Wall Street Journal*, April 22, 2002.

7. Cited in "Corporate Crime and New Organizational Forms," by Steve Tombs in *Corporate Crime, Contemporary Debates.*

8. "Merrill Lynch to Pay Big Fine, Make Changes to Settle Inquiry," *The Wall Street Journal*, May 22, 2002.

9. "White-Collar Defense Stance: The Criminal-less Crime," by Kurt Eichenwald, *The New York Times*, March 3, 2002.

10. Ibid.

11. "Pursuit of corporate crime can't end with Enron," *USA Today*, April 3, 2002.

12. Ibid..

13. "Risk-taking is not a crime," by Merrill Mathews, Jr., *USA Today*, April 3, 2002.

14. Ibid.

15. "Who Should Police The Financial Markets," To the Editor, by Michael G. Oxley, Washington, May 31, published in *The New York Times* Money & Business section, June 9, 2002.

16. "Does Corporate Crime Pay?" by Gene Koretz, *Business Week* , April 14, 1997.

17. "The Earnings Cult," by Harris Collingwood, *The New York Times Magazine*, June 9, 2002.

18. Ibid.

19. Ibid.

20. "How Conservative Philanthropies and Think Tanks Transform US Policy," by Sally Covington, *Covert Action Quarterly*, Winter 1998.

21. "On Camera, People at Andersen, Enron Tell How Close They Were," by Ianthe Jeanne Dugan, Dennis Berman and Alexei Barrionuevo, *The Wall Street Journal*, April 15, 2002.

22. Ibid.

23. Ibid.

[24] "Public's Esteem For Business Falls In Wake of Enron," by John Harwood, *The Wall Street Journal*, April 11, 2002.

[25] Ibid.

[26] Ibid.

[27] "Watson, Who Long Led Dynergy in Enron's Shadow, Steps Down," by Chip Cummins, Jathon Sapsford, and Thaddeus Herrick, *The Wall Street Journal*, May 29, 2002.

[28] "Trying to Catch WorldCom's Mirage," by Seth Schiesel, *The New York Times*, Money & Business, June 30, 2002.

[29] "What If Investors Won't Join the Party?" by Gretchen Morgenson, *The New York Times*, Money & Business, Sunday, June 2, 2002.

[30] "No Safe Haven: Dollar's Slide Reflects Wariness About U.S.," by Jacob M. Schlesinger and Kraig Karmin, *The Wall Street Journal*, June 3, 2002.

[31] "The Corporate Crime of the Century," by Mark Dowie, *Mother Jones Magazine*, November 1979.

[32] Ibid.

[33] "Unjust Rewards: The government continues to award federal business to companies that repeatedly break the law," by Ken Silverstein, *Mother Jones Magazine*, May/June 2002.

John David Rose

CHAPTER SIX
GESTATION OF GIANTS

The power of an idea

Considering the enormous power large corporations wield over nations, states, communities, and individual lives, it's instructive to recall how it all began.

Founders of today's giant corporations didn't start to create monster, industry-dominating global giants. They had an idea, a concept, an itch that they had to scratch.

The majority of new businesses are created to do something - something the founder believes in so passionately that he or she will go through the arduous, lengthy, and frustrating struggle required to get the doors of even a small enterprise open.

To the founder, the *product* is the reason for the business. The sales the business achieves and the money it makes are, at first, important only as affirmations that the product was worth the personal sacrifice required to bring it to the marketplace and as a resource for the founder to continue pursuing his/her vision.

Henry Ford

One of the great "bootstrap" stories of American free enterprise is that of Henry Ford. Born in 1863 of an Irish immigrant farmer father, early on he displayed a natural aptitude for machinery. At the age of 15 he left the farm, went to Detroit, trained as a machinist, and began to tinker with the idea of building a horseless carriage of his own design.

Frustrated in his attempts to get his design into production, he became a racecar driver, building his own mounts. Finally, in 1903, he formed the Ford Motor Company with $28,000 in cash, some his own, some borrowed, and began building and selling his Model A. Six years later he introduced the Model T. With Ford's bold and imaginative promotion behind it, it quickly began to succeed beyond his wildest imaginings.

> The Model T created unparalleled riches, turning Henry into a sort of Midas figure. He hated questions about money, once saying "Oh shit" and turning his back on a reporter who asked how it felt to be a multimillionaire.

> [To Ford] the Model T was more than a car, it was
> a calling, the vehicle Ford believed would take the auto
> industry to the promised land of efficiency and utility.
> 'I will build a motorcar for the multitude,' he said in
> prophetic tones. 'It will be large enough for the family but
> small enough for the individual to run and care for. It will
> be constructed of the best materials, by the best men to be
> hired, after the simplest designs that modern engineering
> can devise. But it will be so low in price that no man
> making a good salary will be unable to own one – and
> enjoy with his family the blessings of hours of pleasure in
> God's great open spaces. [1]

The vision was the motivator, the money an afterthought. Ford was building "a motorcar for the multitude."

George Westinghouse

Ford's story is replicated over and over throughout entrepreneurial and industrial history. Take George Westinghouse, for example, the most prolific inventor in American history. His 361 patents overshadowed even the creative productivity of Thomas Edison. Working in his father's farm machinery shops, he combined an easy familiarity with tools with a creative, problem-solving mind, receiving his first patent at the age of 19 for a design for a rotary engine.

Westinghouse's first commercial success sprung from being a witness to a train wreck. He became convinced there was a better way to force a brake shoe against a wheel than having a trainman run from car to car cranking down a mechanical screw. At age 22 he developed the air brake, using compressed air to apply the brakes simultaneously on every railroad car in a train.

Once focused on a problem area, he was unstoppable in his quest for solutions. He developed equipment to lift de-railed railroad cars back onto the tracks, invented the railroad "frog" which permits the wheel of one rail of track to cross an intersecting track, developed interlocking switches and railroad signaling systems and, in so doing, made railroad travel safe and popular with the public. Later he obtained the rights to Nikola Tesla's patents and spearheaded the development of alternating current as the world's standard. He also created an efficient way to transmit natural gas to home, offices and industry, and invented the first telephone switching system, electric turbines for locomotives and ships, and more. Along the way he founded The Westinghouse Air Brake Company, The Union Switch and Signal Company, and Westinghouse Electric Company.

Westinghouse lost control of all of his companies in the financial panic of 1907 and died of a heart ailment seven years later. Wealth was never his motivation. He saw problems and opportunities that cried out for solution and exploitation. Wrote Nikola Tesla in 1938:

> George Westinghouse was, in my opinion, the only man on this globe who could take my alternating-current system under the circumstances then existing and win the battle against prejudice and money power. He was a pioneer of imposing stature, one of the world's true noblemen of whom America may well be proud and to whom humanity owes an immense debt of gratitude. [2]

Computer Geeks

The age of computers has created another spike in entrepreneurial problem-solving creativity in Steve Jobs and Steve Wozniak of Apple and Bill Gates of Microsoft. Jobs and Wozniak were teenagers when they met and developed their friendship while also developing and selling an illegal "blue-box" device that allowed users to make free long-distance calls. Wozniak, the engineer, and Jobs came together again with the idea of developing a personal computer. Jobs, the visionary and marketer, wanted to bring computer technology to "everybody." Developing a prototype in Jobs' garage, the pair started Apple Computer by selling 50 Apple I computers at $666 each. Six years later Apple was listed among the Fortune 500, the youngest firm ever to hit that prestigious list, and both Jobs and Wozniak were multimillionaires.

Both Jobs and Wozniak resigned from Apple in 1985 to pursue individual ventures. When Apple ran into marketing and financial trouble in 1999, Jobs returned to the firm and guided it through a series of spectacular design and operating-system triumphs, back into financial health.

Jobs assumed the CEO role at a salary of one dollar a year. In the year 2,000 a thankful board rewarded him for a great turnaround effort with an option grant worth $872 million plus a $25+ million Gulfstream V airplane.

Responding in 1995 to a self-published-on-the-Internet article by Dave Winer about Apple (davenet.userland.com) Steve Wozniak wrote:

> I had two goals in life, to be an engineer and to teach 5th grade. For several years I've been teaching computers to not only teachers but also 5th through 8th graders *[in the Los Gatos, California school district].* [3]

Jobs and Wozniak as well as Bill Gates and Paul Allen of Microsoft were in love with computers, not with the money they hoped to make. Their vision was for what they saw as the computer's contribution to the lives of ordinary people and small and big business. The fact that they succeeded in parenting their brain-children into use in tens of millions of homes and offices was the real pay-off. The money was just icing on the cake.

Comics and cartoons

> Try to imagine a world without Walt Disney. A world without his magic, whimsy, and optimism. Walt Disney transformed the entertainment industry, pioneered the fields of animation, and found new ways to teach, and educate. [4]

Unlike those of Ford and Westinghouse, Disney's story has not yet disappeared from common memory. A mid-western boy infatuated with drawing and acting, Walt Disney pursued a commercial art career then began to experiment with animation. After a number of failures and bankruptcies, he began to achieve movie-house distribution and business success with his Mickey Mouse cartoon character, then pioneered the first full-length animated feature, *Snow White and the Seven Dwarfs*. Expanding upon his own love of steam trains, and taking a huge financial risk, he designed and personally oversaw construction of a new form of amusement park, Disneyland, which opened in Southern California in 1955. Disneyland's $17 million investment increased tenfold in value within a few short years and Disneyland became a huge success.

The focus of Disney's initial energies was to improve and perfect the art of animation. Later a vision of a new form of amusement park became his passion. Later still, he focused on finding solutions to the problems of urban America. When launching his Experimental Prototype Community of Tomorrow (EPCOT) in central Florida, Walt told his adoring followers:

> I don't believe there is a challenge anywhere in the world that is more important to people everywhere than finding a solution to the problems of our cities. But where do

we begin? Well, we're convinced we must start with the
public need. And the need is not just for curing the old ills
of old cities. We think the need is for starting from scratch
on virgin land and building a community that will become
a prototype for the future. [5]

Brother Roy O. Disney handled the business end from the time he lent
Walt $350 for the first cartoon. He was President of the firm from 1945
through 1968, and Chairman from 1964 through 1971. Walt didn't want
to be a CEO, although he served as President of the firm through 1938 to
1945, and Chairman from 1945 to 1960, primarily because it was expected
of him. He much preferred the title "Creative Consultant" which he held
from 1960 until his death in 1966.

From imagination to mammon
The pages of business journals are filled with stories of enormously
successful American companies losing their founder's focus and turning
almost overnight into what Carol J. Loomis called, in a 1993 Fortune
magazine article, "Dinosaurs."

The most visible hulks in Dinosaurland — Sears, IBM
and GM — were driven to success by strong executives
with long tenures. General Robert E. Wood ran Sears from
1928 to 1954. The genius of GM was Alfred P. Sloan Jr.
(CEO from 1923 to 1946), and the viziers of IBM - for
57 years, until 1971 - were the Thomas J. Watsons, father
and son.
　　What swept over these companies was profound
change in their markets, to which they were required to
adapt. The three big companies …never seemed to take
off the blinders where reality was concerned. Neither did
these companies fix their gaze on the customer. [6]

In describing General Motors' fall from 4th to 40th largest company
of the world between 1972 and 1992, Ms. Loomis referred to a statement
by a security analyst/GM specialist: "Maryann Keller says that one way
to get ahead at the company (GM) was to display a talent for sprucing up
the numbers." [7]

It is a rare corporation whose founder retains enough stock, not to
mention power and charisma, to offset materially the imperatives of the
market once its stock begins trading on an exchange. When an enterprise

reaches a certain critical mass of assets and stockholders, it takes on a life of its own, separate from the products it produces and sells. It mutates into a "Financial Frankenstein", in the words of the Chairman of the Association of Certified Fraud Examiners, Joseph T. Wells. [8]

Founders of businesses are inventors, creators, and do-ers. They start a business to bring their inventions, creations, or solutions to life. That is their motivation. Granted, they may believe that their creation will become so popular that they will become rich, but the money is not as important as the affirmation, proof that they weren't crazy or obsessed after all.

So long as founders are in control, the organizations they create and the officers and employees they hire reflect their vision, goals, and character. When founders depart, the focus shifts from the *vision* — the product, opportunity or problem the founders were driven to address — to the *money*. As the focus shifts at the top, the culture of the employees down through the ranks also shifts from what's good for the company to what's good for me.

Remember "Thank you for calling United"? In the 1950s and '60s the airlines were struggling to overcome the fear of flying and the dominance of the railroads in passenger transportation. Guiding the battle for customers' loyalty were airline pioneers and founders such as Juan Tripp of Pan American World Airways, William Patterson of United, and C.R. Smith of American. They made sure travel by air was glamorous as well as fast. From the moment you called for a reservation until you departed the plane, cheerful people guided you through your journey. Each airline featured attractive stewardesses in outfits by famous couturiers, meals prepared by the top chefs in the country, even exotic paint jobs for the planes. It was a grand time to be a customer of newly minted competitors in the transportation industry.

Before airlines became dominant in long-distance passenger travel, trains such as the Portland Rose, The 20th Century Limited, and The Yankee Clipper whisked people from small towns to cities courtesy of the Union Pacific Railroad, New York Central, New Haven Railways and others. There were dining cars with heavy silver and smiling and agile waiters, club cars with piano players and singing bartenders, and Pullman cars with helpful porters to make up your bed at night. Travel by train was comfortable and glamorous in the early to mid 1900's. Then the railroads became "successful."

In the dead of a Rocky Mountain winter in the 1950s, I was stranded by a huge snowstorm in Nampa, Idaho. My flight from nearby Boise to my next Coast Guard assignment had been cancelled so I called the railroad. The phone rang and rang and rang. Piqued, I marked the time to see just how long I would have to wait for an answer. Some 17 minutes later (I was persistent for I had no other option) a woman answered, "Union Pacific."

A smartalecky 20-year-old, I replied, "I thought maybe the railroad had gone out of business."

"Well," came the defensive response, "a lady's got to go to the can sometime, don't she?"

That railroad clerk's response has come to mind many times over the years in dealing with firms large and small, some fresh and eager for trade, and others smug in their market position and size. Thirty years later I ran into similar responses in searching for an advertising agency to handle our company's medium-sized account. Calling a series of large firms, I hung up on those whose names I couldn't decipher from the phone receptionist's rapid-fire and careless identification. My assumption was that if they didn't care how they presented themselves to their callers, they wouldn't take much care in how they presented us.

I quickly gave up on those who, after I asked to speak to someone about taking on our account, couldn't figure out what department I ought to be directed to.

We hit pay dirt when the receptionist of one of the largest and most famous ad agencies in the world not only clearly articulated the agency's name but immediately put me through to the firm's president. Out of these and similar observations emerges my theory of "The Stages of Corporate Evolution."

Founder In Charge: Driven by the vision of its founder, beyond the initial cash-inflow worry but before the initial public offering, the concept is proven. The board, executive officers, and employees are enthusiastic and dedicated missionaries for the product as they eagerly seek out and serve their market.

Hitting The Big Time: Once the IPO (initial public offering) has allowed founders and early investors to reap the rewards of their pioneering effort, the focus shifts from product to the firm itself – how to promote it for fastest earnings/market growth, attract capital, and reward investors.

The Founder Departs: The wise board brings up a new management team from within the organization. The average board looks for a "name," a superstar with a strong background in corporate finance. Some of the original vision remains in the older executives of the firm, but the focus inevitably shifts to the bottom line.

John David Rose

The Finance Guys In Charge: By the time the third management team takes over, the firm is rolling along in its chosen industry, snapping up or shutting out competitors. The executive staff no longer has the ability to look creatively at the industry, the market, or the company itself. Their focus is narrowed to that which the financial market itself expects – profit. Only the old timers in the production plants remember the founder's vision. For the officers, board members, and white-collar staff, the company is only a money machine.

Too Rich To Die: Even with executive officers milking the corporation, the company simply has so much money coming in from so many sources that mismanagement and use of corporate resources for selfish purposes is difficult to discover. Eventually, of course, the money machine begins to spin down until it is either taken over by another company or shaken to its roots by product/service/customer driven competitors, such as the American auto industry before the invasion of Japanese makers Honda and Toyota.

There are exceptions to the pattern of corporate evolution, but compare what has taken place with Disney, Westinghouse, and others, where the founders are no longer a force, to that of Apple and Microsoft where the founders are still very much in charge.

In the absence of the founder's vision and presence, a corporation's focus inexorably drifts from the something it was created to do to the money it makes doing it.

Corruptio optimi pessima. [a] When CEOs turn bad.

There are ... pompous, arrogant, self-centered mediocre... people running corporate America.... Their judgments and misjudgments have made me rich.
Attorney Joseph D. Jamail, Jr., after winning a $10.5 billion settlement from Texaco for Pennzoil Company. [9]

[a] Corruption of the best is the worst of all.

Philosophers, prophets, and playwrights tell us that the temptations arising out of enormous wealth and power are beyond the power of mere mortals to resist. The CEO of a large corporation controls more wealth, commands a greater administrative staff, and directs a larger population than many not-so-small countries. More than the power to hire and fire, within the corporate organization itself the CEO can create and dissolve divisions and subsidiaries which in turn enrich or destroy the economies of states and regions. A CEO's decisions, prejudices, and whims can make or break banking partners, suppliers, and vendors, production plants, and communities.

Compensation packages produce more personal wealth than many dictators have ever amassed by stripping their nation's treasury. For example: in just the two years before Global Crossing collapsed, CEO Gary Winnick collected $512.4 million in salary, bonus, and sales of WorldCom stock. CEO Michael Eisner's total take from Disney in 1997 was $580.65 million. These are dynasty-creating sums.

Perks and personal services are defended as helping an executive make the best use of his time, as if each waking moment were critical to the well-being of the corporate enterprise. Being waited on hand and foot with minions bowing, scraping, demurring, and deferring, and knowing that private jet planes and limousines await the snap of one's fingers can "turn a person's head."

Ordinary citizens do not easily obtain appointments with members of Congress, Senators, cabinet officers, heads of government departments, or the President of the United States. CEOs of our largest corporations can and do.

Small employers cannot ask governors to build highways, mayors to move neighborhoods, or legislatures to reduce their taxes. The heads of organizations employing thousands can and do.

It's easy to characterize men and women who allow themselves to be paid these sums as Jabba the Hutt-like monsters, stuffing every dollar that comes within their grasp into insatiable maws and acting smugly arrogant in the conviction that they have earned such treatment and wealth through their brilliance and "hard" work. Yet they believe that they're "worth it" because of the millions or billions the company makes for the stockholders.

The unwillingness to recognize the conceit of these princely salaries simply demonstrates that CEOs are susceptible to the same character flaws, moral lapses, and ethical blind spots as any human granted the power of empire. They would never admit it, but they epitomize the old "power corrupts" saw.

Again the question must be asked: it this a fault of out-of-control humans or the way we have structured corporations?

Mutant Money Machines

In reviewing *Big Blue: The Unmaking of IBM*, by Paul Carroll, and *Soap Opera: The Inside Story of Proctor & Gamble*, by Alecia Swasy, *Newsweek* magazine reviewer Jolie Solomon wrote:

> Are IBM and P&G really filled with unusually arrogant or vile men? Or are they typical of a system that relies on the very slow hand of the market to mete out justice? [10]

Despite their ability to direct the fortunes of these mega-billion dollar corporations while building their own fortunes, CEOs delude themselves if they believe they are truly in command of these financial behemoths. It's "do I run the machine or does the machine run me?"

Consider the CEO of one of our nation's largest corporations as described by *Wall Street Journal* Staff Reporter Matt Murray:

> Twenty-four years ago, A.G. Lafley, then 30 years old and fresh out of Harvard Business School, joined one of America's oldest and biggest companies. His new employer had an imposing $7.2 billion in annual sales, about 53,000 employees and offices or plants in 23 countries.
>
> Today Mr. Lafley is chief executive of the 23rd largest company in the U.S. [Proctor & Gamble Co.] It has about $40 billion in annual sales, 110,000 employees and operates in 70 countries. The question facing Mr. Lafley and his counterparts is: Can anyone run these monsters? [11]

In that brief business biography is revealed the dilemma faced by the chief executive of a corporate monster. He is expected by society to be a "leader," moral and law-abiding, considerate of his fellow man, supportive of his community and involved with its future, and a patriotic and loyal citizen of the nation. Yet not one of those character attributes is critical to the operation of the corporation or contributes to his success in running it.

America's CEOs are generally well-educated college and business school graduates. We may assume most are principled when it comes to dealing with their families, friends, neighbors, and home community. If asked, they frequently express adherence to Judeo/Christian values such as those expressed by Paul in his letter to the Philippians. [b] Many CEOs contribute substantial personal money and time in support of good causes. But personal standards of conduct and ethics are no match for the power of "the market" that ultimately judges a CEO's worth.

Today's corporatized world mimics to a certain extent the nightmare society created by George Orwell in 1984, with giant organizations served by more or less willing human automatons who provide unquestioning service in hope of a life of comfort.

The reality is that all the character attributes which would make CEOs "good" citizens and neighbors are in conflict with what is demanded of them by their corporate positions. When labor costs become an issue, CEO Lafley must find ways to reduce that cost, no matter what affect it might have on the lives of P&G's 110,000 employees and their families. Told he can reduce the cost of producing P&G products and increase the firm's competitiveness and profitability by relocating production facilities overseas, he must do so and ignore the disruption it will cause to the communities which will lose a long-time employer and economic base. It's not a neighborly act, but it's good for the business, and that takes priority.

Should a chief executive need to "work with" competitors to force purchasers to pay a higher price, or to force suppliers of raw materials to reduce their prices, thus protecting the company's market share and margins, he or she must attempt to work around the legal prohibitions against collusion and price fixing.

If a CEO has an opportunity to expand into new territory and it means trading with a nation designated an "enemy" by the government, he must find a way to do so. He may be a loyal citizen, but the corporation he serves does not know what that means.

When a chief executive learns that his company's production processes cause severe health damage to his employees and to children living in the communities where his plants are located, he must ignore the problem until the government orders him to correct it. Why? Because his competitors will not spend the money to correct the problem until forced to do so by the law.

Wrote Johnson and Milburn in their brief on behalf of the Standard Oil Company:

---

[b] "Do nothing from selfishness or empty conceit, but with humility of mind let each of you regard one another as more important than himself."

John David Rose

> There is no rule of fairness or reasonableness which regulates competition, someone is always ready and willing to break or shave the rules to gain an advantage. When people do this in social circumstances we call them "unscrupulous." When business people are this way we say they are "shrewd," or "highly competitive." [12]

Unlike the founder of an enterprise consumed by the creative process of building and selling a vision, executives who follow are captives of the sole corporate imperative: profit. Thus it is not the CEO who is the cruel, unthinking, unfeeling monster. It is the corporate entity which he or she must serve, and the rules of the market that must be obeyed. Economist Milton Friedman put it this way:

> So the question is, do corporate executives, provided they stay within the law, have responsibilities in their business activities other than to make as much money for their stockholders as possible? And my answer to that is, no they do not. [13]

Making money is the only "moral" standard of business. Thus, is it any wonder that so many chief executives and corporate boards give themselves imperial levels of compensation and perks? By what other means can they measure their performance as captains of industry?

"GET SERIOUS, JOHN, WE'RE TALKING BUSINESS ETHICS NOT ETHICS."

[1] *The Fords: An American Epic*, by Peter Collier & David Horowitz, c1987 Summit Books, New York City.

[2] Speech read in absentia, Institute of Immigrant Welfare, Hotel Baltimore, New York, May 12, 1938.

[3] "Steve Wozniak on Apple," by Dave Winer, <http://davenet.userland. com/1995/08/28/stevewozniakonapple> August 28, 1995.

[4] "Walt Disney, Biography," from <justdisney.com> Web site, author and date unknown.

[5] "Walt Disney Biography," unsigned and undated Web site <http:..fuv.hivolda. no/prosjekt/gunnargrodal/bio.htm>

[6] "Dinosaurs?" by Carol J. Loomis, *Fortune*, May 3, 1993, pgs 36-41.

[7] Maryann Keller, GM: Rude Awakening, referenced in above citation.

[8] Op-ed article, "Financial Frankensteins terrorize all Americans," by Joseph T. Wells, *USA Today*, 7/6/2000, p15A.

[9] *The New York Times*, November 21, 1985, as listed in Simpson's Contemporary Quotations, 1988.

[10] "America's Errant Empires," by Jolie Solomon with Robert X. Cringely, *Newsweek*, September 27, 1993, pg. 53.

[11] "As Huge Companies Keep Growing, CEOs Struggle to Keep Pace," by Matt Murray, *Wall Street Journal*, February 8, 2001.

[12] John G. Johnson and John G. Milburn, brief for Standard Oil Company, St. Louis, Missouri, 1909.

[13] Milton Friedman, interview with John McClaughry, contributing editor of Business and Society Review, on the topic of corporate social responsibility.—"Milton Friedman Responds," *Chemtech*, February 1974, p. 72

John David Rose

CHAPTER SEVEN
CORPORATE ETHICS & MORALS

> The modern corporation is not and can not be expected
> to be a 'responsible' institution in our society. For all the
> congratulatory handouts depicting the big firm as a 'good
> citizen,' the fact remains that a business enterprise exists
> purely and simply to make profits.
>
> Economist Andrew Hacker [1]

Good and Evil in Business

"The business of America is business," said President Calvin Coolidge.
Some, including the author, may believe that to be a perversion of its
founders' intent. But the United States is a business-centric nation and,
like it or not, we must acknowledge business for what it is and accept what
it is. What business is not is a charitable endeavor. Business is about
maximizing what is gained and minimizing what is laid out to obtain that
gain. In other words, business is greed made socially acceptable.

What has been forgotten in the nation's love affair with Big Business
is our founders' clear intent when allowing corporations to be chartered by
the state. Acts of incorporation were to be permitted only "in consideration
of services to be rendered to the public." [2]

Although the founders recognized the need, and indeed the right, of
incorporators to profit from their enterprise, the "common good" had to
take priority. Recalling the declaration of the Pennsylvania Legislature in
1834: "A corporation in law is just what the incorporation act makes it. It is
the creature of the law and may be molded to any shape or for the purpose
the Legislature may deem most conducive for the common good."[3]

These were not eyewash declarations but had teeth when it came to the
prioritization of human and corporate citizens before the law. As previously
cited (Chapter 2), within the 1890 New York State Supreme Court decision
to impose a "death sentence" — revoke the corporate charter — on North
River Sugar Refining Corporation was this unequivocal declaration: "The
life of a corporation is, indeed, less than that of the humblest citizen." [4]

When good corporations go bad

Widespread support for business in general, and Big Business in particular, is based on the belief that business executives follow moral standards of the kind espoused at weekly Rotary Club meetings: "Is it the truth? Is it fair to all concerned? Will it build goodwill? Will it be beneficial to all concerned?"

Boosters defending big businesses tend to anthropomorphize corporations as gentle giants "giving" people jobs and willingly pouring taxes into the communities in which they are located.

Defenders of big business often point to the number of "innocent" officers and employees that would be hurt should the corporation be penalized for criminal activities. In a previously referenced "Corporations Aren't Criminals" op-ed piece, law professor John S. Baker wrote: "The Justice Department is proceeding to trial with its criminal case against [accounting firm] Arthur Andersen. Auditor David Duncan has pleaded guilty to charges of obstruction of justice.... But do his actions really indict an organization with 85,000 employees?" [5]

The same question is rarely asked when a large corporation goes bankrupt. Should thousands of employees be thrown out of work because management failed to maintain a going concern? When management breaks "the law of the market" is every employee of the firm more worthy of punishment than if management had committed a crime?

The assumption is, in our free labor market, that employees released from a financial foundering firm will find jobs with others in the industry. After all, the work that they were doing doesn't evaporate. Someone has to pick up the load.

In defending a corporation, lawyers and public relations people generally defend the officers as unknowing victims of wrongdoing by those in lower ranks. Unlike the seafaring tradition, captains of corporations attempt to duck responsibility for the ethical failures of themselves and underlings. If the ship goes down, it goes down without them on board.

This raises the question, who is at fault when good corporations go bad? Is it the officers at the helm or employees in the ranks that go off the track? Or could it possibly be the corporate "culture" that leads both officers and employees astray as suggested by this *Wall Street Journal* report of June 10, 2003, "WorldCom Fraud Was Widespread."

> Former WorldCom Inc. Chief Executive Bernard J. Ebbers, and numerous top underlings and employees

conspired together beginning in the late 1990s to carry out massive and systematic fraud at the company, according to two external investigations....

What emerges is a startling picture that contrasts with the initial image of the fraud as the brainchild of one top manager, Scott Sullivan, the company's chief financial officer, and his immediate lieutenants....

The reports' conclusions that <u>the company had a culture that lent itself to the fraud</u> are likely to add ammunition to the arguments of those who oppose the emergence of the company, now named MCI, from bankruptcy later this year. [6] (Emphasis added).

Corporate philanthropy, executive ego, or cynical public relations?

Consider corporate philanthropy: In its 2001 ranking of America's largest corporations, *Fortune* magazine listed Merck as the 24th largest corporation in the country and the largest, richest, most profitable firm in the pharmaceuticals field. [7] Within the Merck Web site is a page entitled "A message from the Chairman," accompanied by a photograph of Raymond V. Gilmartin, Chairman and CEO of the company. His message begins, "The great humanitarian Albert Schweitzer once said, 'There is no higher religion than human service. To work for the common good is the greatest creed.'" [8]

The Merck organization describes its charitable works in subsequent Web site pages, and then charts 1998 contributions/ donations totaling $221 million.

As the ninth most profitable corporation in America, with well over $7 billion in profits for 2001, Merck can easily afford to contribute slightly more than 3% of its profits to charitable works. Yet profits are not the CEOs to be given away at his discretion. They belong to the stockholders.

Merck & Company trumpet their good citizenship. Each project is no doubt announced with notices to the media and perhaps a special function where recipients express their gratitude. Chairman Galmartin no doubt believes he is acting with high moral purpose to fulfill the company's role as a good neighbor.

At the same time he would be shocked to learn if an employee where he banks had been taking small amounts from his and other wealthy depositors' accounts and donating them to a local soup kitchen. That would be embezzling, a crime.

But is there any difference between a bank employee taking a few hundred dollars in depositors' funds to give to the poor and Chairman Gilmartin's taking $5.3 million of Merck investors' money to give to "civics, culture & environment," as the Web site describes? Both are taking money that does not belong to them to use for purposes of their own choosing.

The point is not as fatuous as it may first appear, but goes directly to the question of ownership of a corporation. Has the corporate list of donations been submitted to the owners? Have they approved? Or have they knowingly given all rights to direct the disposition of their money to the CEO?

Individual proprietors and partnerships may sacrifice profits by paying workers more than the going rate, providing generous health care and retirement programs, or donating to community causes. That's altruism. The money donated to others is taken out of the personal pockets of the proprietor or partners. In an investor-owned organization, however, corporate philanthropy is being generous with someone else's money.

Good manager, loyal employee, or good person?

The morally sensitive corporate CEO walks a fine line between two conflicting imperatives: (a) make money for the investors, (b) be a "good" person.

In his paper, "Management, Morality and Law: Organizational Forms and Ethical Deliberations," included in the collection of papers published in the previously cited *Corporate Crime, Contemporary Debates*, Peter Cleary Yeager of Boston University addresses management's basic conflict:

> In general terms, morality involves considerations of right and wrong in behavior affecting others. The two principal logics in such considerations often compete with each other in moral decision-making.
>
> Consequentialist reasoning is outcome-centered, requiring that action be directed at achieving the best results overall for those affected by them.
>
> In contrast, deontological [moral obligation] arguments are action-centered and involve constraints on the means used to achieve ...outcomes. One notable formulation is Kant's injunction that individuals are never

to be used as means only, but are to be treated as moral ends in themselves. For example, child-labour laws restrict commercial exploitation of children regardless of their potential contribution to market efficiency. [9]

Yeager concludes:

> As instruments of production, corporate bureaucracies are inherently ends-oriented and emphasize efficiency. In the absence of any other moral code and/or legal constraints, they would respect workers' rights and dignity only to the extent that such respect served their own means and ends and would seek to restrict (if not eliminate) consideration of ordinary morality in employees' decision making. [10]

Top executives of an enterprise generally favor what Yeager calls "outcome-centered, utilitarian considerations" when making decisions for the firm. Their ultimate responsibility is, or is supposed to be, to the investors and therefore focused on financial outcomes now and in the future.

Facing the need to reduce costs to keep the firm solvent, a CEO may employ the "lifeboat" allegory to rationalize a course of action. The corporate boat is sinking under its current load. In order that the vessel and its passengers (stockholders) survive, some of the crew must be sacrificed, thrown overboard, "downsized."

The action can be defended morally as long as the captain shares in the misery and is not protected from loss, granted a golden parachute, or given a bonus for "performance."

Down the corporate hierarchy, middle management operates under a more traditional moral code. Again, from Yeager:

> Managers at different ranks are inclined to perceive dilemmas from differing moral angles. For example, many managers describe conflicts between some vital business objective and concerns for the welfare of employees harmed by the policies designed to achieve such objectives. But while top-level managers generally framed these decisions in terms of utilitarian concerns for the organization's ends, middle- and lower-level managers

> [who were] asked to implement such policies as layoffs and increased workloads typically experienced them as hurtful to individuals' ends, implicitly registering deontological concerns with human rights and dignity.[11]

Extrapolating from the two corporate staffs he studied in depth as well as from findings of other studies of corporate lawbreakers, Yeager believes there is little discussion about ethics between top-and mid- and low-level managers.

> In brief, managers commonly indicated that ethical dilemmas were both not publicly discussible as matters of implicit corporate policy and privately inadmissible as matters of personal morality. Moreover, the non-discussibility of ethical conflicts only reinforces the general priority of utilitarian justifications regarding profit-making goals over other moral (and often legal) considerations.
>
> Arguably, the 'inappropriateness' of publicly discussing ethical issues encourages managers to deny the moral implications of their decisions. [12]

The lower-level manager confronted with a moral dilemma also engages in rationalization to relieve him/herself of guilt. A production manager told to ignore quality standards in order to meet a shipping deadline may, says Yeager, consider the matter one of engineering values rather than honesty, justifying his decision in some way, such as, "That thing is way over-built anyway."

"Professional standards" also offer a way out for lower-level managers asked to do something they might otherwise question. If the boss directs it, it must be OK because the boss is a professional and the firm is a professional firm.

Several months before troubles at Enron became apparent, and after learning that the Securities and Exchange Commission was about to mount an investigation of their client, accounting firm Arthur Andersen's Houston office began to shred tons of documents – some 3,400 pounds a day – relating to Enron. David Duncan, one of the firm's youngest partners, earning more than $1 million a year for his work with Enron, directed the destruction after receiving an e-mail from an Andersen lawyer reminding auditors to follow the firm's document retention and disposal policies. Junior staffers and employees, many of them trained in the accounting profession and in Andersen's own employee-indoctrination classes, carried out the shredding.

As reported by *The Wall Street Journal:*

> After doing business for 89 years and being indicted for destroying 'tons' of documents, Arthur Andersen LLP's death sentence may have been sealed by a single e-mail.
>
> A federal jury here on Saturday [June 15, 2002] convicted the embattled accounting firm of one felony count of obstructing the Security and Exchange Commission's investigation into Enron Corp.'s collapse. [13,note]

The answer to our question, "Who is at fault when good corporations go bad," is that immoral or illegal behavior may not be attributable just to the officers. Board members and lower level executives who don't blow the whistle may share the blame. There also may be a corporate culture that influences behavior, that justifies shading or hyping results because of an emphasis on meeting targets above all else. The capacity for humans to excuse and rationalize their misdeeds is and always will be beyond measure and beyond correction.

Small business operates under the gimlet eyes of the involved owners/investors and the social, moral, and ethical influence of its business "family" — lenders, customers, suppliers, employees and community officials. Our largest corporations, however, have grown beyond control of the board, the shareholders, and even government. Shareholders are left with nothing but their faith in the "goodness" of those chosen to guide these economic behemoths.

[Note] This case added a new dimension to the discussion surrounding the question asked at the beginning of this chapter, "Should we prosecute Corporations and/or Individuals?" After the jury had reported that it was unable to come to a verdict, it sent a note to U.S. District Judge Melinda Harmon, hearing the case, asking if all jurors had to agree on a single perpetrator in order to reach a guilty verdict. The judge responded that the jury did not have to settle on a single guilty party, but could return a guilty verdict against the firm if they agreed that several individuals had participated in the decision to carry out the illegal acts.

Morality in the executive suite

> An individual generally indeed neither intends to promote
> the public interest nor knows how much he is promoting it.
> By directing industry in such a manner as its produce may
> be of the great value, he intends only his own gain. But he
> is in this as in many other cases led by an invisible hand to
> promote an end which was no part of his intention.
>
> Adam Smith, *The Wealth of Nations*

In a survey of 401 high-ranking corporate executives commissioned in 2002 by Starwood Hotels & Resorts, 99% said that they are personally honest at business. At the same time, 82% said they undercounted their golf strokes, improved their lie and did other things considered cheating. The excuse was, "This is a social thing, not a corporate report card." [14]

In the largest, most powerful corporations, as in the smallest of small-town retailers, business decisions are made by people, and therefore human moral and ethical standards may temper the business focus on profit — "temper" but not remove it. Not all people live by the same moral code, and even those who profess the same standards of ethics may apply them in vastly different ways.

Consider the difficult ethical problem the executives of DuPont faced with their agricultural chemical Benlate, as related in the pages of *The Wall Street Journal.*

In 1970 DuPont began marketing the fungicide Benlate to the agricultural market. In 1983, Belgian greenhouse owners reported that Benlate was damaging ornamental plants. By 1987, Benlate sales had risen to $100 million, and DuPont began marketing an "improved" easier-to-use version "DF."

Reports of contamination led to a recall of Benlate DF in 1991. Continuing reports of ornamental plant damage led DuPont to suspect problems with the product. When DuPont's scientists reported that Benlate appeared to damage plants at the recommended use levels, the company quietly began paying damages to growers. After paying $500 million in damages and spending $12 million on field tests, it halted payments in 1992, and was hit with hundreds of lawsuits.

During pre-trial discovery, DuPont stonewalled in a strategy laid out by their attorney. "It is a much better litigation position to state that we have looked, are looking, and will continue to look but have had no success, leaving the issue unresolved, than it is to have to admit that we have isolated the mechanism of injury." [15]

DuPont announced it would begin field tests involving 100 scientists, with a panel of six outside scientists to guide and evaluate the results. What DuPont did not disclose was that the six evaluating scientists were each paid $1000 a day by DuPont's law firm after agreeing to "…promote the effective legal representation of DuPont in any pending or threatened legal actions involving Benlate 50 DF." [16]

In August 2001, a Florida jury awarded two growers $29.5 million for damages caused by Benlate and found the company guilty of racketeering and engaging in a pattern of criminal activity in defense of the product. Under Florida law the racketeering charge would triple the damages to nearly $90 million. The following March a Florida judge overturned the racketeering charge, reducing DuPont's penalty to the original $29.5 million. DuPont said it would appeal.

Working under one set of business ethics, the scientists of DuPont who initially raised warning flags about the product's danger told the truth to their superiors even if was not what they wanted to hear. DuPont executives directing the company's defense of a profitable product were working under a different ethic. The lawyer recommending a stonewall defense acted ethically in creating an effective defense strategy even though the strategy was based on influencing the scientists who were to evaluate field trials of the products. Only the scientists who took money and pledged to assist that defense while presenting themselves as unbiased would be considered unethical.

But did DuPont executives directing the Benlate defense consider themselves "honest in business?" Would their actions meet Rotary's standards as being "fair to all"?

Put yourself in this shoe manufacturer's place: Most of your competitors have closed their U.S. operations and now produce their goods in Third World countries for 100 times less than the labor rate you pay. [a] You've grown up with many of the people working in your plant. You see them in church, know their families, watch their kids play ball in high school. If you close the plant and follow the competition overseas, these people will face financial hardship, bankruptcy, and perhaps loss of their homes.

---

[a] In 2002 the average cost of labor in China is 25¢ an hour; in the U.S. $21.39 ($16.65 wages, 3.74 benefits).

99

On the other side of the coin may be your relatives, friends and associates who put money into your business, who invested in it when you were struggling to get it started. Some of them depend on the dividends your company pays. Retired employees rely on the company's retirement program to cover their monthly expenses. To these parties a strong, competitive going concern is more important than where the products are made.

No matter how ethically correct a CEO might be in his or her personal affairs, he/she is held accountable by standards set by a board of directors and the institutions holding blocks of the firm's securities. The smaller operator must answer to the banks, investors, or individuals that provide financing. None of these overseers looks kindly on money spent for the greater good. Social justice is not a quantifiable and spendable result.

In a reversal of what society considers responsible, industrial managers who reduce water, ground, or air pollution from their operations more than the law requires are acting irresponsibly toward the companies' owners.

Yeager quotes a steel executive testifying before Congress in 1977, as it considers amendments to the U.S. Clean Water Act:

> With the sums of money [for compliance] that are at stake here, I think that the people who assume the responsibility for the spending of that money have to have the assurance that the regulations are in fact going to fall uniformly, throughout the industry on a competitive basis, and that they're not — that an individual company is not, in fact, going to invest major funds in compliance with a rule that hasn't been tested, and subsequently be disadvantaged if that's litigated and overturned. I think that's a very real competitive problem. [17]

One of the oldest comedy routines, perhaps not understood in these days of pre-cut, packaged, and plastic-sealed meat, is the butcher putting his thumb on the scales when weighing the meat. The customer got less meat than the scales indicated; the butcher got more profit. The practice continues in more subtle ways.

"Some Dealers in Grain Water It, Making It Weigh and Cost More," was the headline in a front-page *Wall Street Journal* news story. The excuse for the grain dealers' putting their thumb on the scales was explained in the sub-headline, "Saying Dust Control Is Aim, ConAgra Sprays Grain, And Is Being Investigated."

Deep in the belly of a grain terminal… a curtain of water cascades onto a conveyor belt carrying soybeans. The spray, as powerful as a bathroom shower at full blast, is controlled so precisely that the beans absorb the water without changing appearance. By the time an ocean-going vessel has been filled with them, the beans will be 177.5 metric tons heavier. That means $37,000 worth of what the soybean buyer gets is added water. [18]

Grain dust can build to explosive levels. In 1977, *The Wall Street Journal* story noted, "20 grain-dust explosions in the U.S. took 65 lives." The government, in fact, sanctions dust-control watering. Grains themselves contain a certain percentage of moisture. Corn, for example, generally contains 15%. If the moisture level is below that figure grain companies are not allowed to raise it. Doing so is "economic adulteration."

On the other hand, watering grain threatens the U.S. agricultural products trade. According to *The Wall Street Journal*, "South Africa, which monitors crops for dangerous mold, told the U.S. last year it wouldn't import corn from three ports where water is used." [19]

In describing a U.S. Department of Agriculture crackdown on the practice, reporter Kilman also noted that where ConAgra says it uses watering only for dust control, the nation's largest grain dealer, Cargill, Inc., controls dust by spraying a thin film of mineral oil which adds only insignificant weight to the grain.

The temptation to use more water is enormous. Most grain elevators make a profit of just a penny or two on each bushel they handle. An elevator could reap another three cents from a soybean bushel by increasing its weight in water by just half a percentage point.

That would mean chicken growers pay more for feed, millers pay more for wheat and ethanol processors pay more for corn – all eventually coming out of the consumer's pocket. [20]

The moral infection spreads. Reporter Kilman notes, "Outside Nez Perce, Idaho, farmer Bob Branson thinks it would be immoral to raise the moisture of his wheat if it happens to be drier than it has to be. But, he adds, 'we're losing money by selling wheat that the big guys can then wet. If the government doesn't clean this up, we should gear up to do the same thing.'"

The pillar of capitalism – competition

Competition is the pillar upon which the Holy Grail of Capitalism rests. As described by Grolier's Interactive Encyclopedia, "The market system has two distinct advantages over other ways of organizing the economy: (a) no person or combination of persons can control the marketplace, which means that power is diffuse and cannot be monopolized …(b) the market system tends to reward efficiency with profits and punish inefficiency with losses." [21]

On the other hand, "Monopoly is the logical outcome of free market economic organization," writes Charles R. Geisst in *Monopolies in America.* [22] The economic history of the world has been a never-ending cycle of monopoly creation and monopoly busting. One of the main reasons for our founders' distaste for corporations was their experience with "exclusive rights," monopolies granted by the king or parliament to a single individual or organization. Writes *The American Jurist & Law Magazine:*

> [Corporations] are found in all the varieties of formation, from those that had scarcely the shadow of power and being, to the great monopolies, with power to trample down all individual rights that stood in the way of their rapacity. [23]

In the early 1600's, however, the English Courts began disenfranchising monopolies because of their interference with free trade.

> In England, corporations, unless it is expressly otherwise provided by the charter, are now limited and rendered incapable of taking lands without the king's license. [24]

Once corporations were loosed from tight state oversight by Chief Justice Marshall's doctrine on corporations and granted status by the fraudulent Headnote added to the Santa Clara County v Southern Pacific decision (United States Bank v. Dandridge, and Santa Clara County v. Union Pacific Railroad, referred to in Chapter 2), monopolies and trusts began to sprout. The problem grew until, in 1877, the Grangers, an organization of farmers angry over what they believed were unfair prices and practices of the nation's railroads, demanded that the federal government take over regulation of the railroads from the states.

The Interstate Commerce Act of 1887 created the first independent business regulatory commission. Its first act was to ensure "just and reasonable" railroad rates and prevent the formation of monopolies. When that act failed to slow or stop rapacious competitive practices by John D. Rockefeller's Standard Oil in collusion with the railroads, Congress passed the Sherman Anti-Trust Act. Standard Oil was accused of driving rival oil producers and refiners out of business by pressuring the railroads into refusing to carry their products or charging them far higher rates. The Sherman Act specifically targeted Standard Oil in its prohibition of contracts, combinations, and conspiracies in restraint of trade (price fixing), and monopolies or attempts to monopolize.

Against well-financed and highly vocal opposition from the industrial and financial giants of the day, Congress passed the Clayton Act of 1914. Members bolstered their arguments on its behalf by quoting laissez faire champion Adam Smith. "People of the same trade seldom meet together even for merriment and diversion but the conversation ends in a conspiracy against the public or in some contrivance to raise prices." [25] The act broadened prohibitions against monopolistic practices beyond railroads into all other areas of commerce, declaring price discrimination, exclusionary dealing, interlocking directorates, and corporate mergers to be illegal, although not criminal, if they "materially reduced competition or tended to create a monopoly in trade." [26]

A companion to the Clayton Act, the Federal Trade Commission Act of 1914, attacked price-fixing arrangements, false advertising, boycotts, and combinations of competitors. This was followed by the Robinson-Patman Act of 1936, amending the Clayton Act to refine the definition of "unfair" competition.

Business, rather than consumers, are the usual supplicants to Congress for relief from monopolistic pricing and marketing practices. Anti-trust and business regulations are proposed by business interests fearful of monopolists invading their industry.

American tradition reveres competition as bringing out the best in people and products and, in the reverse, holds that "cornering the market" is both legally and morally wrong. As previously noted, a cornerstone of American Capitalism is "...the distribution of goods ... determined mainly by competition in a free market." [27] Competition is implied in the word "free" in our Free Enterprise system and in the "free" market libertarians hold dear. It is what separates the economic model of the United States from the controlled economies of communism and socialism.

The ethics of competition
The ethics of competition? There are none. "There is no rule of fairness or reasonableness which regulates competition," wrote Johnson and Milburn in their brief on behalf of the Standard Oil Company when it was facing anti-trust action. [b] Someone is always looking for a competitive edge. Someone is ready to break or shave the rules to gain an advantage.

The dream of every inventor and entrepreneur is to have a monopoly. One of the first questions asked by venture capitalists when presented with a new business opportunity is how the venture will be protected from competition. Is the idea, product, or process capable of being patented? Patent laws provide the originator with protection against competitors, at least for a certain period of time.

That's the theory. In practice, budding Thomas Edisons have an uphill battle to hold on to their creations or to profit from them. Take for example, the inventor of television.

With the exception of a few older residents of southern Idaho, most Americans believed that David Sarnoff of RCA brought the modern wonder of television to life. The real inventor, however, was an Idaho farm boy, Philo T. Farnsworth, who at the age of 14 got the idea while plowing his father's potato field. Several books have recently been published about Farnsworth – *The Last Lone Inventor* by Evan I. Schwartz (HarperCollins), and *The Boy Genius and the Mogul, The Untold Story of Television* by Daniel Stashower (Broadway Books).

When the Radio Corporation of America heard of Farnsworth's creation of a practical system to transmit and receive pictures over the air, the head of RCA, David Sarnoff, dispatched an engineer to visit the inventor's small lab. The engineer carefully noted what he saw, returned to New York, made a replica, and discovered it solved the primary problem of transmitting/receiving moving pictures and began to seek a patent. Farm boy Farnsworth, however, had beaten them to it.

Instead of negotiating with Farnsworth for a license to use his work in return for royalties, RCA challenged his patents in court while it continued to test and improve on the idea. RCA kept the case from going to final decision for almost fifteen years of litigation, until the court finally determined that Farnsworth, not RCA, was the true inventor. Patents, however, run for only twenty years. Before Farnsworth could profit from his years of struggle, World War II intervened. By the time it was over and

---

[b] John G. Johnson and John G. Milburn, brief for Standard Oil Company, St. Louis, Missouri, 1909.

RCA was ready to introduce television to the nation, Farnsworth's patent had run out. RCA's deep pockets had won.

The lure of monopoly

On the other side of the coin, however, once a firm has created a new product it does everything in its power to extend its exclusive rights beyond the original patent period. The process of creating patentable "improvements" to products whose patents are running out is common to most industries, but has been brought almost to a science in pharmaceuticals.

> Bristol-Myers Squibb Co. is being sued by attorneys general from 29 states, the District of Columbia, the U.S. Virgin Islands and Puerto Rico, who allege that the drug maker illegally delayed for years generic competition to its huge-selling cancer drug, Taxol – costing states and patients billions of dollars.
>
> Yesterday's lawsuit is part of a growing wave of litigation against U.S. drug makers over their use of legal maneuvers to fend off generic competitors to big-selling drugs that are losing patent protection. [28]

Stakes are high for companies such as Bristol-Myers Squibb. Taxol racks up sales of $4 to $5 million a day with huge profit margins. BMS quoted a price of $6.09 per milligram as the Redbook average wholesale price. That works out to $182.63 for a 30 mg. pill, or $1,826.25 per 300-milligram vial — wholesale. To compare, a generic producer reported that his costs of making Taxol were seven cents a milligram, or $6.02 less than BMS's wholesale price. [29]

Pharmaceutical companies defend their prices by pointing to the huge research and development costs they incur in discovering a new drug, testing it, and getting it through the FDA's approval process. A reasonable argument if true, but it is not.

Scientists at the National Institutes of Health discovered the anti-carcinogenic properties of Taxol in the bark of the Pacific yew tree. The NIH licensed the drug to Bristol-Myers Squibb in 1991 for a royalty of 0.5%, a figure so low that members of Congress charged BMS with practically "stealing" the drug from the government agency. BMS quieted their concerns by telling Congress a lie. "Taxol was never patented and no patent is even possible," said Bristol-Myers Vice President Zola Horovitz to a Congressional committee in 1993. The company also promised that generic versions of the drug would be available by 1998.

> Meanwhile, Bristol-Myers lawyers were feverishly working to get two patents on Taxol by claiming the Bristol-Myers's scientists had figured out that the drug could be given during three-hour infusions instead of a more taxing 24-hour infusion. In fact, the three-hour infusion therapy had long been known, but Bristol-Myers didn't disclose to the patent office an earlier study proving three-hour infusions worked.... At the same time, however, Bristol-Myers provided that same study to the Food and Drug Administration to prove that the drug was safe to sell. [30]

Bristol-Myers Squibb defends its price for Taxol, saying it spent over $1 billion on clinical trials. That too is a falsehood. BMS did not sponsor any of the clinical trials used to obtain the original FDA approval for its use in ovarian and breast cancer. The drug was already in government-sponsored clinical trials when Bristol-Myers obtained the license from the NIH. And finally, "For BMS to have spent $1 billion on clinical trials, it would have had to enroll more than 166 thousand patients in trials, at $6 thousand per patient." [31] No record of such a massive trial exists.

Bristol-Myers is not the only company to take advantage of publicly funded research to market expensive new drug therapies. Professor Jerome Horowitz first synthesized Glaxo-Wellcome's anti-AIDS drug AZT in 1964 under a grant from the NIH. A Glaxo subsidiary bought the formula to use on cats. In 1984, when NIH scientists discovered HIV, the lab asked drug makers to send samples of every anti-retrovirus drug they had. The NIH spent millions inventing a method to test the compounds against the virus. Their tests indicated that AZT might attack the virus. NIH asked Glaxo to conduct further lab tests. Glaxo refused. NIH scientists performed the tests themselves, again at public expense, and were able to report to Glaxo that their AZT compound did indeed kill the live AIDS virus. They asked Glaxo to conduct human trials. Glaxo again refused, but within days of the notice filed a patent in Britain for the anti-AIDS qualities of AZT, claiming the discovery as its own work.

Other pharmaceutical firms keep generics at bay with secret and illegal agreements to pay the generic producer not to produce or sell their drug. Generic companies may make more money under these agreements with far less risk and market exposure than if they go into production themselves.

The costs of losing a monopoly is high for drug makers. Eli Lilly's patent on Prozac ran out in August 2001. Generic producers immediately rushed their equivalents into the market, and Lilly suffered an 80%+ drop in Prozac branded sales. [32]

Despite the penalties for collusion, a business executive would be considered incompetent if he/she missed an opportunity to extend important patents through all possible means, "stabilize" the costs for raw materials, come to a negotiating position with labor, or establish "fair" market prices, even if it meant illegally conferring with competitors.

In 1961, Fortune magazine carried a detailed report on the GE/Westinghouse/Allan Bradley, et al price-fixing trial and outcome, "The Incredible Electrical Conspiracy." The author, Richard Austin Smith, summarized:

> No thoughtful person could have left that courtroom untroubled by the problems of corporate power and corporate ethics. We live in a corporate society. Big Business determines institutionally our rate of capital formation, technological innovation and economic growth; it establishes the kind of competition that is typical of our system and sets the moral tone of the market place. The streets of every city in the U.S. are crowded with small businesses that take their cue from great corporations, whether it trickles down from what some executive tells the crop of college graduates about free enterprise or how he himself chooses to compete. [33]

---

[1] "A Country Called Corporate America, *New York Times Magazine*, July 3, 1966.

[2] *Annals of America, Conspectus II*, Chapter 16 "The Corporation," pg. 172-193, "Colonial Corporations 1609-1789.

[3] Carter Goodrich, ed., *The Government and the Economy, 1783-1861,* Indianapolis: Bobbs-Merrill, 1967, p. 44 (Report of the Packer Committee of the Pennsylvania Legislature).

[4] Op Cit   PEOPLE V. NORTH RIVER SUGAR REFINING CORP., 24 N.E. 834 (1890).

[5] Op Cit "Corporations Aren't Criminals," *The Wall Street Journal*, April 22, 2002.

[6] "WorldCom Fraud Was Widespread," *The Wall Street Journal,* June 10, 2003.

[7] "America's Largest Corporations," *Fortune* magazine, April 15, 2002.

[8] "About Merck," <www.merck.com/overview/philanthropy/> pgs 1 and 12 of 14, copyright 1995-2002 Merck & Co.

[9] "Management, Morality and Law: Organizational Forms and Ethical Deliberations," by Peter Cleary Yeager, *Corporate Crime, Contemporary Debates* p148-149.

[10] Ibid.

[11] Ibid, p154.

[12] Ibid, p155-156.

[13] "Andersen Win Lifts U.S. Enron Case," by Jonathan Weil, Alexei Barrionuevo, and Cassell Bryan-Low, *The Wall Street Journal*, June 17, 2002.

[14] "Many CEOs bend the rules (of golf)," by Del Jones, *USA Today*, June 26, 2002.

[15] "On Eve of Trial, Court Documents Show DuPont Knew of Benlate Risk for Years," by Scott McMurray, *The Wall Street Journal*, June 30, 1993.

[16] Ibid.

[17] Ibid, p160.

[18] "Soaking 'Em; Some Dealers in Grain Water It, Making It Weight and Cost More," by Scott Kilman, *The Wall Street Journal*, July 1, 1993.

[19] Ibid..

[20] Ibid.

[21] *Grolier Multimedia Encyclopedia*, 1988 edition.

[22] *Monopolies in America*, by Charles R. Geisst, Oxford University Press, 2000, as reviewed by Albert A. Foer in the Washington Post Book World, August 20, 2000.

[23] "Corporations," *The American Jurist & Law Magazine*, American Periodical Series, 1800-1850, Art. VI, pg 299, University Microfilms, 1964.

[24] Op Cit, "Corporations," *The American Jurist & Law Magazine*, Art VI, pg 303.

[25] *The Wealth of Nations*, Adam Smith.

[26] Ibid.

[27] *Webster's Ninth New Collegiate Dictionary*, "capitalism," p204.

[28] "Bristol-Myers Is Sued by 29 States…", by Gardner Harris, *The Wall Street Journal*, June 5, 2002.

[29] "Disputes involving Paclitaxel…," by James Love and Suzannah Markandya, August 23, 2001, published by Consumer Project on Technology Web site, <http://www.cptech.org/ip/health/taxol/>.

[30] Op cit, "Bristol-Myers is Sued by 29 States…", *The Wall Street Journal*.

[31] Op cit. "Disputes involving Paclitaxel…," from Consumer Project on Technology.

[32] "Antidepresssants Lift Clouds, But Lose 'Miracle Drug' Label," by Erica Goode, Melody Petersen and Andrew Pollack, *The New York Times*, June 30, 2002.

[33] "The Incredible Electrical Conspiracy," by Richard Austin Smith, *Fortune*, April 1961.

John David Rose

CHAPTER EIGHT
DOGS OF MIGHTY APPETITES[a]

> "The notion that a business is clothed with a public interest
> and has been devoted to the public use is little more than
> a fiction intended to beautify what is disagreeable to the
> sufferer."[1]
>
> Justice Oliver Wendell Holmes, Jr.

Crime in the suites

The 1990's was the dot-com decade of corporatism triumphant. Then came "America's Corporate Meltdown" as *USA Today* intoned on its front page.[2] In the midst of capitalism's most disastrous year since the Great Crash of '29, *The New York Times* asked an almost unthinkable question on the front page of its Sunday Money & Business section: "Could Capitalists Actually Bring Down Capitalism?"

> Could the short-term, self-rewarding mentality of a
> handful of capitalists truly destroy capitalism? Bring on
> hundreds of bankruptcies, force banks under, end the
> giving of loans? Destroy America as we know it?[3]

These were not idle musings. In the first six months of 2002, the Dow plunged by over a thousand points, losing close to 20% of its value. Between March of 2000 and March of 2003, NASDAQ lost about 75% of its value. Domestic investors were bailing out of the market. Foreign investors who powered so much of the economic miracle of the 1990's were rapidly pulling their money out of the U.S.

Pundits at first blamed the market slump on the terrorist attack on the most prominent symbols of capitalism, New York City's World Trade Center. But this economic disaster was self-inflicted. Beginning in 2000 and continuing into 2003, investors were hit with revelation after revelation of wrongdoing in executive suites. High flyers of the technology/communications age as well as old-line firms such as Conseco (financial services), United Airlines, Adelphia Communications, Kmart,

---

[a] "They are dogs with mighty appetites; they never have enough. They are
shepherds who lack understanding; they have all turned to their own way,
each one to his unjust gain." Isaiah 56:11

and others began crumbling into bankruptcy. To paraphrase the famous words of Pogo, America's giant corporations had "met the enemy, and it was themselves."

Larceny, bribery, collusion, fraud, corruption, and inhuman heedlessness of the welfare of others – if we were talking of street crime the American people would have been outraged with the moral degenerates committing such crimes. But these were not street thugs and petty thieves. These were the cream of corporate America, the poster boys and girls of the free market.

What had gone wrong? Why had street vendor, flea market, bait and switch venality taken over the executive floors of some of the nation's largest, most respected firms? Who had begun this undeclared, insidious corporate war upon investors, employees, public purses, health, safety, and the world economy?

Americans have been led to believe that our corporate colossi are run by principled people. These were top biz school graduates and financial wizards, cover girls and boys of business pages and magazines. In their interviews they professed deeply held moral values and concern for the welfare of others. This straight-shooter image has been fostered for generations by the nation's business media, the Business Roundtable, Chambers of Commerce, and conservative think tanks deifying corporate gigantism.

Tainted by stories of his own insider trading and that of his vice president, President G.W. Bush assured the nation that the "vast majority" of America's corporate leaders had not succumbed to unbridled greed and had resisted the temptation to "cook the books." Treasury Secretary Paul O'Neill, point person for the White House and Administration, attempted to reinforce the message. "I believe these cases are infrequent, but even a few bad cases can poison confidence in our system. We must take action to restore investor confidence. I think the people who have abused our trust, we ought to hang them from the very highest branches." [4] He then, however, cautioned Congress to move carefully before imposing new regulations on business so as not to slow the engine of economic progress.

Within days of O'Neill's declaration, however, a new record high in corporate fraud was revealed in a $3.9 billion overstatement of earnings by WorldCom, the nation's second largest long-distance and telecommunications company.[b] CFO Scott Sullivan was immediately fired and charged, along with WorldCom co-founder Bernard Ebbers, with financial fraud.

---

[b] Less than a month later, WorldCom's new president announced another $3 billion of misapplied expenses bringing the total to over $7 billion.

As the Dow tumbled to a five-year low, "The Business President," G. W. Bush, went before the nation to reassure the markets. "The business pages of American newspapers should not read like a scandal sheet," he said. "My administration will do everything in our power to end the days of cooking the books and shading the truth and breaking our laws." [5]

Demonstrating a lack of faith in effective government action, investors pushed the Dow down 300 points the very next day.

How the Big Buck Bonanza was born.

In the late 1980's, the public, investors, and even the business media were aghast when executive salaries began creeping toward a stratospheric $1 million, a figure that today would be considered shamefully modest. Reacting to those concerns, the 1992 Congress wrote a provision into the tax bill that prohibited companies from deducting as ordinary business expense executive pay exceeding $1 million.

The first Bush administration (President George Herbert Walker Bush) reacted sharply: "These are decisions to be left to the marketplace, not to legislators and bureaucrats," said deputy secretary of the Treasury John Robson in a speech to an industry group. "Government should not even think about messing around with this stuff." [6] When Congress included the executive compensation provision within a tax bill, President Bush vetoed the measure, explaining that it broke the "read my lips, no new taxes" campaign pledge, a pledge he later abandoned when the federal deficit ballooned skyward.

Congress continued to press for compensation restraints.

Soon after the election of Democratic President William Jefferson Clinton, and over bitter opposition and dire warnings from business interests that America's executives would simply quit working for lack of incentive, Congress passed an executive compensation limits measure. In retrospect, it exacerbated rather than solved the problem.

Section 162(m) of the U.S. Tax Code limited the corporate tax deduction for compensation paid to the CEO and the next four highest-paid executive officers to $1 million per person. "Not to worry," said one executive compensation expert: "Although there has been an awful lot of attention that has been drawn to it, the cap is going to affect very few companies. Only about 20 percent of the largest companies pay basic compensation over $1 million." [7]

But, "the American business community responded quickly to this blow with a subtle, if unmistakable, jeer," wrote Jay Mathews in *The Washington Post.*

The derisive retort seemed to vibrate from every paragraph of the compensation package Spectrum Information Technologies Inc., gave its new chairman, former Apple Computer Inc., chief John Scully, in October.

Scully would not receive a penny more than $1 million in salary from the supposedly chastened Spectrum board.

But by the way, he would also have the option to buy 18 million Spectrum shares over five years, at an apparent paper profit of $72 million. [8]

Spectrum took advantage of an exemption in Section 162(m) for "qualified performance-based compensation." This allowed firms to claim tax deductions for compensation in excess of $1 million if they put in place shareholder-approved plans that linked pay to objective measures of performance administered by a committee of "outside" directors on the Board.

It was a huge loophole that compensation committees and officers immediately exploited. All a board needed to do was set written performance goals for the executive. Even negative goals such as "losses not to exceed…" would serve to make it possible for the officers to "earn" a bonus. Little wonder that executive compensation consultant Graef Crystal wryly noted, "They put in this $1 million cap and then they give you all these wonderful loopholes. Even a person with an IQ of 80 can find a way around it." [9]

Thanks to a budget-balancing tax increase imposed on higher income brackets by the Clinton administration, the federal deficit began to shrink and then turn to surpluses. For the first five years of the 90's, big business enjoyed what seemed to be unstoppable growth. Corporate profits grew 75% and, thanks to "performance-based" bonuses and stock options, executive compensation rose even faster.

The hidden kicker – stock options

Compensation consultants, attorneys, and accountants discovered that stock options were not only a way to award millions to their CEO clients, but a legal way to hide the cost of the awards from their stockholders and lenders.

The practice was immediately attacked by the Financial Accounting Standards Board (FASB) as well as the Securities and Exchange Commission (SEC) as misrepresentation. But under pressure, both the industry board and government agency softened their stance. Thanks to a relaxed set of "Generally Accepted Accounting Practices" (GAAP), companies could award options without revealing the cost in their financial reports. They could also deduct the estimated cost of such awards from their federal and state income taxes.

Many accountants were aghast at the distortion if not outright fraud encouraged by the new standard. CPAs George (Jim) Schneider and Patrick Freer addressed the problem in correspondence directed to the FASB and SEC:

> The cost of stock options never appear in the income statement or in the balance sheet.... In addition, there is a loss of earnings attributed to the reduced shares that would have, otherwise, been issued at market price rather than the shares actually issued at the option price. [10]

The financial statement doesn't reveal the actual cost to the company of stock option grants. Sophisticated investors recognize that options dilute ownership – the value of the company is spread over more shares without a corresponding increase in assets – but have no way of learning how much of investors' money has been given away to the officers.

> Companies [are] allowed to include an annual pro forma theoretical estimate of stock option costs in the footnotes to the financial statements ... [but] the footnote is worthless. On the line indicating options exercised, the number of shares exercised and the exercised price is shown. What is missing: the market price at the date of exercise! They do not want the independent individual investor to have any means of determining the actual cost of stock options. [11]

In their appeal for full and open disclosure — "that compensation costs should be recognized for fixed as well as performance stock options" — Schneider and Freer presented an analysis of 30 Dow Industrial Companies showing a loss of over $90 billion of shareholders' equity over a five-year period ending in 1999. They cited other critics of lax standards:

- "If US corporations properly accounted for the cost of stock options they granted, aggregate published profits would have been 56% lower in 1997 and 50% lower in 1998." (Smithers and Co., LTD, London).

- "Many of the stock options plans in operation involve considerable transfer of wealth from existing stockholders to corporate officers and directors. In any other form of asset ownership, such a transfer without approval of stockholder/owners would be considered theft."
- (Hermes, in a report to NASDAQ). "The big payoff for the managers in all of this is their fat and juicy stock option deals. And, therein lies an even greater deception: the stock options are clearly a form of compensation and, should be deducted from earnings as an expense. But, they are not and investors are screwed." (Martin Weiss' Safe Money Report, Sept. 1999).[12]

When Congress began considering requiring companies to treat stock options as an expense, first Coca-Cola, then *The Washington Post* and a growing string of major firms announced that, henceforth they would do just that. In reporting these decisions, *The Wall Street Journal* presented data from SEC files illustrating how painful the change might be for some companies.

The technology sector complained that it would be particularly hard hit. Microsoft, for example, had reported fiscal 2001 earnings of $7.3 billion. Expensing options would reduce its earnings to $5.1 billion including the loss of a $2.1 billion tax exemption. Some companies that had reported profits in 2001 would have been reporting losses instead. E-Bay, for example, reported fiscal 2001 profits at $90.5 million. With options expensed it would have had to report a loss of $14.5 million. Cisco Systems' loss for the 2001 fiscal year would have increased from $1.01 billion, or 14 cents a share, to $2.71 billion, or 38 cents a share.

Many in industry were quick to defend the current practice. "Our view is that there is no fundamentally sound way to expense stock options without distorting earnings," said Intel spokesman Chuck Mulloy.[13] But as *The Wall Street Journal's* chart and report made clear, not expensing options paints a highly distorted, rose-colored picture of earnings that may well have sucked in investors. [14] To that point a European investment bank, Dresdner Kleinwort Wasserstein, noted that earnings for the S&P 500 would have been 30% lower in 2001 if all stock options had been expensed. Because the practice is not as pervasive in Europe, the company noted that earnings for European companies would have fallen only 10%[15].

The use of stock options in place of cash compensation was common in dot-com start-ups. The potential for future riches was an inducement for staffers to put in eighty+-hour work weeks to bring their new creation to market and, more important to their personal bottom line, to the initial public offering.

The Wall Street Journal wrote:

> Stock options were the near magical currency of Silicon Valley, financing much of the huge success of companies such as Cisco Systems, Inc., and Sun Microsystems Inc. For years, tech companies didn't have to give employees much in the way of real money, because options, tied to the value of the companies' stocks, were so valuable. But that formula depended on a surging stock. [16]

For a few, such as early Microsoft, Netscape and E-Bay staffers, the payoff was real. Except for top executives and the venture capitalists who'd put in the first money, the profits for late-comer staffers were only paper. Their stock was restricted from immediate trade. For lower level employees, paper fortunes vanished as quickly as they had appeared, while the car and house payments eagerly undertaken in the heady days of dot-com enthusiasm continued.

"Before Telecom Industry Sank, Insiders Sold Billions in Stock," was the front page headline of *The Wall Street Journal,* August 12, 2002.

> All told, it is one of the largest transfers of wealth from investors – big and small – in American history. Hundreds of telecom executives, almost uniformly bullish, sold at least some portion of their stock and made hundreds of millions, while many investors took huge, unprecedented losses. And the economic and personal damage in jobs lost and bankruptcies is far worse. [17]

Stock options were also defended as giving ownership to the rank and file and, in fact, there has been growth in such plans. However, according to a survey by the National Center of Employee Ownership, 70 percent of stock options in publicly traded companies are given to managers, and 50 percent of those to senior executives. The average value of option grants to senior executives is $512,000; the average for hourly workers is $8,000. As Corey Rosen, Executive Director of NCEO put it: "Options for ordinary employees can work out to a new car, college tuition, a down payment on a house, a great vacation, and maybe even a more secure retirement. Options for executives can amount to enough money to fund a small country." [18]

Since Section 162(m) was enacted, attempts have been made to close the non-reporting loophole. Each time the correction has been fought off by business organizations, large accounting firms and, most notably, the Business Roundtable. As pointed out by accountants Schneider and Freer and *The Wall Street Journal*, CEOs and boards of directors used stock options to hide the enormous amounts of money they were awarding to their executives. The result:

> The shareholder now has a spurious income statement that increases income from a tax reduction and at the same time excludes the cost giving rise to such reduction! [19]

Whether the options are granted to employees or executives, the inability of investors and stockholders to know the cost of those options guarantees a false and misleading financial statement.

The other pay-for-performance link – sales
Investigators looking into the use of stock options quickly discovered another accounting trick used to boost executive pay – performance bonuses linked to sales. These may be appropriate if the sales are real. Often, however, they are phantom sales reported only to trigger executive options.

The sales practices of two drug companies, Bristol-Myers Squibb and Merck & Company, were put under the microscope by SEC investigators intrigued by Merck's reporting as revenue on the books some $14 billion in prescription co-payments. Co-payment amounts from consumers are retained by the prescription-filling pharmacy and do not flow back to Merck. The company insisted that booking of the phantom revenue was proper. But then it was learned that pay-for-performance bonuses for Merck's senior executives are determined by comparing growth in revenues and earnings per share to those of competing pharmaceutical firms. The extra $14 billion in revenue – over 10% of the company's total sales for the year – would be calculated into the bonus formula for senior executives.

Bristol-Myers Squibb also came under scrutiny for potential overstatement of sales when its chairman announced that the company's revenue would fall in 2002 because wholesalers were holding hundreds of millions of dollars worth of "excess" inventories of B-MS products sold to them the preceding year. As with Merck, executive compensation at Bristol-Myers is also linked to sales. In addition to his $1.25 million in salary and bonus, the CEO, Richard J. Lane, had been awarded $2.145 million in restricted stock through the performance formula. When the chairman of the board announced the reduced revenue figures based on real rather than phantom sales, Lane departed the company.

"O.K. guys, now lets go and <u>earn</u> that four hundred times our workers' salaries."

Meanwhile, in the trenches

Fortune 500 executives and those in high-tech/dot-com/ communications enjoyed rapidly ascending incomes and perks in what was called "The New Economy" of the 1990s. White- and blue-collar workers in more traditional industries didn't fare so well. While corporate profits rose 75% between 1990 and 1995, layoffs rose 39%. Hundreds of thousands of workers were put out on the street. Those who kept their jobs averaged increases of a little over three percent per year. At the same time CEO compensation climbed 92%, from an average of $1.95 million in 1990 to $3.75 million in 1995. People were beginning to grumble.

In April 1996 *Business Week* magazine featured a special report, "How High Can CEO Pay Go?"

> When United Technologies Chairman Robert F. Daniell strolls into the Carlton Hotel in Washington... for his company's annual meeting, he should expect to see nothing but a sea of happy faces.
>
> After all, the company's stock outpaced the market last year, throwing off a return of 55% to shareholders in 1995 alone. Net income rose 28%, to a near-record $750 million on $22.8 billion in sales. So no one is likely to grouse about the $11.2 million in pay Daniell got last year.
>
> Yet back in the factories and offices of the far-flung conglomerate, some employees are stirring – as they are at companies large and small across the country. In an era of massive downsizings, stagnant wages, and ever more burdensome workloads of layoff survivors, employees are feeling disenfranchised, discouraged and angry.
>
> Listen to a United Technologies Corp. manager in the trenches who has seen his company downsize by some 30,000 employees in the past six years.
>
> Despite consistently good performance reviews, this $67,000-a-year manager with nearly two decades of service to the company has averaged a mere 4% pay raise in each of the past three years. "At the same time, the CEO is paid millions, and his salary is going up much higher than anyone else's," he adds. "It makes me angry and resentful." [20]

Despite worker complaints, many compensation experts felt that all was well. *Business Week's* report quotes Arnold S. Ross, a New York pay consultant: "If you produce, you get paid the big bucks. Right now, the system is working better than anywhere else in the world. More than ever, pay is tied to performance." [21]

One example cited by the magazine was that of Lawrence M. Coss, CEO of Green Tree Financial Group based in Minnesota.

> [Coss] garnered $65.6 million last year – a tidy sum for a CEO of a consumer-finance company with net income of only $254 million. But look at Green Tree's performance: Its market value has grown to $3.6 billion from $330 million in the past five years. Earnings per share have grown at an annual rate of 44% since 1990. Coss's compensation, the

company insists, is a near-perfect example of how pay for performance should work. [22]

What neither the company nor the magazine pointed out was that Coss's compensation represented fully a quarter (25.8%) of the company's net income for that year. Nor did they note that the glowing praise for his "pay for performance" was issued by the company, not its investors.

Two years later the directors of Green Tree Financial may have wished they could reclaim Coss's extravagant award. The share price dived almost 20% on revelations of "accounting problems." In 1998 the troubled company was sold to a competitor.

Executive compensation became an issue in the political campaigns of 1996. Both an ultra-conservative presidential candidate, Patrick J. Buchanan, and an ultra-liberal, Jesse Jackson, called for CEO compensation to be set as a ratio to the wages of workers. The idea wasn't new to them. It had its first airing in *The Maximum Wage* (The Apex Press 1992) by Sam Pizzigati, a union publicist. Pizzigati contended that "linking the income of the rich to that of the poor would insure that a rising economic tide lifted all boats, not just the yachts." [23]

In 1992, when the average CEO at a Fortune 500 company earned 197 times as much as the average worker, radical reformers suggested that CEO compensation packages should be capped at 10 or, at absolute maximum, 25 times the minimum paid to the workers. Moderates suggested that a ratio of 50 to one might be more appropriate. Thus in a plant where the janitor earned $20,000 a year, the CEO's compensation would max out at $1 million. Or if the firm paid its CEO the 1992 average of $4.06 million, the janitor would take home $92,000.

By 2001, average CEO compensation had risen to 531 times the pay of the average worker. If the minimum wage had moved up at the same rate as CEO pay in the 1990's decade, it would have risen to $25.20 per hour. [24]

Proponents of "income-equalizing" suggest that the poor and middle class need an income sufficient to sustain consumer demand, whereas executive greed strangles the free market. The business community saw it differently. "'This is just another manifestation of the politics of envy,' said William A. Niskanen, chairman of the Cato Institute and once President Reagan's chief economic adviser." [25]

By 1999, however, the concerns of investors over executive compensation began to be heard. "Who Profits If The Boss Is Overfed?" asked the headline of *The New York Times'* "Investing" column, "The Stockholders Could Go Hungry." [26i]

Soaring CEO pay was defended as an incentive, however. Executive thoroughbreds were expected to devote 60-80 and more hours a week guiding their multi-national conglomerates through the maze of global commerce. Interviewed by writer Reed Abelson, compensation consultant Graef Crystal expressed an opposing view, that executive pay "doesn't really motivate the CEO. They are already working as hard as they can."[27] Based on his study of the relationship of pay to performance he cited 58 companies whose pay packages included what he considered overly high salaries, bonuses, and stock option awards.

> Mr. Crystal found that those 58 companies, on average, significantly underperformed both the overall market and other companies in their respective industries. They lost, on average, 1.5 percent for the twelve months ... compared with a 12.2 percent gain for the average of companies in the Standard & Poor's 500 index, regardless of market capitalization. Roughly two-thirds of the stocks dropped in price. [28]

Another rationale for high compensation packages was that extraordinary pay is required to keep a CEO from jumping ship for a better offer. Boards also provide lavish "retention" bonuses to justify enormous executive pay packages. Not true and unnecessary writes "Economic View" columnist David Leonhardt of *The New York Times.*

> Since 2000, a year in which executive turnover spiked, 77 of the 200 biggest companies have hired a new boss, according to Pearl Meyer & Partners, a compensation consultant. How many of those companies had to do so because their chief executive took another corporate job? Two.
>
> Most departing chiefs retired and remained on their company's board, according to news accounts. A good number were forced out. [29]

Senator John McCain, Republican of Arizona, proposed that top executives be required to hold all their company stock until they leave their jobs. Leonhardt agreed. "If boards were wise...they will [sic] realize that finding a new company to run is not easy. Bank One and Citigroup already have stock-holding rules for top executives, and neither has suffered an exodus." [30]

CEO Sweepstakes: Can You Top This?

By the year 2000, the average annual compensation – salary and options — for a chief executive of a major American corporation was $27 million. But, "Will Today's Huge Rewards Devour Tomorrow's Earnings," asked *The New York Times* Money & Business "Report on Executive Pay."

> Over the last five years, America's companies have handed over a large portion of themselves to the executives who run them.
>
> As top executives (and other employees) continue to exercise their rising pile of options over the next decade, other stockholders will see their stakes watered down. Already, companies have spent billions of dollars in recent years – and taken on rising levels of debt – buying back shares to minimize the dilution. For the repurchasing to continue at the present pace, a recent Federal Reserve study warned, companies would have to devote virtually all of their future earnings to buybacks. [31]

When CEO compensation packages began to exceed the $100 million mark, even Big Business's cheerleaders began to turn sour. The June 25, 2001 issue of *Fortune* featured a series of blunt and no-holds-barred "Executive Pay" reports. "This Stuff Is Wrong," headlined a series of interviews reported by writer Carol J. Loomis, with the subhead: "That's the conclusion of most of the insiders who talked to *Fortune* – candidly – about CEO pay. And you know what's even worse? They don't know how the overreaching can be stopped." [32]

From a well-paid CEO who had served on several "big time" boards:

> Compensation committee members are not malevolent. I've seen situations that are f—d up, and yet the directors think they're doing a hell of a job. They delude themselves. They think things are being done right and fairly – they don't think they're being had – when actually the excesses they're approving are just mind-boggling. [33]

From another corporate executive with wide experience serving on boards:

"Compensation committees are really in the pockets of CEOs. There are all kinds of cozy relationships involved. And when a CEO wants the rules changed as to how people are paid, the rules simply get changed. [34]

The CEO of one very successful *Fortune 500* company acknowledged:

The scandal of what goes on in compensation is how much is paid in the many, many instances when it isn't at all deserved. But a sub-scandal is the lack of a charge against earnings when stock options are issued. Companies go along as if these things are free, when actually they cost the shareholder enormous amounts. If you think how much more money CEOs have gotten because there isn't an earnings charge for options, it blows your mind. [35]

Before the scandals of 2001-2 became public, WorldCom's Chief Financial Officer had been considered a "good guy" by Wall Street and his peers.

Many Wall Street professionals thought Scott Sullivan was one of the best chief financial officers around. 'Scott was well regarded as a straight shooter who had his arms around a lot of details,' said Lehman Brothers analyst Blake Bath....

People who know Mr. Sullivan said he is likely to be deeply upset by the collapse of the company and his apparent role in it. Some investors believe Mr. Sullivan slid into his current predicament out of a desire to come through for Mr. Ebbers, who had always been able to rely on him to make the numbers work. [36]

Sullivan was, as *The Wall Street Journal* described, "handsomely rewarded for his work," earning a salary of $700,000, plus a $10 million retention bonus.[37] Perhaps even more embarrassing to the ex-CFO than his firing was the characterization of his financial manipulations as unsophisticated compared to the intricate financial creations of Enron. WorldCom had simply reassigned ordinary operating expenses to the "capital expense" column for a period of 15 months. Sullivan apparently intended to hide the obvious in a write-down of goodwill.

While compensation for WorldCom's CFO and CEO were generous – CEO and co-founder Bernard Ebbers had raked in over $30.7 million in salary, bonus, and stock-option grants in 1998— their compensation package was modest when compared to some of the highest of high rollers.[38] In the year that Enron's complex financial fabric unraveled, 2001, CEO Kenneth Lay was awarded $67.4 million in salary, bonuses, and restricted stock, plus an additional $70 million in loans. The company's CFO, Jeffrey Skilling, received compensation of $40 million that year plus $19 million in stock options. Wrote *The Wall Street Journal:*

> Representatives of Enron Corp.'s laid-off workers and pension-plan participants reacted with outrage to Enron's disclosure yesterday that it made $745 million of payments and stock awards to senior executives in the year prior to the company's bankruptcy-law filing. [39]

In awarding their CEOs princely sums, boards of directors could point to the yardsticks set by Disney's Michael Eisner. He took home $500 million from the sale of stock options. In 2000, Citigroup gave CEO Sandy Weill $151 million. Jack Welch of GE had taken home a pay package of about $125 million and Oracle's Larry Ellison, $92 million. Steve Jobs of Apple won the compensation sweepstakes with an options grant from Apple of $872 million. "The No. 1 earners in each of the past five years got packages valued cumulatively at nearly $1.4 billion, or $274 million on average," wrote *Fortune* Magazine's Geoffrey Colvin in "The Great CEO Pay Heist," [40]

It wasn't only giants anointing their CEO with a king's ransom. When insurance company Conseco, 239th on the 2002 Fortune 500 list, ousted its founder, chairman and CEO Stephen Hilbert in early 2002, "he walked away with a hefty $72.5 million severance package," reported *The Wall Street Journal.* "Even as his company went into a devastating tailspin, the documents show he received a total of $57.4 million last year." [41]

Bad apples in the Big Business Barrel continued to ferment during the summer of 2002. Adelphia was forced into Chapter 11 on disclosures that the founding Rigas family had borrowed $3.1 billion using company assets as collateral. Adelphia had also subsidized their many other ventures, including the purchase of the Buffalo Sabres hockey team. Martha Stewart was charged with insider trading along with family members of ImClone Systems founder and CEO Samuel Waksal. Prominent money-manager Alan Bond, a former regular on TV's "Wall Street Week With Louis Rukeyser", was convicted of allocating winning trades to his own account while charging the losers to his clients. It was discovered that Perot Systems, under CEO and former presidential candidate Ross Perot, designed and sold an energy management and cost-control system to the State of California, then turned around and sold ways to scam the system to California's energy providers such as Enron and Reliant Energy.

As Global Crossing underwent bankruptcy proceedings in the spring of 2002, the company told the court that it was covering $8.8 million in taxes due on $10 million in personal loans made to CEO John Legere. Legere had received a $3.5 million signing bonus when he joined the company just six months prior.

In the three years before he resigned as CEO of Tyco International Ltd., Dennis Koslowski took home more than $300 million. He used company funds to buy an $18 million New York City apartment, then was charged with borrowing company funds, interest free, to buy artwork and evade sales taxes on the purchases by having empty shipping crates sent to the company while the real artwork was sent to his home.

E*Trade's CEO became the stock brokerage industry's highest paid with a package valued at $80 plus million. The package included forgiveness from the company of a $15 million loan plus $15 million in taxes paid on the loan, plus $29 million in restricted stock and $1.87 million in stock options.

Few of the huge compensation awards had any relationship to success. Many of them were awards for failure. WorldCom's directors, "frustrated with the company's tanking stock price, Mr. Ebbers' $366 million personal loan from the company and the wide-ranging investigation by the Securities and Exchange Commission," asked CEO Ebbers to step down.[42] When Michael Ovitz resigned from Walt Disney Company after only 16 months with the company, he walked away with a buyout worth more than $90 million – a compensation package of more than $5.6 million for each month on the job. That was in 1996, when $90 million was real money.

As previously noted, excessive executive compensation has been of concern in the halls of Congress and in the editorial rooms of the business media itself. "These Raises Are Insane!" headlined Fortune magazine's September 30, 1996 issue. [43] Two years later the magazine asked, "Can Even Heroes Get Paid Too Much," in its June 8, 1998 issue. [44] And in May of that year, in "Revealed: Boardroom Secrets," *Fortune* writer Geoffrey Colvin described how boards become cheerleaders for their CEOs instead of watchdogs for the stockholders. His conclusion, based on a study by James D. Westphal of the University of Texas: "Boards that are more independent seem to exert less power over the CEO. The more independent a company's board … the higher its level of diversification and the <u>higher</u> and <u>less</u> at risk the CEO's pay." [45] (Colvin's emphasis).

There is a very direct cost to the shareholders for compensation excesses, especially in the granting of stock options, as per this unusually frank announcement by Electronic Data Systems.

> Electronic Data Systems Corp. said its departing chairman and chief executive officer, Lester M. Alberthal Jr., will receive $35 million in converted stock options, a consulting contract and other benefits.
>
> The company said the cost of the compensation to Mr. Alberthal … will reduce its third-quarter profit by five cents a diluted share. [46]

Pharaoh-sized executive compensation again raises the question: who owns a corporation?

[1] Tyson vs Banton, 1927.

[2] *USA Today*, June 27, 2002.

[3] "Could Capitalists Actually Bring Down Capitalism," by Kurt Eichenwald, Money&Business, *The New York Times*, June 30, 2002

[4] "Treasury Secretary Criticizes Misconduct," *The Wall Street Journal*, June 14, 2002, and "Treasury secretary blasts lack of ethics," by Martin Crutsinger, The Associated Press, June 14, 2002.

[5] "Bush Crackdown on Business Fraud Signals New Era," by Jeanne Cummings, Jacob M. Schlesinger, Michael Schroeder, *The Wall Street Journal*, July 10, 2002.

[6] "Bush Aide Blasts Moves To Curb Pay. Robson Calls SEC, Congress Out Of Line," Knight-Ridder, as published in *The Washington Post*, June 11, 1992.

[7] Ibid.

[8] "Firms Find Ways Around Salary Cap; Stock Options Are Used To Increase Executive Compensation." By Jay Mathews, *The Washington Post*, November 27, 1993.

[9] Ibid.

[10] "Stock Options: Greed, Arrogance, and Power," by George J. Schneider CPA and Patrick E. Freer CPA; an unpublished letter to Securities Exchange Commission, Financial Accounting Standards Board, Senate Banking Committee and others, August 20, 2001, provided by the authors.

[11] Ibid.

[12] Ibid.

[13] "For Silicon Valley, Stocks Fall Upsets Culture of Options," by Rebecca Buckman and David Bank, *The Wall Street Journal*, July 18, 2002.

[14] "Following Coke's Lead Could Bring Big Changes," A *Wall Street Journal* News Roundup, July 16, 2002.

[15] "Accounting Panel Approves Change," by Silvia Ascarelli and Ken Brown, *The Wall Street Journal*, July 17, 2002.

[16] Op Cit. "For Silicon Valley, Stocks Fall Upsets Culture of Options," by Rebecca Buckman and David Bank.

[17] "Before Telecom Industry Sank, Insiders Sold Billions in Stock," by Kennis K. Berman, *The Wall Street Journal*, August 12, 2002.

[18] "Reforming Stock Options in the Post-Enron, Post-WorldCom Era," by Corey Rosen, The National Center for Employee Ownership (NCEO), Web site www.nceo.org, undated.

[19] Ibid.

20 "How High Can CEO Pay Go?", by John A. Byrne, *Business Week*, April 22, 1996.

21 Ibid.

22 Ibid.

23 "Corporate Greed, Meet the Maximum Wage," by Steven Greenhouse, *The New York Times*, June 16, 1996.

24 "Bush: Corporate Confidence Man," by Charlie Cray and Lee Drutman, CommonDream.org, www.citizenworks.org, July 9, 2002.

25 Ibid.

26 "Who Profits If The Boss Is Overfed?", by Reed Abelson, "Investing," *The New York Times*, June 20, 1999.

27 Ibid.

28 Ibid.

29 "Once Upon A Time, A Restless C.E.O.," by David Leonhardt, *The New York Times*, July 28, 2002.

30 Ibid.

31 Will Todays Huge Rewards Devour Tomorrow's Earnings?" by David Leonhardt, *The New York Times*, Money&Business, April 2, 2000.

32 *Fortune* magazine, June 25, 2001.

33 Ibid.

34 Ibid.

35 Ibid.

36 "Wall Street Thought Highly Of WorldCom's Finance Chief," by Shawn Young and Evan Perez, *The Wall Street Journal*, June 27, 2002.

37 Ibid.

38 "Executive PayWatch,", AFL-CEO Web site, www.aflcio.org/cgi-bin/ downloaded April 12, 2000.

39 "Enron Awards To Top Officials Provoke Outrage," by Mitchell Pacelle, *The Wall Street Journal*, June 17, 2002.

40 The Great CEO Pay Heist," by Geoffrey Colvin, *Fortune* magazine, June 25, 2001.

41 "Conseco Paid Ex-CEO $72.5 Million, But He Owes $162.5 Million for Loans," by James P. Miller, "Who's News" column, *The Wall Street Journal*, May 3, 2000.

42 "WorldCom CEO Suddenly Quits Amid SEC Probe," by Rebecca Blumenstein and Jared Sandberg, *The Wall Street Journal*, April 30, 2002.

43 "Wall Street Pay: These Raises Are Insane!, by Shawn Tully, *Fortune* magazine, September 30, 1996.

44 "Can Even Heroes Get Paid Too Much," by Thomas Stewart, *Fortune* magazine, June 8, 1998.

[45] "Revealed: Boardroom Secrets," by Geoffrey Colvin, *Fortune* magazine, May 25, 1998.

[46] "EDS Chairman Compensation To Lower Profit," by Evan Ramstad, *The Wall Street Journal*, August 10, 1998.

CHAPTER NINE
THE OTHER GUYS

If you can meet with Triumph and Disaster
And treat those two imposters just the same...

IF by Rudyard Kipling

Spurred by the lure of huge bonuses for "performance," chief executives sought opportunities to boost the bottom line. Some, as investors were to discover in 2002, simply "cooked the books." In the mid-90s, however, the fashion was to downsize domestic operations and send the work to wherever the least expensive labor could be found.

Typically, when a company announced "restructuring" with layoffs, its stock price would shoot up as investors saw a potential for added profitability, as in this story in *The New York Times* business section: "Moves by Campbell Soup Send Shares Surging to New High." [1] The story reported on the firm's $160 million restructuring plan, the $210 million purchase of a German soup business, a $2.5 billion stock repurchase plan, an increase in its advertising budget, and the dismissal of 650 workers including 11 percent of its headquarters staff. Once that pattern had been established in one firm in an industry, other companies are almost forced to do the same. The result? The U.S. Labor Department reported that one out of every 14 jobholders — a total of 8.4 million people — was laid off or otherwise lost their jobs involuntarily in the years 1993-1995.

There are, thankfully, exceptions to short-term myopia.

Malden Mills of Methuen

On December 11, 1995, a fire burned most of Malden Mills to the ground and put 3,000 people out of work. Most of the 3,000 thought they were out of work permanently. A few employees were with the CEO in the parking lot during the fire and heard him say 'this is not the end.' With these words began a saga that has made Aaron Feuerstein a legend among American leaders and a hero to his employees. [2]

Aaron Feuerstein became a hero to the entire nation following the disaster by insisting he would rebuild the plant and keep the 96-year-old family company going. In his late 60's, the mill owner could have taken the tens of millions in insurance money and retired comfortably. Instead, he kept all 3,000 employees on the payroll with full benefits and set about rebuilding the mill.

Asked why he was rebuilding instead of retiring he simply said he was doing what he believed was the honorable thing to do. Later, when he was being lionized on national television and honored at a string of ceremonies, he said he hoped that his loyalty to his workers and community would be an example for all corporate executives: "I feel that I am a symbol of the movement against downsizing and layoffs.... People see me as a turning of the tide." [3]

Certain elements of Feuerstein's story as told by *The Boston Globe* not long after the fire, are especially germane to any discussion of capitalism and corporatism:

> Samuel Feuerstein, who died in 1983, left his son Aaron, a twofold legacy: responsibility for an Orthodox synagogue that had grown to be the largest in New England, and for a textile operation that had remained in the region long after others had moved south.
>
> In the last two years, both temple and mill have burned down.
>
> Yesterday, Feuerstein sat in a makeshift office ... and once again vowed to rebuild.
>
> In the days since the fire, he has repeated that pledge many times. He has already made sure his employees were paid on time. He has given them Christmas bonuses and promised them another month's pay. He has told customers that partial production should resume within a month.
>
> Feuerstein said it was a 2500-year-old quote from the Jewish tradition that has kept him strong in recent days. 'When all is moral chaos, this is the time for you to be a mensch.'
>
> In Yiddish, the word 'mensch' means more than just a man. It carries a sense of righteousness that friends, family and co-workers say has been the driving force in Feuerstein's life.
>
> Chuck Henderson, president of Chuck Roast Equipment Inc., in Conway, N.H., recalls how Malden

Mills extended generous credit when his own outdoor equipment company was foundering a few years ago.

The credit line saved his company, he said. 'That's the kind of guy Aaron is,' Henderson said. 'If he's got half a loaf of bread, he's going to share it around.'

Speaking yesterday of his charred factory, Feuerstein said he expects the new mill to be up and running in time for the High Holy Days next fall. The desire to rebuild as quickly as possible, he said, is as much about looking after his employees as it is about profits. [4]

Feuerstein's righteousness was expensive. In 2001, reported *Fortune* magazine, the mill was down to 1,200 employees and the 76 year old mill owner was forced to file for Chapter 11 bankruptcy. *Fortune* asked him:

"Is Chapter 11 proof that you made mistakes recovering from the fire?" His reply: "Had I replaced the factory exactly as it was before the fire, I would have had enough insurance. But I wanted everything to be the absolute latest and best. As a result we spent millions over what we were insured for." *Fortune*: "Have customers shied away?" Feuerstein: "The CEO of one of our largest customers called to tell me his company is behind me 100%. He said, 'You're going to have all our business. We owe it to you.' And I said, 'Why do you say that?' Back in the early '90's when they had similar trouble, we helped them. And I had plumb forgotten. When you treat people the way you ought to treat them, later on it comes back to you." [5]

Certain key points stand out in the Feuerstein story. First, he had not relocated his mill as had most of the New England textile industry to regions of lower labor costs and taxes. Second, he was close to the community, a contributor to it rather than, as is most often the case today, demanding tax rebates and other government aid as an inducement to keep the mill in place. Third, when he had the opportunity to take the insurance money and run, he stayed. Employees of the mill took precedence over self. Fourth, he knew his employees, what they did in his mill and how they did it, because he walked through the plant frequently. He was in touch with the people, the production processes, and the products. Fifth, he knew his customers on a personal level, and they knew him.

Little wonder that the media leapt upon Feuerstein's story. It presented reaffirming relief to the "greed is good" fashion of business in the mid-1990s. It also presented fodder for business consultants, such as the "Quality Monitor Newsletter" of the Organizational Productivity Institute, Inc.

> Aaron Feuerstein spent millions keeping all 3,000 employees on the payroll with full benefits for 3 months. Why? What did he get for his money? Is he a fool? Did he have some dark motive? Here is Aaron Feuerstein's answer: 'The fundamental difference is that I consider our workers an asset, not an expense.' Indeed, he believes his job goes beyond just making money for shareholders, even though the only shareholders of Malden Mills are Feuerstein and his family. 'I have a responsibility to the worker, both blue-collar and white-collar,' Feuerstein added, his voice taking an edge of steely conviction. 'I have an equal responsibility to the community. It would have been unconscionable to put 3,000 people on the streets and deliver a death blow to the cities of Lawrence and Methuen. Maybe on paper our company is worth less to Wall Street, but I can tell you it's worth more. We're doing fine.'[6]

A final point: Aaron Feuerstein also knew his stockholders. They were "family" in every sense of the word. [a]

Cole Hardwood

On an early summer Saturday afternoon in 1998, a fire swept through Cole Hardwood, Inc., of Logansport, Indiana. All 10 buildings of the company, 140,000 square feet, were lost to the flames, including 8 million board feet of fully processed lumber. They lost their office, their planing mill, and retail store. But "we never lost heart" owner Milt Cole writes in the Cole Hardwood Web site. [7]

---

[a] On May 9, 2003, The Wall Street Journal reported that Feuerstein needed $92 million by July 31 to buy his business back from lenders. The nation's economic slump of 2000-2001 had forced the firm into a second Chapter 11 bankruptcy in late 2001. As of the May 9th report he'd raised all but $10 million.

In July of that year, Milton Cole was featured on a National Public Radio broadcast in an interview with Noah Adams, senior host of "All Things Considered." From that interview:

> *Introduction*: "Noah talks with Milton Cole, the owner of Cole Hardwood. Cole decided to rebuild his business after a devastating fire, even though it would be more financially lucrative for him to simply collect the insurance money and retire."
>
> *Cole*: "It happened about 3 p.m. on June the 13th."
>
> *Noah*: "This fire was on Saturday, and on Monday you got all your employees together there at the yard and you say 'we're going to rebuild it, right?'"
>
> *Cole*: "That's exactly right. Saturday night I went home from the fire, while the fire was still going on. I couldn't take any more. I went home. That evening if you would have asked me if I was going to rebuild I'd probably said 'no.' But after I got a good night's sleep, I got up Sunday morning, I was re-energized and ready to go. And so I knew I was going to rebuild."
>
> *Noah*: "Did you sit down at the kitchen table and try to figure it all out?"
>
> *Cole*: "No, not really. I just knew I was going to do it. I just care too much for my people."
>
> *Noah*: "How can you afford to pay them all the way through the rebuilding process?"
>
> *Cole*: "Well, we're probably running about seventy-five percent efficient right now. I just feel they've made it and now … we've done very well and I'm just willing to share."
>
> *Noah*: "Could you have decided on that weekend or the Monday … could you have met with your insurance people and they could have said, 'well, that's it, it's a total loss,' and shut it down and give you a check?"
>
> *Cole*: "Oh yes, we could've. But I chose not to do that. It was certainly not money. You could take the money and live very good the rest of our lives. But we live very good … and the extra money wouldn't do anything to change our life style. We're living as good as we care to. We just enjoy sharing." [8]

Milton Cole didn't get the same national acclaim as did Aaron Feuerstein, even though the motivations of both were identical. In the face of business disaster and the opportunity to cut and run with the money, both men arrived at the same conclusion: people come before personal wealth.

Perhaps their perspective differed from that of CEOs of other corporations faced with similar ethical dilemmas because they knew their employees as real people, not just numbers in an operating expenses budget or files in human resources records.

The Next New New Thing

The Jim Clark story is far different from that of Aaron Feuerstein or Milton Cole. Clark is not of the old school of traditional industry and business, but at the cutting edge. Some would say Clark is the cutting edge.

The founder of Silicon Graphics, Netscape, and Healtheon, "he was built to work on the frontier of economic life... He was designed for rapid social and technological change. He was the starter of new things," wrote Michael Lewis for *The New York Times Magazine.* [9]

Clark grew up poor in Plainview, Texas, was expelled from high school, and was a problem recruit for the Navy who tested him and discovered an aptitude for math that Clark didn't know he had. Encouraged to go to college, within eight years Clark had a college degree in math, a Masters degree in physics and a Ph.D. in computer science. He failed at two marriages, landed and was fired from several teaching jobs, and finally ended up teaching computer science at Stanford University where, says Lewis, he was miserable. He concluded that he had achieved nothing in his 38 years.

Clark re-invented himself, according to Lewis, quickly became the most sought-after computer science professor at Stanford and put his students to work on a little idea he had, a computer chip "geometry engine," that would simulate 3-D graphics in real time. "In 1981 it became the basis for a new company, founded by Clark and his students, called Silicon Graphics [which] became a multi-billion-dollar company and Clark became a multimillionaire."

And yet, writes Lewis, "The man was still miserable!" Clark didn't enjoy being part of a large corporation and made life difficult for himself and everyone else within the company.

In his misery he landed on a new idea, to turn the television in everyone's home into an interactive "telecomputer" through which one could communicate with friends and businesses, and even go shopping.

Clark's depression turned into hyperactivity. He spoke at trade shows, hit the media circuit, and, with his passion, conviction, and commitment to the project, convinced Time Warner to pay $30 million to Silicon Graphics to build the telecomputer and test it in 4,000 homes in Orlando, Florida. Just before the test, however, Clark suddenly quit Silicon Graphics to start his own company. How did he justify leaving Silicon Graphics and Time Warner in the lurch? As Clark explained: "The guy who finds the new new thing and makes it happen wins. The engineers who help him do it finish second. The financiers and the corporate backers, the suckerfish of economic growth, finish a distant third."

Casting about for his "new new thing," Clark found a new love, the internet, and a new partner, Marc Andreesen, author of what turned out to be the first "browser" application, "Mosaic." Clark and Andreesen formed Mosaic Communications Corporation.

Clark, from an interview with *Wired* reporter Michael Goldberg:

> Of course I knew what the Internet was. But I hadn't thought about what the implications were in terms of its growth rate. You would be astounded at the number of terabytes of data that are served by Mosaic today, daily, running on numerous platforms. It's sort of the standard network tool. [10]

Mosaic became Netscape, which Clark and Andreesen gave away free to users of the Internet while selling a version of the program to companies for their own communications. Asked by *Wired* if he could do with Netscape what he did with Silicon Graphics, turn it into a billion-dollar company, Clark responded: "The vision is really Marc Andreesen's, not mine. And I think he can strike fire."

Use of the Internet exploded and, by 1995, Netscape controlled over 80% of the browser market, a market share soon to be challenged by Microsoft. Netscape made Clark a billionaire several times over, but he quickly found other opportunities for his creative energy: Healtheon, later WebMD, and then in 2001, a network security startup, Neoteris. Was wealth his objective? Writer Michael Lewis didn't think so.

> One evening not long after the Healtheon offering, as we sat in his kitchen, I reminded Clark that he had said that once he became a real, after-tax billionaire he'd retire.... I asked the obvious question: 'Would you want to have more money than say, Bill Gates?'

'Oh, no,' Clark said, waving my question to the side of the room where ridiculous ideas gather to commiserate with one another. 'That'll never happen.' A few minutes later, after the conversation had turned to other matters, he came clean. 'You know,' he said, 'just for one moment, I would kind of like to have the most. Just for one tiny moment.' [11,b]

Not giving back, paying back

"This is a story about a very generous man named Jim Rogers," wrote *New York Times* reporter Diana B. Henriques in the paper's November 29, 1998, Personal Business section.[12]   The Jim Rogers referred to is owner and chairman of Sunbelt Communications, owner of KVBC and eight other Rocky Mountain television stations. Rogers, a lawyer by training, had just pledged $50 million to the University of Arizona Law School. At that time this was the largest gift ever made to a law school in America.

Then in 1998, he doubled it to $100 million and iced the cake with a $15 million "challenge" grant to encourage other givers, plus an additional $15 million for other programs at the University. Then he made a pledge of $28.5 million to the University of Nevada at Las Vegas' Law School.

As might be expected, U of A's Law School was immediately named "The James B. Rogers College of Law." But being memorialized was not Jim Rogers' objective. "I think we should abandon the concept of giving," Rogers told reporter Henriques. "The concept implies that success is due to your own hard work." But, insists Rogers, "Your success is the convergence of a lot of lucky events – you were born in America, with a good brain, with parents who taught you good values – none of which you had any control over." After you've acquired all the toys, said Rogers, "what you have left, you hold in trust for the public [and] I'm holding my money in trust for education."

Writes Henriques, "In 1971 [Rogers] and some business partners filed an application to take over an existing television license in Las Vegas. In late 1978, after years of litigation involving the former owner, the application was approved and Mr. Rogers, at 40, became a broadcasting executive – just as his region's growth broke into a gallop. 'We caught lightning in a bottle,' he said."

---

[b] As of June 2003 Clark's Healtheon was still running in the red. His webMD, linking insurers, doctors, and patients online has lost $3 billion on revenues of $517 million, but had a base of 250,000 doctors and 1,000 hospitals using the software and was gaining favorable Wall Street attention. His newest startups were "myCFO" and the "Smartpipes" internet network.

In dollar figures, Rogers, age 60 at the time of *The New York Times* story, is worth about $500 million and says he intends to give away about 75% of it to promote education. "Leaving children wealth is like leaving a case of psychological cancer," says Rogers, telling Henriques that his wife Beverly and three children support his plans. Denying a religious motivation for his charity, advisors believe it comes from "moral compulsion" and "a belief in the impact law can have on society."

Rogers himself attributes his benevolence to a long-time Las Vegas friend who named him his executor and gave him explicit instructions for his funeral. As Henriques relates the story: "Behind the hearse was to be a Wells Fargo armored truck… bearing a sign that read, 'I've changed my mind; I'm taking it with me.' Mr. Rogers got the hint."

Giant killer

In 1990, a 20-year-old Finnish college computer sciences student, Linus Torvalds, created a computer operating system "kernel" (the essential or core operating language) by hacking an early version of Unix. He called it Linux and distributed his creation on the Internet asking other hackers to look at it, test it, and improve upon it. He licensed his creation – his source code – free to all comers with only one caveat: Linux always had to remain open and visible. Programmers could use it, change it, de-bug it, improve upon it, and modify it for their own purposes, but they could not patent or keep their modifications secret. Within a few years, thanks to contributions of computer geeks around the world, Linux became an almost bulletproof crash- and bug-free operating system.

Torvolds' first copyright strictly prohibited commercial re-sale. Users could use or modify the program, but they could not distribute it or their modifications for money. He later eased that requirement to a Public License that allowed computer software developers to use Linux in commercial applications, so long as the code remained visible and accessible.

"Making Linux freely available is the single best decision I've ever made," asserted Torvolds. "Essentially, making it free is what made a difference between a system that was something one person was able to write in half a year, and a system that rivals (and surpasses) commercial operating systems." The advantage to a free system is "that it allows more developers to work on it, and extend it. However, even more important than that is the fact that it in one fell swoop also gave me a lot of people who used it and thus both tested it for bugs and tested it for useability." [13]

Within eight years of its introduction, Linux began to threaten Microsoft's lock on computer operating systems. Wrote *Time Digital,* "IBM, Dell, Intel, Oracle and Compaq are gearing up to support Linux.

As it gets easier to install, Linux is going to make serious inroads into the consumer-oriented PC market." Linux has become the world's fastest growing server operating system. It's also rapidly being adapted and adopted by such firms as Amazon, Ameritrade, Google, and other high-intensity users.

Commercial developers took Torvalds' Linux and adapted it for various uses with a number of features, some of which were patented (or protected under copyright). This did not go down well with open-source purists whose mantra, "No more monopolies; no more price gouging; no more technology lock-ins", was aimed at Microsoft, Apple, Sun, and all developers of proprietary software.

Torvalds, however, is a pragmatist; in his words:

> That which works, works. When it comes to software, I much prefer free software, because I have very seldom seen a program that has worked well enough for my needs, and having sources available can be a life-saver. However, that doesn't mean that I'm opposed to commercial software. Commercial software development has some advantages too – the money-making aspect introduces some new incentives that aren't there for most free software. And those incentives often make for a more polished product. [14]

Linux could have made Torvalds a very rich young man. But wealth appears to be low on his list of priorities.

> I've been employed by the University of Helsinki, and they've been perfectly happy to keep me employed and doing Linux. So in a sense I do get my pizza paid for by Linux indirectly. The cyberspace "earnings" I get from Linux come in the format of having a network of people that know me and trust me, and that I can depend on in return. And that kind of network of trust comes in very handy not only in cyberspace.
> …The act of making Linux freely available wasn't some agonizing decision that I took from thinking long and hard on it; it was a natural decision within the community that I felt I wanted to be part of. [15]

The Altruism Virus

Torvalds not only became godfather of the open source movement, but those who followed with commercial Linux-based products appeared to have caught Torvalds' altruistic spirit. One of these, Red Hat Linux, headquartered on the Centennial Campus of North Carolina State University, Raleigh, notes in its Web site that it too shares the source code of its products. "Red Hat engineers assemble the Linux kernel and other elements of the Linux operating system.... Then they add new features, test for compatibility – all while sharing the software with customers, partners and software vendors, and members of the open source community in a structured feedback cycle." [16]

A year 2000 start-up, VA Linux Systems of Sunnyvale, California, also calls itself a standard-bearer of the open source movement. Unlike most Linux development firms, VA Linux sells complete computer systems loaded with the Linux operating system rather than the current industry standard Microsoft Windows. Its founder, Notre Dame and Stanford graduate Larry Augustin, took his small company to an initial public offering in December 1999, and watched its per/share price rocket to $320, then drop to just above $100. *A New York Times* Private Sector story on the company by Lawrence M. Fisher which ran on February 6, 2000, ended with this quote by the founder: "Mr. Augustin tells employees not to think about VA Linux's share price, and he tried to take his own advice. 'I didn't start this thing to cash in and get out,' he said. 'I started this to build a real company.'" [17]

By July 2002, VA Linux stock was quoted in the 80-90¢ range.

EToys R Bust

"When you get an M.B.A., to be creative you've got to start a business," explained Toby Lenk, CEO of now defunct eToys. "When you do that, you're at the top of the food chain in terms of respect. It was alluring to think about eToys as a much bigger business. It was the excitement of the hunt, the chase, the competition." [18]

Lenk was featured by *The New York Times Magazine* because he knew, as their headline put it, "How to lose $850 million – and Not Really Care." Writer Michael Sokolove provided a short-form history of Lenk's quick rise to the top of the "food chain," his fall, and how it all didn't matter too much.

While employed at a comfortable six-figure salary at Disney as Vice President for Strategic Planning, Toby Lenk became intrigued with the idea of selling toys online. He applied his Harvard M.B.A. skills and training by conducting thorough and painstaking research on the idea. He studied Toys "R" Us, Hasbro, children's books, and software and created a strategic business plan, then founded eToys with $900,000 gleaned from 35 investors.

As Sokolove relates:

> After surprising initial success in the 1997 holiday season, venture capitalists poured an additional $28 million into the business. Lenk anticipated about $10 million in revenue for the final, all-important holiday quarter of 1998; eToys did $23 million. The following year, final-quarter revenues soared to $107 million. "The venture capitalists had already been swirling," Lenk recalls. "Then the investment banks started calling. And it was like, you know, everybody could sense a money-making opportunity. And then we had the whole press buildup, the David versus Goliath storyline. The Wall Street Journal, CNBC, started talking about upstart eToys taking on Toys 'R' Us. I never had any intention of taking on Toys 'R' Us."

In the spring of 1999 eToys launched its initial public offering with an opening share price of $20. The first trade came in at $79. The stock fluttered up to $85, then closed at $76.56. The market, noted Sokolove, had valued two-year-old eToys at $10 billion, "two and a half times greater than the bricks-and-morter giant Toys "R" Us." Lenk's 10.5 million shares made him a rich man, with a net worth close to $800 million.

But, as Sokolove concludes:

> Lenk entered into a strange relationship with this windfall. Mostly, he tried to ignore it. Sometimes he got mad at it. When a banner updating the eToys stock price went up on the company's internal home page, he ordered it taken down. He bristled when employees, all of whom held pre-I.P.O. stock, showed up at work in fancy new cars. Over time, he would come to believe that the stock market bubble ("this craziness, this frothing") had doomed an idea that would have survived a normal market.

Lenk didn't sell high, didn't sell when the market began to tumble, didn't sell at all. "I never felt comfortable with this whole notion of, 'I'm gonna make my $100 million and the hell with everybody else,'" he told Sokolove.

> Just before eToys filed for bankruptcy in March 2001, its stock plunged to 9 cents a share before being ignominiously de-listed by Nasdaq. When the company finally did expire, Lenk – the "captain of the ship," as he likes to say – went down with it. At the end he was still holding 10 million shares.

Some of Lenk's venture capitalist bankers made several hundred million dollars profit from the venture. Some family members parted with part of their stock and made money. Lenk and several of his top people, however, made a conscious decision not to part with any of their shares when they had the opportunity. "But Toby Lenk couldn't cash in as his company tanked – on some level it wasn't even a conscious choice," writes Sokolove, "because if he had, what would that have said about him?"

Why him? Why them?

The past two chapters have touched upon a few examples of egregious as well as laudable CEO behaviors making one ask: "What factors makes some corporate leaders voraciously greedy and others indifferent to personal wealth and thoughtful for the welfare of employees and investors?" Within the world of great and small corporations there are without a doubt a million shades of gray between the black and white extremes. There seems to be no easily identifiable cultural, educational, religious, ethnic, or professional factor that determines who wields the scepter of CEO-hood in benign or despotic fashion. Some of the most barbarous actions described were done by people who should have known better. Some of the grandest gestures were made by those from the same heritage and cultures.

Of the malefactors, the mystery is what gives these highly privileged people permission to break the rules they were taught in home, school, church and other social intercourse? As related in Chapter 4, chemical company executives and the trained physicians they employed agreed to a monstrous pact of silence even after witnessing proof of hideous disfigurement and long- term health damage to the workers in their vinyl chloride plants.

To sell accident insurance as State Farm did, collecting premiums from people trusting that the "good neighbor" would stand with them should an accident occur, and then to use faked-up "peer" reviews to deny payment for legitimate medical claims is repulsive and as evil as the actions of any thief stealing bread from the mouths of widows and orphans.

To accept tens of millions of dollars when your corporate ship is foundering under your command, is akin to a captain commandeering a lifeboat for himself then smashing the lifeboats of passengers and crew before jumping ship. Yet that is exactly what Jeffrey Skilling and Ken Lay of Enron, Dennis Koslowki of Tyco, Bernard Ebbers of WorldCom, and dozens of other executives are guilty of doing.

Yet if any one of the perpetrators of those acts was upbraided as being cruel and greedy, they would be outraged. In their heart of hearts, they believe they did nothing more than what anyone else might do given the same circumstance and opportunity.

And they would be right.

[1] "Moves by Campbell Soup Send Shares Surging to Reach a High," by Glen Collins, Business/Financial Desk, *The New York Times*, September 6, 1996.

[2] "Malden Mills; A Study in Leadership," by Art Boulay; from the October 1966 *Quality Monitor Newsletter*, Organizational Productivity Institute, Inc.

[3] "The Risks of Keeping a Promise; In Becoming an Icon, a Mill Owner Bets His Company," by Louis Uchitelle, *The New York Times*, July 4, 1996.

[4] "Methuen's Unstoppable Hero Aaron Feuerstein Tempered By Fire, by John Auerbach and John Milne, Globe Staff, *The Boston Globe*, December 15, 1995.

[5] "Looming Problems; Corporate kindness might cost Aaron Feuerstein his family's mill," by Julie Sloane, *Fortune Small Business*, March 1, 2002.

[6] Op cit, "Malden Mills: A Study in Leadership," by Art Boulay.

[7] <http://www.colehardwood.com/>.

[8] Extracted from "All Things Considered," National Public Radio, July 23, 1998.

[9] "Jim Clark Is Not So Much an Internet Entrepreneur as the Embodiment of a New Kind of Economic Man," by Michael Lewis, *The New York Times Magazine*, October 10, 1999.

[10] "Why Jim Clark Loves Mosaic," by Michael Goldberg, *Wired* magazine, October 1994.

[11] op. Cit, "Jim Clark Is Not So Much an Internet Entrepreneur..." *The New York Times Magazine*, October 10, 1999.

[12] "Determined To Share The Wealth," by Diana B. Henriques, *The New York Times*, November 29, 1998.

[13] "The Father of Linux," *Time* Digital, undated.

[14] "The Pragmatist of Free Software," by Hiroo Yamagata, Tokyo Linux Users Group (TLUG), September 30, 1997 <www.tlug.gr.jp/docs/linus.html>.

[15] "What motivates free software developers?" unsigned and undated interview with Linus Torvalds, by First Monday, <www.firstmonday.dk/issues/issue3_3/torvalds/>.

[16] "What is Red Hat Linux," Red Hat Web site <www.redhat.com/about/> undated.

[17] "A View that Needs No Windows," by Lawrence M. Fisher, *The New York Times*, February 6, 2000.

[18] "How to Lose $850 million – And Not Really Care," by Michael Sokolove, *The New York Times Magazine*, June 9, 2002.

John David Rose

CHAPTER TEN
WHO OWNS A CORPORATION?

> Corporations are legal entities which are separate and distinct from their owners; they are, in fact, "persons" created by state law. Corporations are owned by investors (shareholders) and generally managed by an elected board of directors and its appointed officers.
>
> West Legal Studies

Who owns General Electric, Disney, Enron or any of the publicly held *Fortune* 1000 corporations? If your answer is "the stockholders", think again. Stockholders are no more owners of these huge corporations than casino players are owners of the crap tables at which they place bets.

> "Own (transitive verb) 1 a: to have or hold as property: *POSSESS* b: to have power over : *CONTROL*." [a]

But if stockholders don't own a corporation, who does? Find the answer to that question and you'll have the answer to outrageous CEO compensation, stockholder fraud, and corporate crime.

One *owns* only what one has power over, what one controls. Conversely, one does <u>not</u> own what one does <u>not</u> control. So the answer to the question "Who owns General Electric, General Motors, Union Carbide, State Farm, etc." is most definitely not what is written in law books and assumed by the majority of shareholders. Pin any corporate attorney down and he/she will be forced to admit that shareholders do not hire or fire company officers, have no control over what the CEO is paid, what the directors are paid, whether the company should keep or break the laws of the land, or even whether to report a corporation's financial results honestly.

The fact is that stockholders have absolutely no control and thus no real ownership of the major corporations whose stock they hold.

What is the real status of stockholders? An illustration:

---

[a] Webster's Ninth New Collegiate Dictionary,

Financier and political dabbler Ross Perot was once General Motors' largest shareholder with more than 11 million shares. In the early 1980's he attempted to shake up what he considered to be a badly managed organization.

GM's board resisted Perot's interference. In 1986, at the expense of the other shareholders of the company as well as workers dependent upon the GM retirement fund, the Board of General Motors bought Perot's stock and silence with a deal that included a $7.5 million fine if he continued to speak out against GM's management. [1]

A more recent (2003) example was an attempt by former board member and the largest individual stockholder Selim K. Zilkha to replace the board of El Paso Corporation.

> Over the past several years, the incumbent Board of Directors has created the financial equivalent of the "perfect storm" in which El Paso Corporation now finds itself — a condition brought about by risky investments, excessive borrowing, dubious accounting practices and egregious executive compensation. During this turbulent period that has seen the company's market value decline nearly 90%, El Paso's management has enriched itself while El Paso's shareholders have suffered devastating losses. [2]

Zilkha's ire was fed by his own personal losses, some $500+ million, as the value of El Paso stock had plummeted from $75 to a low of $4 a share in two years. Over the same period the President and CEO of the company, William Wise, had received over $39 million in salary, cashed out stock options in excess of $11 million, and had another $29.5 million in options yet to be exercised.

El Paso spent an estimated $10 million fighting Zilkha, so it's no surprise that, despite the support and assistance of other major shareholders including New York pension funds, the AFL-CIO retirement fund, and another large individual investor, the proposal failed. As Russell Gold of *The Wall Street Journal* reported:

> El Paso Corp., dragged down in recent years by a disastrous move into energy trading, said that it narrowly beat back a dissident director slate.... The company's own nominees for the board were elected by 52.5% of shareholders voting. [3]

The following day the lead editorial of *The Wall Street Journal* applauded the effort while pointing up the problem.

> Hats off to Oscar Wyatt and Selim Zilkha, two aggrieved El Paso Corp. shareholders, for their efforts to hold the company accountable to its owners. For one thing, their narrow defeat in this week's proxy vote demonstrates what's wrong, and getting wronger, with our approach to corporate governance. [4]

Attempts of shareholders to influence corporations, and their inability to do so, is a long-standing problem. Most large corporations, however, don't even notice when shareholders are upset.

> To gauge the depth of shareholder activism, *The Wall Street Journal* identified a number of sizeable companies with long-term problems and tried to determine whether their CEOs were facing increased pressure from directors or shareholders. Generally speaking, the answer was 'no'. [5]

The *Wall Street Journal* article, which noted that even big institutional funds can't keep close watch over more than a few of their largest holdings, concluded:

> In any case, the weapons such shareholders can wield — the threat of bad publicity or a proxy fight on corporate-governance issues — aren't very powerful. [6]

Only in the most unusual circumstance can a shareholder have an opportunity to influence corporate management. But because conventional wisdom staunchly holds to the myth that stockholders own a corporation, it is worth repeating their real status: with the exception of small or closely held or "family" corporations, <u>individual shareholders have absolutely no control over what they supposedly own.</u> Even large institutional shareholders have a voice only if they choose to expend the energy and considerable sums of money it takes to be heard.

The reality is that it is enormously expensive for a major stockholder or fund, and virtually impossible for an individual stockholder, to mount a challenge to management. Management holds all the cards, from its own treasury to shareholder mailing lists. Dissidents must rally stockholders to their cause through paid advertising. Even when major stockholders and funds are involved, the task is rarely accomplished.

Shareholder complaints over excessive executive compensation and stock option plans are a fairly new phenomenon. Strategic Compensation Research Associates based in New York City conducted a study between July 1997 and June 1998 of shareholder complaints over executive compensation. Historically, they noted, from five to 10 percent of shareholders voted "no" on executives' stock compensation plans. In 1998, however, shareholder votes against management moved up to an average of 13.8%. At 270 companies more than 30% cast "no" votes.

Shareholder influence on management rarely goes beyond a letter or question at the annual meeting. Corporate attorneys and consultants strongly resist even those ineffectual articulations of shareholder concern as "micro-management."

In response to the flurry of 2001-2002 corporate scandals, *Wall Street Journal's* "Political Capital" columnist, Alan Murray, wrote: "Capitalism has never depended on trust in corporate managers to put the shareholders' interests above their own." [7] Indeed? Was *The Wall Street Journal's* columnist suggesting that people buy stock with the objective of making management wealthy and consider themselves fortunate if there is something left over for themselves?

Murray then disingenuously suggested: "Instead the key to successful capitalism is having owners of capital who look after their own interests."

A number of political figures responding to the 2002 Enron-stimulated revelations of corporate misdeeds also attempted to put the blame on heedless, lazy stockholders. Yet as sharp-eyed and attentive as shareholders might want to be there is no window in the wall between stockholder and management where shareholders can truly "look after" their interests. Once shareholders have traded their money for a stock certificate they have but two choices: hold or sell.

The stockholders' perspective

I recall a conversation overheard as a boy between my father, president of a small Delaware-incorporated, Idaho-based corporation and an older brother who later took over the company after my father died. With youthful enthusiasm, my brother pushed to use the company's surplus and borrowing power to build new production facilities in a promising region of the country. Dad resisted, balancing the potential growth that might be achieved with the needs of several of the original investors in the firm. One of his descriptions stands out in my memory, that of the widow of one of the original founders who, my father believed, was very much dependent upon the quarterly dividend checks paid by the company.

The discussion continued for several days with others of top management joining in. Sixty-some years later I don't recall the outcome of the discussion, but the concern for the welfare of stockholders is indelibly imprinted.

It is, of course, impossible for the CEO and Board of Directors of, say Aetna Insurance, to know the personal financial situation of the tens of thousands of holders of its 142.6 million shares of common stock (as of 12/31/2000). The basic principle remains the same, however. Aetna's $47 billion in assets, and everything it earns and owes is the shareholders, not the management's.

"It was early in the 20th century that power began shifting away from the shareholders who own a company to the manager who runs it," said Richard Sylla, a professor of business history at New York University's Stern School of Business, as quoted in Gretchen Morgenson's "Market Watch" column in *The New York Times*. [8]

> For most of the 1990's, shareholders had little reason to carp about the stewardship of their assets by company executives. Stock prices were rising; shareholders were content. But much has happened since last year's annual meeting season, not the least of which is $5 trillion in lost stockholder wealth. [9]

Morgensen reported that "the number of shareholder proposals related to executive pay is up 24 percent this year (2001)," according to the Director of Corporate Governance at the Investor Responsibility Research Center in Washington, and that "shareholder opposition to companies' stock option plans that dilute existing owners' stakes is also rising." Morgensen concluded, "It is high time these people are held accountable." [10]

Holding chief executives and their boards of directors accountable, however, is difficult if not impossible for shareholders. Professor Sylla stated:

> As they [companies] grew, so did the gulf between owners and stewards; although shareholders began agitating during the 1980's takeover era, owners today still have little say in the way their businesses are run. [11]

The largest blocks of stock are managed by institutional investors – mutual funds and retirement funds. Yet even they exercise little influence over management. At best they can voice disapproval after the fact by selling their holdings of the company's shares. But it would take unprecedented coordination, perhaps collusion, among a significant number of large-block-holding institutional and fund managers to force any corporation's management to change how it operates.

The Informed Investor

What stockholders know of "their" company is provided officially by its quarterly and annual reports. The CEO or chairman of the board offers an assessment of the firm's progress. The treasurer provides the financials. The accounting firm (and the CEO, thanks to Congressional action following Enron et al) attests to their accuracy. Unofficially, investors may learn of important actions by their company through the business news media, brokers' reports, and free-lance newsletters.

Annual and quarterly reports present a one-dimensional, unchallenged picture of the corporation's position. Nothing in corporate charter or reporting practices allows for the presentation of views other than that of management. Shareholders are thus led to believe that the board and management stand in complete and unanimous agreement.

As for the board members themselves, the average shareholder knows only what may be learned from an abbreviated biography (generally only a business history) of each member. Only when stockholders force a proxy battle is more than one slate of candidates offered. At all other times stockholders are presented with one candidate for each opening. They may vote for, vote against, or not vote at all for each or all. The same options are offered for the one accounting firm candidate presented.

The CEO votes not only his own shares but shares that have been "pledged" to management by the company's pension fund, officers, board members, and shares held in trust. If there appears to be a potential source of disagreement at a coming annual meeting, or when a stockholder insurrection is suspected, the CEO may contact holders of large blocks of stock to enlist their votes for management.

As noted in the El Paso example above, managers of funds with large blocks of shares have a far greater opportunity to affect the outcome of corporate elections than individual shareholders, but that power is rarely exercised. Nell Minow, expert on corporate governance and editor of the newsletter of The Corporate Library, explained why in a Public Radio International "Sound Money" interview during the height of the Enron/Global Crossing/WorldCom scandals.

One of the great frustrations for me in my earlier career as a shareholder activist was that I could never get any interest from the mutual fund guys. They're really the one-night-stand of the corporate finance community because they never stick around long enough to care enough about whether companies are planning well for the long term. And so we would try to get them to support us – I felt like the little red hen: "Who will help me bake my cake?" I'd say, Look, this company's got O.J. Simpson on their audit committee, there has to be a problem there. And they would say, "Well, we don't know if we're going to own this stock by the time the annual meeting comes up in four months. What do we care? [12]

Fund managers' indifference to corporate policy may change, at least while the memory of the meltdown of 2002 is fresh. According to a "Business & Investing" page feature by Robert D. Hershey, Jr. in *The New York Times:*

Mutual funds used to avoid direct confrontation with the management of their portfolio companies when they were unhappy about, say, executive pay or director independence. Instead, the funds would quietly sell their shares.

But many of the biggest fund companies, including Fidelity and Vanguard, are beginning to publicly oppose management on matters of corporate governance. [13]

Noting that "managers have gotten burned" by the likes of Enron, WorldCom, Tyco International, Global Crossing, and Adelphia Communications, Hershey quotes an investment consultant:

A growing number of investors are thinking they're not big enough by themselves to make a difference and are interested in having mutual funds step up and be their spokesman. [14]

Warren Buffet's "Berkshire Hathaway has jettisoned at least one stock because of over its high executive compensation," [15] writes Hershey, and other fund managers have refused to support management's slates of directors and voiced publicly their concern with stock option accountability issues.

Yet even when funds use their voting power, their votes remain unrevealed to stock/fund holders, and they want it to stay that way, reports Tom Lauricella and Michael Schroeder in *The Wall Street Journal:*

> The mutual fund industry for the most part argues that investors don't have a right to know how their fund managers vote on individual proxy issues.... Indeed, while pushing for increased disclosure from the companies they invest in, fund companies have been battling attempts for greater openness on their part – as in the case with proxy votes and more frequent disclosure of portfolio holdings. [16,b]

In the final analysis the only avenue for individual investors to express displeasure is to sell the stock. But it would take hundreds of thousands of stockholders selling millions of shares almost simultaneously for the officers in a widely held corporation to take notice. Fund and pension managers controlling huge amounts of a corporation's stock have more of an opportunity to break through corporate indifference and speak of their concerns directly to a CEO or board member. Yet, if jawboning doesn't have any effect, the only real leverage fund managers can apply is to do as Warren Buffet has done and drop the company from its portfolio. Movement in a stock's price caused by large amounts of stock being dumped on the market may get a board's attention.

But if shareholders exert no influence, are not listened to and have no control, and therefore don't own the corporation, who does?

---

[b] In September 2002, the Securities and Exchange Commission considered for the first time requiring mutual funds and other investment managers to disclose how they vote. The industry is strongly opposed to the rule. A public-comment period follows such announcements and several months may elapse before the rule is finalized, modified, or dropped.

Do directors direct or are they directed?

"All those in favor say 'Aye.'"
"Aye."   "Aye."   "Aye."
"Aye."   "Aye."

Ultimate accountability to stockholders or members is vested in the board of directors, who may subsequently grant certain authority to officers, agents, and employees as permitted under the corporate charter, bylaws, and applicable laws. The executive or general manager, in turn, is accountable to the board and initiates action within the boundaries of authority granted by the board. [17]

The description of board authority above is echoed in some form in most corporate charters. Control of a corporation is vested in the board of directors. Thus, if control implies ownership and ownership demands control, it follows that the board of directors owns the corporation.

But do they really?

"Dissenting Directors: Should You Shut Up, Quit, or Fight?" writes Julie Connelly in *Corporate Board Member:*

> The duty of a director is clear – in concept anyway. You serve as the shareholders' surrogate and are obliged to speak up when you disagree with a management decision that's important to the company's future.
>
> The reality, however, is that when a director actually does dissent, the crystalline concept of disinterested duty promptly fogs. [18]

In theory the board represents the stockholders. "In theory" because members' loyalty often lies elsewhere. In many companies the CEO is the primary recruiter of new board members. New members are often recommended and recruited by serving members. Meetings are called and convened by the CEO. The CEO controls the agenda. The CEO sets board members' compensation.

> For companies thinking about raising board salaries, there's a delicate balancing act. "If you pay them too well, you raise questions with the public. If you don't pay them well enough, how do you get good people to sit on the board?" says Jannice Koors, a partner at compensation consultants Pearl Meyer & Partners. [19]

Members are given or afforded opportunities to acquire the company's stock on favorable terms proposed by the CEO and ratified by themselves. They deal with the CEO and other board members on a person-to-person basis in social and professional gatherings. To do their job they attempt to know the company, its culture, its executive staff, and each other. Unconsciously or deliberately they align themselves with the officers of the company and each other, developing a collegial if not fraternal relationship.

On the other hand, connection between boards and stockholders is tenuous at best. Except for other board members and the company's officers, they may not know or ever meet face-to-face any of the stockholders in whose interests they are supposed to labor. The connection is made even more slender because board members are not dependent on the corporation's success or failure for their livelihood. They may profit from its success and may lose some money if it fails, but more often than not losses are confined to "house" money, stock they were given as compensation for their membership.

Given the circumstances of their appointments and relationships as members of "the team," directors may find it difficult to voice their doubts or concerns to management. Even more difficult is questioning the judgement and integrity of fellow members serving on the compensation or audit committees. Again, from "Dissenting Directors: Should You Shut Up, Quit, or Fight?:[20]

> When directors discover they are lonely voices crying in the wilderness... they have an equal number of choices. The first is to shut up in the interest of harmony – and a widely held view says that boards should be instruments of consensus whose decisions must be unanimous. If individual directors find that untenable, they can exercise their second option and resign. The third option is the most controversial: Go public with a disagreement and hunker down for what might turn out to be a nasty fight.

From an ethical standpoint an individual director is in a most difficult position. Stockholders understand and corporate charters declare that the board has ultimate responsibility. They are collectively charged with preserving and building shareholder value. Management, they are told, works for them. Yet board members are covered by insurance that protects them against lawsuits from stockholders and other stakeholders of the company and, other than a loss of face, board members who observe or are co-conspirators in sinking a corporate vessel are not much at risk of getting their feet wet.

Board members generally believe that management has more day-to-day working knowledge of the company's affairs and a better opportunity to assess the company's capabilities and weaknesses than they. To voice doubts about a company's direction may be committing the sin of micro-management. Thus, before raising a question, directors ask themselves if they are interfering on the basis of limited and incomplete knowledge or truly fulfilling their obligations to the shareholders?

Important decisions made by boards are rarely concise matters to be quickly plumbed and voted up or down. Most issues have layers of history and management decisions made over a period of months or years. Quoting from "Dissenting Directors...":

> A board's three major responsibilities are deciding whether to merge or sell the company, hiring or firing the CEO, and determining the CEO's compensation. After that, a

157

director is in the murk of management's prerogative to
run the business. [21]

Without a doubt there are thousands of hard-working, knowledgeable boards doing yeoman service for their corporations while keeping shareholder interests uppermost in their deliberations. But boards are not made effective because of the structure of the corporate charter, customs of corporate governance, or legal definitions of control and responsibility. They are effective in spite of a lack of clear guidance.

Good directors overcome the enormous contradictions of their position with little more than their own consciences to keep them focused on their constituency. "Good" boards leap over the hurdles of ill-defined responsibility and accountability to make meaningful contributions. It comes down to the character of the directors involved.

Addressing the inability of boards of directors to control bad-boy CEOs, Minow noted:

I don't understand how you take these extraordinarily accomplished people who all want to do the right thing and somehow you put them around a boardroom table and their I.Q. drops fifty percent and their courage flies out the door. And yet that happens over and over. We've been focusing a lot this year on the problems with the accountants, the problems with the analysts and the problems with corporate managers but, of course, at the center of all of those relationships is the board of directors. And if they don't do a good job, nothing is gonna work. [22]

The men and women serving on major corporate boards are usually working executives themselves, perhaps chairing their own company's board and frequently serving on multiple boards. They are ostensibly appointed (or elected, if you will) for their experience and hands-on wisdom. They generally own stock in the company. They are aware of and sensitive to their ultimate responsibility to the shareholders, and understand that the success or failure of "their" company will reflect for good or ill on their own reputations and standing among peers.

So what factor turns "extraordinarily accomplished people" as described by Ms. Minow into less than effective shareholder representatives? Directors are generally given stock options in an attempt to buy their attention and to link them closer to shareholder concerns. It doesn't, however, appear to have had the desired result. Directors have their own businesses, are comfortably retired, and have other sources of income and security. Their interest in the corporation on whose board they serve is no doubt real, but not as impassioned as for their own company and interests.

In point of fact, a board doesn't own a corporation. Its control is a slender reed easily bent or broken.

CEOs "own" the company

Blue- and white-collar workers, executive officers, members of the board of directors, stockholders, community and state public officials, suppliers, and customers are lumped together under the term "stakeholders." All are affected by the success or failure of the corporate venture. Legally. only one of the above "owns" the corporation, the shareholders. But legal ownership and proprietary ownership that arises out of control are quite different.

Control of a large, publicly and widely held corporation most often rests with the Chief Executive Officer – sometimes identified as the president and sometimes the chairman of the board. Sometimes one person holds both titles. Although "hired" by and technically responsible to the board of directors, the CEO is, much like the captain of a ship, in total and unquestioned command of the enterprise. The directors are aboard for the ride and have the right to suggest or question policy or, in extremis, fire the CEO. But the manner in which directors are chosen, employed, and compensated – by the CEO and not the shareholders – means they are as much under his influence as he is under theirs. This lack of a clearly delineated and mutually accepted chain of command for all practical purposes allows the CEO to "own" the corporation.

The only constituency to whom CEOs are *legally* responsible is the directors. In practice, however, CEOs have but one audience to satisfy: the financial market — "Wall Street." Wall Street measures the success or failure of a CEO by one and only one standard: profit. Moreover, because of the fluid nature of the market, with corporate shares a parity product defined by price alone, a CEO's success is judged primarily on quarterly earnings – a three-month period.

In current practice, the company (the CEO or sometimes the CFO – chief financial officer) provides the financial market with an estimate of earnings for each quarter as well as the year ahead. Financial market "analysts" then use their knowledge of the company, the market, the nation's and world's economy to predict whether the company will make, exceed, or fall below the company-provided estimates of earnings. The system has its flaws, as suggested by *The Wall Street Journal:*

> Heinz suffers from a problem that, except for a few exceptions, is plaguing the food industry: Sales are growing as fast as ketchup coming out of the bottle. Companies respond by obscuring things with numerous restructuring programs, divestitures, write-downs. 'It's a bit of a shell game,' Mr. Leach [analyst for Bank of America] says. 'Heinz is one of the poster children for this phenomenon. In my coverage, only two companies, Wrigley and Sysco, put out press releases where you can figure out what they actually earn' [23]

CEOs play a constant shell game with the financial markets, tempting them with favorable numbers that appear to be makeable to the outside analyst, yet holding something back to cover a possible shortfall or becoming a hero by "beating the numbers."

None of this contributes to the well being of the company, its employees, suppliers, or customers. A short-term focus benefits only in-and-out traders, not investors holding for long-term growth. It takes away any incentive for the CEO to equip and direct the firm for the long haul.

It's important to remind ourselves that none of the money changing hands in daily stock market trades flows into the company's treasury. Stock market trades are nothing more than wagers between unconnected individuals. They neither take money out of or put money into a company's treasury unless the company sells its treasury stock. When the company sells its own stock it is trading shares of ownership in the company for cash. The more shares out, the smaller share of the company's assets represented by each share.

Increasing stock prices benefits only sellers. Although, in making an acquisition using a combination of stock and cash, an increased stock price may help a company acquire another for less cash outlay. (This is not the book to cover puts, calls, short sellers, arbitrage, etc.) Which brings us back to concerns about executive stock options discussed in Chapter 7. When officers and directors of a company are granted options to purchase their company's stock at a certain price – the "strike" price — they have an incentive to do everything possible to push that price higher, even at the cost of the company's long term sustainability.

In "Good Timing: CEO Stock Option Awards and Company News Announcements," Professor David Yermack of New York University documented how companies time the release of executive stock option grants to occur before the release of favorable quarterly reports. [24] When the company's stock price goes up – because of favorable earnings estimates (or dishonest booking of revenues, expenses, and other shenanigans), option holders may exercise their right to buy at the lower price and thus enjoy a windfall profit. They exercise their options; the company sells the stock to them from its treasury at the original striking price. The option holder may then "flip it" – immediately selling all or part at the elevated market price. No risk, all gain for the option holder. For shareholders it's the reverse – all risk, all loss. Their share of ownership in the company is diluted by the number of shares optioned and released to the market at less than what the company could have sold them for on the open market.

Before Enron, Americans generally and small investors in particular assumed that officers of our largest corporations were motivated to act honorably, if not always successfully, to further the interests of the corporation and thus the shareholders. Their personal success was assumed to be linked to that of the company whose fortunes they guided.

The great scandals of 2000-2002 revealed more than just out-of-control avarice in executive suites. It exposed a basic and major structural flaw in the corporate form of enterprise.

Simply put, the CEO has all of a corporation's wealth and resources at his command. But the corporation doesn't control the CEO. Shareholders don't appoint or elect the CEO. The board does. Board members are not appointed by the shareholders, but by the CEO. As long as the CEO doesn't press too far, he controls through loyalty, persuasion, tradition, familiarity, compensation, and perhaps even coercion. The only body that can direct, discipline, or dump him is the board. If the CEO has any leadership capability at all, the board is under his thrall.

From *The Wall Street Journal:*

> Jack Welch did a lot of good for a lot of General Electric shareholders and employees as CEO. But that makes it all the more unfortunate that his contribution will be tarnished by the public airing (in a divorce settlement) of a retirement package that makes him seem greedy, or at least too attached to the playthings of corporate opulence.
>
> These bennies, if not their dollar value, were detailed in a 1996 proxy statement.... But it still raised shareholder eyebrows anew to learn the extent of GE-paid services that Mr. Welch is entitled to, from cars to airplanes to financial planning, home gadgets and use of a GE apartment. What? No retinue of grape peelers? [25]

Mr. Welch took to the "Letters to the Editor" section of *The Wall Street Journal* to defend his retirement package and defuse the anger mounting against him personally and expansive retirement packages in general. In his letter, "My Dilemma – and How I Resolved It," Mr. Welch wrote:

> The simple truth is: There was not a single day in the past six years [since the retirement contract was settled] that I thought it was improper, and I don't believe it is improper today.
>
> [However], I've asked Jeff [new GE Chairman Immelt] and the GE board to modify my contract by eliminating everything except the traditional office and administrative support given for decades to all retired GE chairmen and vice chairmen.
>
> In the new contract, I will pay the costs for my use of all other facilities and services provided by GE such as planes and the company apartment. I estimate that I will be paying GE between $2 million and $2.5 million a year for those services. [26]

What is most revealing in Mr. Welch's statement is what is <u>not</u> addressed. There is no acknowledgement that the ever-waiting cars, planes, apartments, staff, etc. while he was CEO were not <u>proper</u> expenses for the company to pay. If anything, the statement assumed that whatever sums GE spent for his comfort and convenience were appropriate. That having to drive and park his own car, fly commercial, buy club memberships and sports tickets, or call the florist himself were beneath the high station to which he'd arrived. The cost of these executive prerogatives was at least the $2-2.5 million a year Mr. Welch is now agreeing to pay out of his own pocket and, if all the executive "necessities" and niceties were added up, it would probably come to much, much more.

Mr. Welch is not alone in thinking that attention to the personal comfort and convenience of executive officers before and after retirement is an appropriate expense for shareholders to cover. *Wall Street Journal* reporter Joann S. Lublin delved into other CEO retirement packages in "How CEOs Retire in Style." [27] The article detailed retirement perks such as club dues, lavishly designed and furnished offices, automobiles provided for life, financial planning, and college tuition for the children. "Advisory" and consulting fees were generous. Gerald Levin, ex-CEO of AOL Time Warner will earn $1 million a year for five years for five days' work a month as an advisor. Louis V. Gerstner, Jr., CEO of IBM will consult with his company for 10 years at the rate of $600 an hour.

The "Money & Business" section of The New York Times noted in "Perks From Tuition to Bodyguards," that companies don't have to disclose CEO privileges and what they cost. It's merely lumped within "Other Compensation" in the annual report. Examples of Other Compensation include company-provided clothing, the incremental cost of the Chairman using his own New York apartment, a sum to educate an officer's children, legal fees in case a "Golden Parachute" deal is taken to court, a security-trained driver and 24-hour bodyguard service, and even continuing education. [28]

The two-edged going-public sword

The reason for "going public" is commonly stated as raising capital to "grow" the business. More frequently the more important agenda is to allow the firm's venture capital partners to reclaim their capital and make a quick and substantial profit – the reason why they invested. At the same time the creators/founders get a payoff from their "sweat equity", and employees who have taken stock options in lieu of salary enjoy the fruits of their labor.

In the dot-com crash in the second half of the year 2000, however, many of the highest flyers in the technology sector plummeted 90% or more from their market peak. Billions in paper profits evaporated. Within the space of a few weeks, sometimes a few days, many whose stock options ballooned into hundreds of thousands, sometimes millions, of dollars found themselves dramatically poorer.

Not everyone took the same hit. Some heads of high tech companies sold their founders' shares and options at the peak of the market, "Leaving Shareholders in the Dust", as the *New York Times* "Money & Business" section noted. [29]

Reporter David Leonhardt described how one CEO, David Rickey of Applied Micro Circuits, kept promoting his company's stock even as he was quietly selling the majority of his own holdings. "I dare you not to own my stock," he told a CNBC audience during an interview not long after Applied Micro Circuit's stock had fallen 67% in six weeks. "What Mr. Rickey did not say," the story continued. "was that he had already come close to accepting his own dare. Between July 2000, when Applied Micro Circuit's stock was trading at $100, and March 2, when it was trading at

$29, Mr. Rickey had sold 800,000 shares in the company, or more than 99 percent of his stock, making $170 million in the process." [30]

Leonhardt then noted:

> In an inversion of the notion that corporate managers should align their interests with shareholders', Mr. Rickey and many technology executives unloaded many shares during 2000 — as other investors were taking a beating — and thus becoming some of the year's most lavishly rewarded managers. [31]

While it's rarely commented upon, a key reason for companies to go public is to dilute ownership and give management a free hand. A CEO dealing with 10 or 100 shareholders — often the original investors and their family members — must consider every decision in light of how it will affect the owners. Once that number reaches into the thousands and tens of thousands, individual shareholders become powerless.

Founding shareholders give up control in favor of making their holdings marketable because there is little or no market for the stock of a closely held corporation. Taking the company public lets them recoup their original investments and, with good financial press, profit substantially from a run-up in the price.

Who Really Owns a Corporation?

It should be clear by this point that stockholders of all but closely held corporations do not control and therefore do not own the companies whose stock they hold. It's also clear that boards of directors do not own the companies on whose boards they sit, even though a very active, involved board may provide a certain amount of influence.

Control over a corporation is in the hands of the chief executive officer. He can direct how it spends its cash, buy and sell its assets, open, close, and move headquarters and production facilities, decide what to make, how and where to sell it, and how much to charge for it.

Because control is ownership, then the CEO owns the corporation. Final proof is the compensation package. As any small business owner can tell you, only the owner has the right to dip into the cash register for as much as he or she wants.

Executive (Over) Compensation

America's industries were founded by headstrong, independent promoter/innovators such as Henry Ford, I.B.M. founder Thomas J. Watson,

Eastman of Kodak, Walt Disney, and thousands of other lesser-publicized lights who poured their intellects and energies into making their ideas take hold and flourish. Within the last twenty years Ted Turner (CNN, Turner Network), Bill Gates (Microsoft), and Craig McCaw (McCaw Cellular Communications) fought their way through financial, competitive, and marketplace minefields to create new giants of commerce.

Few would argue that creators, inventors, and founders of companies are worth every dime they are rewarded. Succeeding executives, however, no matter how talented, experienced, skilled, or aggressive, are hired hands. They are captains of ships of enterprise they didn't design, build or pilot on their maiden voyages. "The entrepreneur has skin in the game, so he has a downside," says Howard Stevenson, professor at the Harvard Business School. "It's not like when you sign up for Disney and don't stand to lose even a million if it goes wrong, and it does go wrong, and you [referring to Disney CEO Michael Eisner] make $70 million after nine months." [32]

"There is a limit to what hired hands ought to get," says Dean Phypers, a director of AIG, Bethlehem Steel, Cambrex Corp., and Church and Dwight," in an interview for Fortune magazine. "And in the last five to ten years with stock compensation and a wild market, many CEOs have found it." [33]

In a survey of 200 companies by Executive Compensation Advisory Services, in the year 2000 the average CEO enjoyed a 22% raise in salary and bonus, $1.7 million in stock – a 14% increase from the preceding year — plus $14.9 million worth of stock options. In comparison, typical investors lost 12% of their portfolios in the year 2000, the average hourly worker received a 3% raise, and salaried employees about 4% more.

Average CEO compensation packages of $22.8 million a year pale when compared to the really high flyers. GE's John F. Welch, Jr., took home $144.5 million. Citigroup CEO Sanford I. Weill was paid a mere $19.9 million in direct compensation plus an additional $3.7 billion (yes, billion) in profits realized from his stock options after having been given $28.3 billion (yes, billion) in the company's equities.

The average blue collar worker in one of these organizations earns around $12.50 an hour on the job while the CEO is paid $2,603 for every minute awake and asleep of every day of the year. Even the financial media has questioned amounts paid to top executives, laying the blame on incestuous relationships among boards and management.

In *Fortune* magazine's "Revealed: Boardroom Secrets," Geoffrey Colvin writes: "Directors mostly aren't paying for what shareholders want, which is a higher total return." [34]

"Top performers deserve top dollar — no question about it," wrote Thomas A. Stewart in a following Fortune magazine article. "But there comes a point where that logic breaks down." [35]

Stewart quotes Howard Stevenson, professor at the Harvard Business School: "Above $5 million I have serious questions. That's the equivalent of earnings on between $50 million and $100 million in capital. That's $13,000 a day." [36]

"Plato told Aristotle no one should make more than five times the pay of the lowest member of society," says Graef Crystal, a compensation consultant interviewed by Stewart. "J.P. Morgan said 20 times. Jesus advocated a negative differential — that's why they killed him." [37]

Today the United States has the widest gap between rich and poor of any industrialized county. One percent of the population controls 40% of the nation's assets. What is called the "social contract" that bound our near classless society together from the post-depression years through to about the beginning of the Vietnam War has been broken. More billionaires have been created in the last 15 years than at any time in our history. "If the past thirty years have demonstrated anything about business, it is that the avarice of corporate leaders is practically unlimited," wrote John Cassidy in the September 23, 2002, *The New Yorker.* [38]

Does the sudden increase in wealth for a few Americans at the top of the ladder bear a relationship to the six-fold increase in the number of full-time, year-round workers living in poverty? Is there really a "trickle-down" from the lofty income heights? Apparently not. As one-tenth of one percent of Americans enjoyed unprecedented prosperity, the number of working poor grew from 459,000 in 1998 to 2.8 million in the year 2000.

Current CEO compensation packages go far beyond taking care of a dedicated corporate manager and his family in his declining years. The hundreds of millions flowing into private hands (much of it put in offshore banks to escape taxes) is creating dynasties rivaling if not exceeding those of the Robber Baronies of Carnegie, Mellon, Vanderbilt, and Rockefeller of the 1800's. As the nation learned at that time, enormous wealth equals enormous power to influence elections, presidents, congresses, and the courts. The nation attempted to rein in that power during the Great Depression with the creation of regulatory agencies such as the SEC.

In the 1990's however, Wall Street's lobbyists pushed through Congress the 1995 Private Securities Litigation Reform Act. The "reform" was putting a limit on private and class action lawsuits, effectively removing a key deterrent and remedy for securities fraud. The result was a diminished

SEC, an explosion of corporate deceit, investor losses in the billions and, in mid-2002, a market dipping perilously close to one-half its previous value as investors lost confidence in corporate honesty.

Deregulatory zeal has undone the Glass-Steagall Act, also Depression-era spawned, which kept banks out of the brokerage and insurance business. The results have not been pretty, write Jathon Sapsford and Paul Beckett in *The Wall Street Journal:*

> A few years ago, J.P. Morgan Chase & Co. poured money into the telecommunications and cable businesses. Though the bank didn't expect to make much money on the loans themselves, it anticipated a huge payback from investment-banking business the companies would send its way in exchange for credit.
>
> The payback came this week – in the form of $1.4 billion in costs related to souring loans.
>
> At the end of last month, Moody's Investment Service placed the long-term debt of J.P. Morgan on credit watch for a possible downgrade, in part because its strategy of using commercial-banking relationships to boost investment banking has met 'mixed success so far.'[39]

"We're giving entrepreneurial profits to people who aren't entrepreneurs," says Michael Josephson, president of the Josephson Institute of Ethics and the Character Counts! Coalition. "If we had to freeze pay at $3 million, could you get 500 good CEOs? I think so."[40]

In studying the relationship between pay and performance, compensation consultant Crystal found that companies that significantly overpaid their chief executives "significantly underperformed both the overall market and other companies in their respective industries. Roughly two-thirds of the stocks dropped in price."[41]

The payoff for munificent compensation is supposed to come from the CEO's ability to outperform the market. A study by Watson Wyatt Worldwide, a management consulting firm in Bethesda, Md., confirmed Crystal's observations. They found that companies that grant the largest number of stock options substantially underperform companies granting less. To illustrate: from 1989 through 1992, Aetna Chairman and CEO Ronald E. Compton was given 107,400 option shares. At the same time the insurance giant performed dramatically below the S&P 500 and Dow Jones Insurance Index.[42]

Yet, for all their power and riches, CEOs may not have the final say as to when and how they will leave their corporate thrones. In the rarified world of executive suites, the most glittering of superstar CEOs may be shuffled out the door at the slightest sign of a financial hiccup.

The real seat of power

Who calls the shots when a CEO fails to meet profit expectations? The answer is complicated. As related in "Corporate Governance":

> InstitutionalInvestors hold about 50% of all listed corporate stock in the United States (about 60% in the largest 1,000 corporations). They have assumed the role of "permanent shareholders." As early as 1988 the <u>Department of Labor (DOL) </u>set forth the opinion that, since proxy voting can add value, voting rights are subject to the same fiduciary standards as other plan assets.... However, if votes are not disclosed, how can these standards be enforced?[43] (Author's emphasis).

Institutional investors could wield real control over corporations if they would exercise it. When institutional investor or funds take a position in a stock, they command substantial numbers of votes through proxy. If motivated, they could not just encourage but enforce social responsibility upon much of corporate America. They don't, however, because their reputations as fund managers rest only on the return on investment they produce, not on social or ethical issues. ROI is the sole criteria by which they are judged.

Thus it finally comes down to this: the real wielders of power over corporations are nameless, faceless Wall Street "gnomes" laboring in front of multiple computer screens to squeeze every last cent of gain into the fund they manage. They know little more than what they read in the financial and business press about the companies whose stock they trade. They may have no knowledge of the products of those companies, couldn't name the communities in which production facilities are located, wouldn't know the CEOs or directors of the boards if they were riding in the same elevator. Odds are they, personally, don't own a single share of many of the stocks they trade. But they monitor every analyst's analysis, peruse every quarterly report, compare "their" stocks' performance against those of competitors, the industry, the indexes, and the expectations they have been given by company officers. When they detect something that indicates that one of "their" holdings will not meet their profit expectations, that CEO's head may go on the chopping block.

From an Associated Press report:

> Eastman Kodak Co. is looking for a new chairman after directors fired Kay R. Whitmore Friday, saying he failed to cut costs or boost profits fast enough to satisfy investors.[44]

The dismissal came after Kodak laid off 2,000 employees and announced cuts in research spending. The principal of a fund holding $4 million of the company's stock, told the AP, "We believe there is a clear need to move faster and further on operating cost efficiencies and enhanced earnings." Considering that individual shareholder concerns are rarely addressed by corporations, who, then, are the "investors" referred to in the Associated Press report above if not the funds?

When traders sense a company's profit performance is slipping, they dump their holdings without a second thought. Before selling they may alert their supervisors who may give the Chief Financial Officer or other well-placed insider a call to inquire as to what is causing the slippage. The trading supervisor may then suggest that the board might look into the matter. For all the deference paid to the niceties, however, when traders begin to dump a company's stock the board is forced to act.

Forced changes of watch demonstrate the reach of these unrecognized wielders of power behind corporate thrones.

In 1992, the board of directors of giant American Express Corporation (market capitalization 4/11/2001, $51.3 billion, #74 in Fortune 500) came under fire from major institutional investors for not performing up to the investors' expectations. With hardly a nod to the niceties, the board forced out its president of 15 years along with directors who resisted the move.

The CEO's abrupt departure was totally unrelated to the quality of work by thousands of American Express employees or the quality of service provided to its millions of customers. It was forced by investment fund managers with little or no personal financial stake in the fortunes of the firm.

In one two-year period, between 1991 and 1993, before the Enronization of corporate America, the CEOs of some of the world's largest corporations were abruptly shown the door: Robert C. Stempel of General Motors Corporation, Paul E. Lego of Westinghouse Electric, and John F. Akers of IBM. The combined assets of these three companies was almost $300 billion in 1991, representing more wealth than the international reserves of France, Germany, Italy, and Japan combined.

If the head of any of those countries had been summarily removed it would be splashed on the front page of every newspaper in the world. The United Nations and the state departments of the civilized world would be in a state of confusion. Armed forces might be put on alert.

Yet, despite the enormous implications and potential impact on the nation's economy, most corporate coups d'etat don't make the evening TV news or front page in morning papers.

"Of course, you could try another bank, if there were any other banks."

[1] "GM Boots Perot," *Newsweek*, 11/15/86.

[2] "El Paso Narrowly Defeats Dissident Director Slate," by Russell Gold, *The Wall Street Journal*, June 18, 2003.

[3] Ibid.

[4] "A Welcome Brawl," Review & Outlook editorial, *The Wall Street Journal*, June 19, 2003.

[5] "Weak Force: Shareholder Activism, Despite Hoopla, Leaves Most CEOs Unscathed," *Wall Street Journal*, 5/24/93,

[6] Ibid.

[7] "Street Flees Responsibility With Rush on Washington," Political Capital, by Alan Murray, *The Wall Street Journal*, July 16, 2002.

[8] "Holding Executives Answerable to Owners, in "Market Watch," by Gretchen Morgenson, *The New York Times* Money & Business section, April 29, 2001.

[9] Ibid.

[10] Ibid.

[11] Ibid.

[12] "Sound Money," with host Chris Farrell, Public Radio International, June 29, 2002.

[13] "Investor Angst Prompts Funds to Speak Up," by Robert D. Hershey Jr., "Business & Investing" section, *The New York Times*, July 7, 2002.

[14] Ibid.

[15] Ibid.

[16] "SEC to Consider Rule on Voting By Mutual Funds," by Tom Lauricella and Michael Schroeder, *The Wall Street Journal*, September 16, 2002.

[17] "Criteria for Separating Cooperative Board and Executive Decision Areas," adapted from Leon Garoyan and Paul O. Mohn, "The Board of Directors of Cooperatives, University of California, Davis, 1976, found on University of Wisconsin Center for Cooperatives <http://www.wisc.edu/uwcc/infor/criteria.html>.

[18] "Dissenting Directors: Should You Shut Up, Quit, or Fight?" by Julie Connelly, *Corporate Board Member*, September-October 2002.

[19] "Board Compensation Becomes Balancing Act," by Robin Siden, *The Wall Street Journal*, August 30, 2002.

[20] Op. Cit, "Dissenting Directors: Should You Shut Up, Quit, or Fight?"

[21] Ibid

[22] Ibid

[23] "Playing Catch-Up," in "Ahead Of the Tape, Today's Market Forecast," column by Jesse Eisinger, Money & Investing section, *The Wall Street Journal*, September 10, 2002.

John David Rose

[24] "Good Timing: CEO Stock Option Awards and Company News Announcements," by David L. Yermack, *Journal of Finance* 52, p449-476, June 1997.

[25] "Jack's Booty," unsigned editorial, *The Wall Street Journal*, September 10, 2002.

[26] "My Dilemma – And How I Resolved It," by Jack Welch, "Opinion" page, *The Wall Street Journal*, September 16, 2002.

[27] "How CEOs Retire In Style, by Joann S. Lublin, *The Wall Street Journal*, September 13, 2002.

[28] "Perks From Tuition to Bodyguards," by Geraldine Fabrikant, *The New York Times*, September 15, 2002.

[29] "Leaving Shareholders in the Dust," by David Leonhardt, *The New York Times*, "Money & Business" section April 1, 2001.

[30] Ibid.

[31] Ibid.

[32] "Can Even Heroes Get Paid Too Much?, by Thomas A. Stewart, *Fortune*, June 8, 1998.

[33] Ibid

[34] "Revealed: Boardroom Secrets," by Geoffrey Colvin, *Fortune* magazine, May 28, 1998, page 199.

[35] Op Cit."Can Even Heroes Get Paid Too Much?" by Thomas A. Stewart

[36] Ibid.

[37] Ibid.

[38] "The Greed Cycle: How the financial system encouraged corporations to go crazy," by John Cassidy, *The New Yorker*, September 23, 2002.

[39] "Linking of Loans To Other Business Has Perils for Banks," by Jathon Sapsford and Paul Beckett, *The Wall Street Journal*, September 19, 2002.

[40] Op Cit. "Can Even Heroes Get Paid Too Much?, by Thomas A. Stewart.

[41] "Who Profits If The Boss is Overfed?", by Reed Abelson, *The New York Times*, "Investing," June 20, 1999.

[42] "Aetna Proxy Statement, Notice of Annual Meeting, 1993," Aetna Life and Casualty Company, March 26, 1993.

[43] "Corporate Governance – Enhancing the Return on Capital Through Increased Accountability," by James McRitchie, Editor, revised 12/23/2001, www.corpgov.net

[44] Associated Press, 8/9/93.

CHAPTER ELEVEN
WHERE DID WE GO WRONG?

*"What is the finest game? Business. The soundest science?
Business. The truest art? Business. The fullest education?
Business. The fairest opportunity? Business. The cleanest
philanthropy? Business. The sanest religion? Business.*

Edward E. Purinton, The *Independent*, April 16, 1921

Americans have a love affair with business. So much so that one could almost believe Americans invented it, from capitalism to the stock market, from the corner store to the corporation.

Ancient Rome, however, was "mother to the modern capitalist," writes business-historian Miriam Beard, although "she has been a singularly severe stepmother as well. For more than any other city, she has scorned trade and sought to bar the trader from advancement to power and salvation."[1]

Before the world became enamoured of business, people of business had been reviled and scorned as leeches feeding upon honest craftsmen and artisans and profiting from the labor of others. Even the church got into the act, as Beard notes:

> After the Empire collapsed, the Roman Church took up
> the task of subduing the profit maker. She was determined
> to prevent him from breaking through the ordered system
> of mediaeval society, by his boundless 'avaritia.'[2]

Somewhere in the 16th and 17th Centuries, business and the Christian church came together.

> All through the ages, from the dissolution of antique
> capitalism to the latest crisis of modern capitalism, [a]
> Christian institutions, whether Catholic, Calvinist or
> Methodist, have exercised a profound modifying and yet
> fostering influence upon commerce and the characters of
> those engaged in it. Christianity, which as ever sought

---

[a] Beard was writing this in the 1930's, during the Great Depression.

to moderate the profit-seeking of the business man, has assisted him to develop finance and industry. It was the curious destiny of this greatest spiritual force in the Western world to prepare mankind for materialism and mechanization. Yet it has exerted ceaseless pressure on the money-makers to consider the effects of their activities upon society and their own souls.[3]

In contemporary America, religion and business are often linked. Witness the following samples of among 30 listings in a popular Internet bookstore: *Business Buy the Bible: Financial Wisdom of the Ancients:* Offers ideas for becoming wealthy and using the Bible for guidance in earning, saving, spending, and investing in service to God, and *Corporate Giants: Personal Stories of Faith and Finance.*

Once the labor battles of the 1890's to 1930's had been fought and the forty-hour week and unionization of industry grudgingly accepted, the middle-class climbed out of the Great Depression and began to enjoy the fruits of the post-World War II economy. Attacking business or capitalism in the 1940s and '50s became near-heresy. With the beginning of the Cold War it became un-American. Social Science school-books featured belching smoke stacks of industry and steam trains on their covers. Where communist Russia's poster people were a hammer- poised worker at the anvil of industry and a babushka-hooded peasant woman swinging a scythe in the field, magazine covers in the U.S. celebrated main-street merchants and briefcase-toting executives.

The bulbous tycoon, sharp trader, and sly finger-on-the-scales butcher were accepted as common to the human condition. As Carl Dreher wrote in a 1936 *Harper's Magazine:*

No one who has to earn a living can shake the dust of business off his feet.... For most of us complete integrity, in the sense of one-hundred percent consecration to elevated objectives, is an unattainable luxury and pharisaism to boot.[4]

In our veneration of business and business people, Americans rarely mark the difference between businesses owned, run, and conducted by our friends and neighbors in our communities and the mega-monster corporations dominating entire sectors of the world's economy. Yet, as the preceding chapters have made plain, there is a difference.

The difference is more than size

During the past fifty years, industry in corporate form has moved from the periphery to the very center of our social and economic existence. Indeed, it is not inaccurate to say that we live in a corporate society.[5]

William T. Gossett, former Vice President,
Ford Motor Company, 1957

The small business [b] owner/manager deals directly with employees, customers, and suppliers on a daily basis. Simply to remain in business, his or her business ethics must be acceptable to the community in which he or she lives, works, and trades. But pressure to stay within the community's code of ethics does not exist for executives of corporations dealing with people at a distance. They may employ tens of thousands of people in far-flung facilities, deliver product through an extended supply chain to a mass market, deal with vendors through a purchasing department, but it all goes through surrogates. They make their decisions shielded by the wall of corporate anonymity, with enormous legal resources, political, and financial power to keep them from seeing or sensing the human costs.

By definition, business of any kind, big or small, is not a charitable institution. Its anti-social aspects, however, are restrained when business is conducted by individual proprietors, craftsmen, and professionals dealing face to face with their customers. The impulse to take advantage is held in check by the personal nature of each transaction. "If I cheat her, she'll tell her friends. I'll lose not only her trade but the trade of everyone she talks to." Enlightened self-interest overcomes innate avarice.

In a world where producer, seller and buyer, lender and borrower never meet face to face — the world of mass production, mass marketing, and mass financing — Rotary Club ethics are easily forgotten.

Salomon Smith Barney, like so many firms on Wall Street, seeks to please its clients. When it was still Salomon Brothers, it offered one of those clients, Bernie Ebbers, the C.E.O. of WorldCom, the opportunity to buy more than two hundred thousand shares in the initial public offering of a telecommunications company called Qwest.

---

[b] For these purposes we define "small business" as those with less than $50 million in gross sales.

At the time the I.P.O. market was lucrative, and a bet on Qwest was a virtual lock, so Ebbers bought in. Three days later, Qwest's stock price was up twenty-seven percent, and Ebbers began selling. In the end, he cleared almost two million dollars.

As it happens, while Salomon was making Ebbers richer, he was sending a lot of business its way. Between 1997 and 2001… WorldCom paid Salomon a hundred forty million dollars in fees for its underwriting of the company's debt and equity, and another seventy-six million in fees for its advice on mergers and acquisitions. [6]

Writing the above in a *New Yorker* piece entitled "The Bribe Effect," author James Surowiecki then points out, in fairness, that the giving of gifts — from the chiropractor's knotted ball-point pen to World Series tickets to a favored client – is an accepted and time-honored sales practice.

So what makes Wall Street's particular brand of bribery such a big deal?

It's a big deal because the deals are so big. When it comes to bribery, size does matter. A free Linkin Park CD is one thing; eleven million bucks is another. [7]

Beyond the ethics of bribery, Surowiecki and others point out, real damage was done to unknowing and innocent parties. He describes how underwriters like Salomon, in order to increase the attractiveness of these special inducements, would price initial public offering shares for much less than fair market value. This cheated start-up companies of significant amounts of capital that might later make the difference between success and bankruptcy.

A Congressional house panel investigating links between IPO allocations and investment bank fees found that "investment-banking relationships led to overly optimistic research reports," and "companies were brought to market prematurely in an effort to generate investment-banking fees. Most had insufficient assets and revenue to remain viable." [8]

The difference between your local Chevrolet dealer offering "cash back" on the purchase of a new car, and what investment bankers such as Salomon and Goldman Sachs Group did to companies like Qwest and others, was that, in Surowiecki's words, "banks were making bribes with other people's money."

As might be expected, Surowiecki noted, "Salomon insists that the transactions had nothing to do with each other – that there was a quid and quo, but nary a pro in between." [9] *The Wall Street Journal* reported a Goldman spokesman protesting, "The suggestion that Goldman Sachs was involved in spinning or other inappropriate practices around IPO allocations is simply wrong." [10]

Protestations of innocence are standard in situations such as these, advised by corporate lawyers in preparation for a defense against criminal charges and civil lawsuits. But did the executives who put the IPO allocation "sales incentive plan" into motion or approved it when suggested by others understand the deception they were perpetrating against people looking to them (and paying dearly) for their professional assistance in obtaining working capital? It's difficult to believe that allocations of IPOs were determined by underlings, or that the CEOs were naively unaware of the impact on a chief executive of a possible new client who gains a windfall of millions of dollars.

> *Untruthfulness and dishonesty were with me, as with most people, called into being in so immediate, so contingent a fashion, and in self-defence, by some particular interest, that my mind, fixed on some lofty ideal, allowed by character, in the darkness below, to set about those urgent, sordid tasks, and did not look down to observe them.*
>
> Marcel Proust "Remembrance of
> Things Past, The Guermantes Way, Part I"

High position or low, there is simply no limit to our efforts to justify and excuse our actions. Its not that people who rise to positions of power in business are unusually immoral, unethical, or unconscionably greedy. It's that they have become corporatized and absorbed into a world of different standards and goals. They are insulated from gimlet-eyed oversight and the ethical standards regulating human interaction.

Competition – the wonder-cure in all supply and demand economic discussions — works two ways. We most often think of it as a force to stimulate invention, improve products, keep quality high and prices low. But competition is also the force that drives rivals across moral lines. Were Salomon Barney and Goldman Sachs the first companies to woo and win investment banking business with IPO allocations? Probably not. But once one of the major players in a field creates a new way to attract business, the others must follow. They cannot be left behind, ethics be damned, for the judge of corporate goodness – the "market" – punishes those who fail to keep up.

Society's only protection against destructive profiteering on the one hand is open competition. When other entrepreneurs see an opportunity to improve quality, reduce price, or deliver a better product to serve a need, the public good is served. On the other hand, society's protection against a competitive race to the bottom of the ethic standards ladder is (a) the marketplace of public opinion leading to (b) government regulation.

The problem is that public opinion is a weak, belatedly informed, and inconsistent watchdog of corporate misbehavior. Yes, there is a non-government-controlled "free" press. Dissenting opinions can be found. But 80 to 90% of our mass media is controlled by fewer than a dozen corporations.

Public opinion is manipulated, distorted, and, when necessary, suppressed by those who control the media. [c] The primary information-gathering and dissemination sources for the 250 million people living in the United States are in the hands of a few players, all of whom are in business to make a profit from advertising dollars spent by major corporations. Biting the hand that feeds them is not in the best interests of either management or investors. Thus the status quo rules until an overwhelmingly aroused public demands that it not.

Curiously, the above does not hold as true in the field of business journalism. If *The Wall Street Journal*, for example, doesn't track and report business bungling, misdeeds, and crime, it is of no value to the audience it attempts to attract and serve. Investor/business readers read

---

[c] An example of this control was demonstrated during the debate over the 2003 attack on Iraq. One in four Americans opposed the war, yet "were more than six times as likely to see a pro-war source as one who was anti-war; with U.S. guests alone, the ratio increases to 25 to 1" according to a study conducted by Rendell and Tara Broughel of FAIR (Fairness and Accuracy In Reporting), published in the May/June edition of FAIR's magazine Extra!.

The spring 2003 discussion surrounding FCC (Federal Communication Commission) rule changes permitting greater consolidation of media was practically ignored by the three television networks – primary beneficiaries of the changes – until an internet-based campaign raised the awareness of the public, resulting in over 700,000 messages to the FCC opposing the rule changes and causing Congress to hold after-the-fact hearings.

business and financial newspapers and magazines not for their cheerleading of free-market causes — that's reserved for the editorial pages — but for factually reporting things that might cost or make them money. *The Wall Street Journal,* as Ralph Nader pointed out, is the *True Crime Reporter* of American business.

Whenever a large organization or industry is caught playing fast and loose with the truth or other peoples' money, there are enthusiastic calls from business and free-market supporters for "self-regulation." But self regulation doesn't work. Never has, never will. After 2,000 plus years of Ten Commandments-directed self-regulation the world still need police, jails, and the SEC.

> An individual generally indeed neither intends to promote the public interest nor knows how much he is promoting it. By directing industry in such a manner as its produce may be of the greatest value, he intends only his own gain. But he is in this as in many other cases led by an invisible hand to promote an end which was no part of his intention.
>
> Adam Smith, *The Wealth of Nations*

Adam Smith's famous invisible hand is just as apt to push present chiefs of industry into fraud as honest productivity.   Under the pressure of villainous competition, good apples may join bad apples at the bottom of the moral barrel. It's not a lack of character. They have no choice. The financial market demands it. Their stockholders demand it. Capitalism demands it.

Profit is the sole reason for being in business; return on investment is the sole reason for capitalism. The CEO who stays honest while competitors eat his lunch will not be a CEO for long. Honesty in business is the best policy until a dishonest competitor starts outselling your sales force. Then you either close up shop or match him in the moral muck.

The only chance honest business people have to keep from being dragged down to the lowest ethical level is a well-umpired game. Individual companies, even leaders, can't keep the industry honest without the help of strong, well-enforced government regulations to compel honest competition. Nor can a single business sector – the accounting industry, for example — coerce honesty in corporate reporting without the strong fist of the law to back it up.

The 2001-2003 epidemic of accounting scandals finally produced criminal action against some perpetrators, as seen in this *Wall Street Journal* report of June 18, 2003:

> Rite Aid Corp.'s former chief executive, Martin Grass, faces as many as eight years in prison after pleading guilty to two conspiracy counts in a massive accounting fraud at the drugstore chain....
>
> By pleading guilty, Mr. Grass becomes the first CEO of a major company to be held criminally liable for accounting fraud in the recent wave of corporate scandals....
>
> "We hope we've gotten the message across to corrupt officials," said [U.S. attorney] Thomas Marino. "We won't tolerate this and we're coming after you." [11]

The case against deregulation

What we need is an Andrew Jackson to stand, as Jackson stood, against the encroachments of organized wealth.

William Jennings Bryan's "Cross of Gold" speech,
Democratic National Convention, 1896.

Capitalism cannot exist without well-enforced commerce and banking regulation. Post-communist Russia is a prime example of the crime and chaos created when trying to force free-market capitalism into an unprepared and unregulated nation. Even in a mature capitalist economy such as our own, when government oversight is weakened or disarmed, corporate crime explodes.

In the Market Meltdown of "ought-two", investors suffered a $7 trillion dollar loss of wealth over a period of just thirty months. The stock market went into its worst slump in 30 years. A Niagara of money flowed out of the country as foreign investors pulled billions out of a business environment they could no longer trust. From *The Wall Street Journal:*

> What Stock Investors Need First, Trust in Firms' Numbers.
>
> The bad news could be that the fix won't be quick.
> Of the major forces shaping the market now, two of the

180

most important – disagreement about how much stocks are really worth and a lack of trust in corporate numbers – could take months, or perhaps longer, to change.[12]

Regulatory laws put into place in the 1930's in hopes of preventing another market crash have been under constant and massive attack by corporate interests ever since they were enacted by Congress. Attesting to the success of those regulations is the strong economic and industrial growth the nation enjoyed from the 1940's through the 1960's. (Granted, World War II contributed to it as well). Yet business fights regulatory restraint even when it's in its best interest. Deregulation is the ever-present objective of business-sponsored organizations such as the Business Roundtable and National Chamber of Commerce. Industry groups and large corporations use political campaign contributions and constant lobbying to free themselves from regulatory fetters.

The story is always that business people know best how to regulate themselves. and that government interference diminishes entrepreneurial creativity and economic growth. "Unleash the economic power of business," is the cry. So what happened when accounting standards were eased, banking regulations removed and SEC oversight of the markets reduced? The market meltdown of 2001-2002. Deregulation is not an economic stimulus when it destroys investors' confidence in the market.

In one of his many books about poverty in Appalachia, Kentucky lawyer, historian and legislator Harry M. Caudill wrote in 1976:

> A foolish American myth has it that the rich and super-rich are entrepreneurial Daniel Boones who… fare forth to wrest fame and fortune from other like-minded souls. With some notable exceptions, nothing could be farther from the truth. In the main the rich are the clever and adroit who understand the purposes and functions of government and bend it to their purposes. Government becomes a device which they use to expand their fortunes, then hide behind to make certain their gains remain intact.[13]

Small businessmen and start-up entrepreneurs are the first to benefit from a level playing field of fair competition. But fair competition is the last thing Big Business wants. "We all try to impose our will on decision makers in the White House," said a lobbyist for Ashland Oil, as reported in *The Wall Street Journal*. "We all take advantage of what we can."[14]

Despite lip service to the free market, established businesses work hard to protect themselves from open-market pricing, often using government regulations to protect their turf against competitors. Officials of town and county boards, state legislators, Congress, and the President are besieged by businesses, small and large, individually or through associations, asking for protection from "unfair" competition.

For example, in March of 2002, at the strong "suggestion" of large U.S. steel makers who believed they were being subjected to unfair price competition from foreign producers, President G. W. Bush raised tariffs on foreign steel. As reported in *The Wall Street Journal*, Thomas Usher, chief executive of U.S. Steel Corporation told the Senate that the increased import levies "will only result in modest and reasonable price increases." [15]

The action was also taken with an eye on the slim, one-vote Democratic majority in the Senate and the 2002 elections. The President hoped to attract the support of steelworkers and their unions in a number of states with close races.

What was given to one industry, however, had unintended consequences for many others. Wrote *The Wall Street Journal*:

> Less than three months after the Bush administration suggested its stiff new tariffs on steel imports would have only a limited impact on prices, the levies are sending waves of pain through America's manufacturing sector – including steep price increases, supply shortages and layoff threats.
>
> 'This has never happened before – people are breaking contracts all up and down the supply chain,' said Richard McClain of Chicago-based Metalforming Technologies, Inc., a 1,400-employee concern that makes automobile parts. He is also having trouble getting enough steel. 'If we can't get steel, we'll have to cut jobs,' he said. [16]

The $500 billion savings and loan scandal of the 1990's wasn't a minor legal peccadillo created by a few bad apples in the world of high finance but the direct result of deregulation of the savings and loan industry by Congress.

When drivers fill their tanks at the corner station, the only assurance they have that they received the amount shown on the pump is regular state inspection of the pumps. The only guarantee a buyer of bread has that the advertised "One-pound Loaf" weighs 16 ounces is through government regulation. The only assurance airplane passengers have that the plane in which they ride has been safely constructed and maintained is FAA regulation and certification.

It's often said "big corporations can't afford to cheat." As the preceding chapters have made obvious, they can and do.

Who (or what) is running the country?

There's an enormous gulf separating the decision makers of our largest corporations from the people whose lives they affect and sometimes control. When you consider the power these huge economic machines hold over our communities, states, nation, and world this creates a major problem. *Fortune* magazine's "Top 1,000" corporations represent less than 2/1,000ths of a percent (.000182) of the 5.49 million companies filing federal corporate taxes in 2001. Yet they employ about 27 percent of our non-farm, non-government workforce (30 million, out of 109.7 million).

Many of the world's medium to large corporations intimidate the communities, cities, and states where their plants are located simply by dropping a hint that they might move to another location. Regret may be expressed for the thousands of employees thrown out of work, banks left holding mortgages, retailers without customers, etc., but corporations must make their decisions to go or stay based only upon what location will produce the greatest profit.

A large corporate production plant in a community or state is a mixed blessing. When significant numbers of citizens depend on one corporation for their livelihood combined with the "multiplier effect" of that payroll on retail businesses, banks, mortgage lenders, utilities, etc., that employer has not only enormous economic power but political muscle as well. A employer is usually not bashful about using that power to gain tax and other concessions.

"Business or Blackmail, Desperate town gives concessions to paper company," reads a *Newsday*.com headline.

> To keep their [International Paper Co.] mill alive, Essex County taxpayers floated $35 million in tax-exempt bonds to help underwrite the cost of modernizing the mill's pollution control equipment.

> The state gave the company $500,000 to help it upgrade the mill's machines…. And Ticonderoga town leaders agreed to reduce the plant's property tax assessment by $29 million, a 30% decrease, to help the mill survive.
>
> All told, the company has taken $1 million worth of subsidies and tax breaks from Gov. George Pataki's administration without creating a single job in return, according to state documents. Instead, International Paper has closed or downsized four plants around the state, laying off 467 workers, state records show. [17]

Upgrading a mill's machinery is a normal cost of business. This is a capital expenditure anticipated in depreciation schedules and written off against taxes. Why should the public and other businesses subsidize a normal business expense? And why should the public pay extra to keep an industry from polluting its air and water?

Through giveaways such as the above, *Newsday* notes that big business has shifted a greater share of the cost of government from their books to individual taxpayers.

> Business taxes now account for 13 percent of [New York] state revenues, 6 percentage points less than corporations paid in 1994. Conversely, personal income taxes now comprise 60 percent of state receipts, 10 percentage points more than when [Governor] Pataki was elected. [18]

In an attempt to woo Amazon.com, the city of Huntington, West Virginia, population 60,000, spent $4 million of taxpayers' money to renovate several floors of a downtown office building, including $1.5 million to buy new computers for the firm.

Ironton, Ohio's population had dropped from about 14,000 in 1980 to under 13,000 in 1990. On the promise of 600 jobs, Cabletron Corporation talked local officials into building the company a new office building. Two years after the building was complete, Cabletron laid off the 300 people it had hired (half the promised number of jobs), closed the office and moved it to another state. [19]

Financially strapped Toledo, Ohio, desperate to keep DaimlerChrysler's Jeep plant in the city, produced a $300 million package of local, state, and federal subsidies, plus ten years exemption from property taxes, plus site preparation of the land it bought for the company (destroying a neighborhood of 83 homes), and accepted responsibility for all environmental liability the plant might incur. Because of the new plant, DaimlerChrysler was able to reduce its Toledo workforce by 700 jobs. [20i]

In 1977, the Marriott Corporation announced that its Bethesda, Maryland, headquarters were too small to hold its 3,800 employees, scheduled to increase by 700, and initiated a search for a new location. CEO Bill Marriott informed the media that the company would be willing to locate to another state if the price was right. With lower tax rates than Maryland, neighboring Virginia jumped at the opening.

Playing the two states against each other, Marriott finally agreed to stay in Maryland based on an offer of $33.68 million to $44.17 million in state and county tax abatements including school taxes. Writes Robert Weissman of "Focus on the Corporation":

> Unfortunately, Marriott's corporate blackmail of Maryland is now the norm in corporate location decisions.
>
> In many cities and states, virtually no major building is built, no large corporate headquarters lease renewed, no Fortune 500 factory opened, without a slew of tax breaks and related subsidies. The most outrageous example… is the New York City gift to the New York Stock Exchange – a subsidy of $600 million to $900 million to keep the Exchange from migrating to New Jersey. [21]

Corporate hardball is not confined to industry. Three companies, Cargill, ConAgra, and Tyson/IBP, control 75% of the meatpacking market. Livestock ranchers have long complained of the stranglehold these three firms have on the prices they get for their livestock. Even as the price of meat climbs at the supermarket, the price cattle ranchers get for their stock has gone down, with the packing companies taking an ever-greater share of the difference.

To control livestock prices, corporate packers began operating their own ranches and feeding lots. They'd transfer animals to their packing plants near or at cost, setting the price that independents had to meet to stay in business. Many of them didn't.

After ranchers presented their plight to Congressional representatives, in February 2002 the Senate voted to keep a provision in the 2002 Farm Bill prohibiting corporate meatpackers from owning or feeding livestock[d]. Then, reported the *Plains Truth* newsletter:

> Smithfield Corporation took out a full-page ad that threatened to shut down a South Dakota hog processing plant because Senator Tim Johnson (D-SD) sponsored the packer-feeding ban. Dennis Weise, president of the South Dakota Farmers Union called Smithfield's threat corporate blackmail. 'This is blackmail on our whole political system,' said Weise. 'It's not only a blackmail on Senator Johnson, but on South Dakota's farmers and ranchers.[22]

We don't own them. Do they own us?

In its early stages the corporate entity is controlled by its human founders and their human standards of right and wrong. Once the organism attains sufficient size with ownership sufficiently dispersed, the opportunities for human input to alter the course of the creature from its single-minded focus on profits or to consider larger goals of human society is lost. Like Dr. Frankenstein, we have achieved the semblance of life for our corporate creatures but cannot give them a soul. Our paper creations grow beyond our control and have become our masters.

Like the fictional dragon of *Jason and the Argonauts*, when a corporation's head is cut off – it loses a chief executive — it simply grows another. Should it lose a limb — a line of business — it acquires or creates another. Corporations are not limited by physical or mental constraints to a finite number of interests and activities. They enter any field of endeavor or market and undertake any task their human managers believe holds out a promise of profit.

Corporate control of labor is now more subtle than in the 1800's and early industrialization years. In place of goon squads and lockouts, companies suppress worker unrest with threats that they will close or move the plant overseas. Legislation and court decisions that allow companies to permanently replace strikers have deprived employees of the only card

---

[d] The House version of the 2002 Farm Bill did not contain the packer-ban provision. The meatpacking lobby vowed to strip it in conference committee from the final bill and were successful in doing so. The final bill, passed in April 2002, did not contain the packer-ban provision.

they had to play — the ability to band together to force a company to enter negotiations.

America's defense corporations actively pursue sales to the nation's enemies for, as one of America's most gifted journalists, Lewis Lapham, wrote in an article entitled "After 1984":

> The frontiers run between markets and spheres of commercial interest, not along the boundaries of sovereign states. If a company is large enough and rich enough ... the company, of necessity, conducts its own foreign policy. [23]

Expanding on the theme, author Phillip Bobbitt [e] wrote in a *Time* magazine essay:

> In the 21st century, what might be called 'market states' could replace nation-states. Market states will have the same borders and political systems as nation-states but will shift important responsibilities from government to the private sector; multinational corporations will become surrogate agents of government... blurring the boundaries between political and corporate leadership.
>
> The U.S. is already evolving into a market state, though the process will take decades to complete. For example, a market state shifts reliance from the law and regulation-based approach of the nation-state to the incentives of the marketplace. [24]

Once a corporation grows large enough, rich enough and dispersed enough it can conduct its own foreign policy, demand changes in the nation's monetary and tax policies and poison the environment with little fear of punishment. Our largest corporations are now more powerful than the governmental bodies that regulate them. Their influence corrupts legislative bodies, regulatory agencies and the system of justice that might bring them to heel.

Mega-corporations continue their relentless march toward ownership of the wealth of the world. Out of the reach of shareholders, exceeding the powers of boards of directors, beyond the reach of government itself, they may now own us, not we them.

---

[e] *The Shield of Achilles: War, Peace and the Course of History*, Alfred A. Knopf, 2002.

[1] *A History of Business, Vol I, From Babylon to the Monopolists*, by Miriam Beard, University of Michigan Press, 1938; Chapter II, "Rome and the Rise of Finance – Capitalism," pg 30.

[2] Ibid.

[3] Op Cit. *A History of Business, Vol. I*, "Christianity and Business," pg 54

[4] "What Business Kills," by Carl Dreher, *Harper's Magazine*, June 1936.

[5] William T. Gossett, 1957, quoted in *The Annals of America, Conspectus I*, Encyclopaedia Britannica, Inc., 1968, Chapter 16, "The Role of the Business Corporation in American Life."

[6] "The Bribe Effect," by James Surowiecki, *The New Yorker*, October 7, 2002.

[7] Ibid.

[8] Goldman Gave Hot IPO Shares To Top Executives of Its Clients," by Randall Smith, *The Wall Street Journal*, October 3, 2002.

[9] Op cit, "The Bribe Effect," by James Surowiecki.

[10] Op cit, "Goldman Gave Hot IPO Shares...." By Randall Smith.

[11] "Rite Aid's Ex-CEO Pleads Guilty," by Mark Maremont, *The Wall Street Journal*, June 18, 2003.

[12] "What Stock Investors Need: First, Trust in Firm's Numbers," by E.S. Browning and Gregory Zuckerman, *The Wall Street Journal*, July 17, 2002.

[13] *A Darkness at Dawn*, Harry M. Caudill, 1976.

[14] *The Wall Street Journal*, October 13, 1992.

[15] "U.S. Feels the Pain of Steel Tariffs as Prices Rise, Supply Is Reduced," by Neil King, Jr., and Robert Guy Mathews, *The Wall Street Journal*, May 31, 2002.

[16] Ibid.

[17] "Business or Blackmail?, by Jordan Rau, *Newsday*.com, March 18, 2002.

[18] Ibid.

[19] "Corporate Blackmail," by Aaron Myers, *Huntingon News*, February 5, 2001.

[20] "State and Local Corporate Welfare," by Ralph Nader, Ralph Nader for President Web site <www.votenader.com/press>, undated.

[21] "Marriott: corporate schoolyard bully, by Robert Weissman, Focus on the Corporation, March 12, 1999 <corp-focus@essential.org>.

[22] "Packer Feeding Ban, COOL Pass With Farm Bill," from *The Plains Truth* newsletter of the Northern Plains Resource Council, January/February 2002 edition.

[23] Lewis H. Lapham, "After 1984," *Harper's*, September 1988.

[24] "Get Ready for the Next Long War," by Philip Bobbitt, *Time*, September 11, 2002.

CHAPTER TWELVE
WHATEVER HAPPENED TO FREE
ENTERPRISE?

*Free men engaged in free enterprise build better nations
with more and better goods and services, higher wages
and higher standards of living for more people. But free
enterprise is not a hunting license, and it is the hallmark
of contemporary management that it recognizes the
individual and social responsibilities which go hand-in-
hand with freedom.*
California Governor Ronald Reagan [1]

The United States is the richest, most powerful nation in the world. Is
that the result of the concentration of economic power in a few corporate
giants or has it occurred in spite of them?

Some defenders of Big Business point to the high standard of living
enjoyed by 40% of Americans, those (in 2001) with incomes above
$58,800. Detractors point to the 60% of Americans earning an average of
$22,300, barely above the poverty threshold of $18,200 (family of four) [a].
They might note that a minimum-wage earner can't afford to rent a two-
bedroom home anywhere in the U.S. and, in many places, two jobs aren't
sufficient. [2] Or that 11% of our total population, 33 million Americans,
don't have access to enough food to meet their basic needs. Or that one in
every five children in this country – some 13 million – don't get enough
to eat. [3] Is starvation in the midst of plenty a failure of Christian charity or
the failure of free enterprise and capitalism? Or is starvation in the midst
of overwhelming abundance for some the result of political and legislative
choices imposed on the nation by big business interests? Would the nation
and capitalism be far stronger and far better off today if we had not allowed
a few monster corporations to become such dominant players? Like any
"what if," the question is beyond our ability to prove or disprove. But the
conditions that exist because of corporate domination of our society are not
beyond measure. Witness the examples in previous chapters of corporate
crime, malfeasance, and fraud culled from the thousands reported every
year.

---

[a] 2002 income levels from Institute on Taxation and Economic Policy, Tax
Model, April 2002.

Controlled enterprise

For much of the world, including the United States, "free" enterprise is a myth, the exception rather than the rule. In place of the feared socialism, our economic policies are directed by our largest corporations. In place of leadership provided by democratically elected officers, policies are determined in the executive suites and corporate boardrooms. The result is a national policy that assists and protects the wealthy while it endangers and ignores the poor. Entrepreneurial opportunities are limited, small business and individual taxes provide the majority of support for government.

Consider the following 10 bits of data:

1. The federal corporate rate for taxes is 35%. Among the Fortune 500, the 250 largest paid a federal tax rate of just 20.1% in 1998. Instead of paying $257 billion to the IRS they paid $159 billion – a loss of $98 billion to the U.S. Treasury. [4] "One obvious group of losers is the general public, which pays more for – or gets less in – public services," writes USA Today. [5]
2. In 1998, General Motors reported a $952 million profit. Instead of paying federal income taxes, GM received a $19 million rebate for an effective tax rate of –2%.
2.A. One of General Electric's competitors in kitchen appliances, Maytag, paid 35% of its profits in taxes from 1996 to 1998. GE paid an average of only 8.1% while receiving over $6.9 billion in tax breaks.
2.B. Abbot Laboratories paid 29% of its profits in taxes from 1996 to 1998, while Pfizer paid only 3.1%. [6]
3. Large contributions from small groups of donors determine the outcome of elections. Candidates who are given the most money win 90% of their races. Almost a third of campaign contributions come from donors who live out of state. [7]
4. In 1972, corporations paid 24.2% of federal income taxes collected by the IRS; individuals paid 75.6%. In 2002, corporations paid 6.3%, individuals 86.3%, yet the federal corporate income tax rate had not substantially changed. [8]
5. The number of farm families in the U.S. has shrunk by 300,000 over the past 30 years. Four corporations now control 82% of the beef cattle market. Five corporate packing firms control 55% of the hog industry. Family farms – 94% of all farms – receive only 42%

of farm income. In 1996, a 250-pound hog sold for $51. In 2002 it costs $38 to raise a hog and yet it sells for only $31 – the price set by the major packers.

6. In 1992, the five largest grocery chains captured 19% of all grocery business; by 1998 they controlled a third of the business and 42% by 2000. It's estimated that those five chains will control 60% of the business within a few years. [9]

7. Suicides have replaced equipment-related death as the number one cause of farm deaths. [10i]

8. In 1998, the Huffy Bicycle Company shut down its last three remaining U.S. plants and laid off the last of its 1800 workers, moving production to China, Mexico, and Taiwan. The U.S. workers cost Huffy $11 an hour in wages plus $6 in benefits. Chinese workers are paid 33 cents an hour and have no benefits.

9. In 1998 and 1999, the U.S. lost 483,000 manufacturing jobs. Between 1990 and 1999, employment in the shoe industry dropped 60%, from 62,700 jobs in 1990 to 24,800 today (2000). The Pou Yuen company of China employs over 100,000 workers assembling Nike, Timberland, Reebok, and New Balance sneakers and shoes for export to the U.S. [11]

10. "This is a free-market economy," declared New York City Mayor Rudolph Giuliani. "Welcome to the era after Communism." The Mayor then pushed through a $900 million subsidy for the New York Stock Exchange, gave CBS $10 million in tax breaks, provided sales-tax exemptions, property-tax abatements, and discounted electricity prices for ABC, NBC, Ziff-Davis, McGraw-Hill, Reuters, Conde'Nast, Time Warner, and Rupert Murdoch's News America.

But it's not just the federal government under the foot of Big Business as the following illustrates:

11. In the 1960's, General Electric Company promised the city of Crotonville, New York, that it would provide steady employment and economic prosperity if Crotonville would approve a GE plant on the banks of the Hudson River. waive its environmental regulations, and allow GE to discharge PCBs into the river. In the 1980's GE closed the plant, fired all the workers and left the town with a $2 billion cleanup bill, an unusable plant site and a polluted river. [12]

"This corporate socialism is for the rich only," wrote Ralph Nader. "Small and medium-size businesses don't qualify. These subsidies create competitive advantages for large corporations, which use the same city services as smaller businesses but don't pay a proportionate share of the taxes that finance them."[13]

Not one of the governmental policies illustrated by the 11 items above stemmed from a concern for the welfare of the public, out of a desire to stimulate competition, invention or free enterprise. Each one is the result of well-funded and intense lobbying of Congress by corporate interests, created for their specific benefit without regard for the public good.

What is "the public good?"

There is no doubt but that the corporate form of organization is an essential tool of capitalism. It is also apparent that by the year 2000 the "tool" was jamming the gears of our democracy. Once the Marshall Court ruled that a corporation was a "citizen" with all the rights of a human being, compounded by the fraudulent headnote on the court's decision in *Santa Clara County vs. The Union Pacific Railroad*, the founders' structure of public control over corporate existence began to crumble.

Our founders allowed corporations to exist as long as they served "the public good." Profits were anticipated – how else would those with capital be enticed to provide it — but public gain, not private profit, was the reason for allowing their formation.

But what is "the public good?" Is it opportunity for the many or great riches for a few? Is it a level playing field among competitors or "them that has, gets?" Is it the stimulation of invention or protection of the established? Is it encouragement for the entrepreneurial spirit or the raising of roadblocks to upstarts? Is it to encourage consolidation among many providers of similar goods and services or dispersion among many competitors? Are a few hundred industrial-size hog farms of 5,000+ animals essential to provide pork at a reasonable price, or can thousands of family farms raising a few animals each provide sufficient pork as well as a stronger family farm community? In short: are the lowest possible prices critical to the publics' welfare, or will our economy be stronger and society more healthy by paying a little more to trade with our neighbors and buy the work of our countrymen?

When the nation was young and our founders set the rules, "public good" was defined as that which was good for society. Today it is "what's good for General Motors."

Of the 5.49 million chartered corporations paying federal tax, 99.81% are not included in the Fortune 1,000. Only a very few can afford to employ lobbyists to influence legislation in Congress or the states. Most small businesses limit their political activism to contributions to industry or business organizations whose policies and direction are most often driven by the largest corporations in the field.

There are those who say that "small" business" provides more jobs than the *Fortune* 1000. Whether or not that proves out statistically, it's obvious that America's small businesses are both the economic and ethical backbones of the nation. Founders, owners and managers of small to middle-size enterprises like Aaron Feuerstein of Massachusetts' Malden Mills, Indiana's Milt Cole of Cole Hardwood, and Jim Clark of Silicon Valley, are viscerally committed to their businesses. They are involved with and connected to their employees, communities, suppliers, and customers. They are not quick to pull up stakes and move their production plants to gain competitive advantage. They are personally at risk if they cook the books or dip too deeply into the till. When disaster strikes, or competitors eat into their sales and revenue stream, they either find a way to rebuild and compete within the moral framework of their community, or they reluctantly close up shop.

These are the people, entrepreneurs, businesses, and corporations our free enterprise capitalist system should serve and encourage.

Historian David M. Potter asserted in his book *People of Plenty* (published 1954) that in America "liberty" and "equality" mean the same thing, the freedom to grasp opportunity and advance economically without social barriers to advancement. [14] The strength and power of the United States as an economic force and a political idea does not reside in its "upper crust" but in its solid middle-class filling. If anything has been a constant in the American vision people it is that this is and must be remain the "land of opportunity." [15]

"Corporate" co-opts "Business"

Influenced by 50 years of a pro-business, anti-government drumbeat by corporate media, corporate-sponsored think-tanks, and corporately funded "public-interest" organizations, a significant number of middle and upper-class Americans are convinced that America's billion-dollar corporate enterprises are more to be trusted with their future than the democratic government they elect.

In over-a-cup-of-coffee discussions among the middle-class, reverence for business wins hands down over respect for the role of government in balancing private and public interests. Anti-government sentiment and humor is repeated as gospel by hundreds of thousands of small business owners and even by much of the wage-earning public. "What's the world's biggest lie? I'm from the government and I'm here to help you."

Continually reinforced by mostly anti-government, libertarian-leaning Talk Radio, the working class has given up its traditional loyalty to itself in favor of an undefined and poorly understood "free market." Witness the continuing decline in union membership, the unquestioning acceptance of business deregulation, the disdain shown for universal healthcare ("socialized medicine"), and lack of concern over efforts to "privatize" Social Security.

Conservative and business organizations contend that the interests of business are under constant attack from consumer organizations, tort attorneys, and government regulators. An example is this October 2002, *Wall Street Journal* headline and report: "The Regulators: Did Washington Help Set the Stage For Economic Woe?" [16]

The headline implies that "Washington" was at fault for the nation's economic problem, yet the story itself is a tale of a long-term and very effective lobbying effort to tear down regulatory walls created to protect the public. The story began:

> In an unseasonably warm February morning of 1987, three bank executives squared off against the Federal Reserve board in a crowded hearing room in Washington, D.C. Their mission was to persuade the Fed to start tearing down the half-century old regulatory walls between the business of banking and business of selling stocks and bonds.
>
> Paul Volcker, the Fed's gruff chairman, was leery. He worried that easing the limits set by the Glass-Steagall Act of 1933 posed dangers: lenders recklessly lowering loan standards in pursuit of lucrative public offerings; banks marketing bad loans to an unsuspecting public.
>
> Thomas Theobald, then vice chairman of CitiCorp, countered that three 'outside checks' on corporate misconduct had emerged since the financial shenanigans of the Roaring Twenties had led to Glass-Steagall. He cited 'a very effective' Securities and Exchange Commission, knowledgeable investors, and 'very sophisticated' rating agencies. [17]

The Wall Street Journal's reporter concluded that "The erosion of that landmark law [Glass-Steagall Act] was one of many steps that added up to a free-market sweep of Washington over the past century. When a government regulator attempted to defend her agency's oversight of the financial markets ...

> a crowd of regulators watched in silence as Robert Rubin stared across the table... at Brooksley Born, head of the Commodity Futures Trading Commission. Mr. Rubin, President Clinton's venerated Treasury Secretary,[and former co-chairman of Goldman, Sachs & Co.] curtly informed her that she had no right to pursue her plan to explore whether more regulation was needed of the market for over-the-counter derivatives.
>
> Mr. Greenspan, sitting to Ms. Born's right, chimed in with a warning that she risked disrupting U.S. capital markets.
>
> And yet Ms. Born worried that leaving derivatives unregulated also carried huge risks. Because they weren't subject to rules that applied to other securities, little was disclosed about the transactions. That made it easier for traders to take big risks, or fraudulently manipulate deals.
>
> Wall Street went into lobbying overdrive, as leading derivatives underwriters such as J.P. Morgan, heavy derivatives users like Enron, and nearly a dozen financial trade organizations pleaded with the Fed and Treasury to stop Ms. Born. They then asked Congress to block the study. [18]

Wall Street's effort to gut Glass-Steagall came home to roost quickly when New York Attorney General Elliot Spitzer began delving into financial house practices in 2002. First Goldman Sachs came under the gun, then Merrill-Lynch paid $100 million in fines for the firms' misleading use of stock analysts' research to benefit their investment banking clients. Later it was the mutual fund industry under fire first for failing to disclose hidden fees, then for making illegal "after-hours" trades.

In addition to the coercion felt by federal agencies, state and local governments come under enormous pressure from corporations dangling the promises of jobs and economic growth. For example:

In 1974 the State of Michigan passed Act 198, which authorized municipalities to grant tax abatements with the approval of the State Tax Commission. Within ninety days of the passage of the legislation, G.M. was knocking on the door of the Ypsilanti township government seeking abatements for its Willow Run plant and accompanying Hydra-Matic plant. 'From 1975 through 1990 ... General Motors requested and received tax abatements on facilities investments in those two plants of over $1.3 billion.'[19]

In February 1992, G.M. announced it was closing its Willow Run auto assembly plant. At its peak it had employed 42,000. A stunned Ypsilanti community and state were given little solace in the knowledge that G.M.'s transmission production facility, employing some 5000, would remain.

Public money used to subsidize private enterprise ranges from the obvious – tax abatements for industry, crop/price support to dairy farmers, foreign trade advertising support — to invisible. Farms and industry pay far less per gallon of fresh water than home-owners. Industries frequently pay little or nothing to dump their waste into public landfills and waterways. Smokestack industries spew billions of tons of waste into the air, not only without charge but complaining bitterly if they are asked to clean up their discharge.

The public, not industry, pays for the down-stream/down-wind pollution damage to forestry, crops, animals, and health. Where railroads pay to build and maintain rights of way, interstate highways are funded by the federal government and maintained with dedicated taxes.

With almost universal agreement that our federal tax code is unfair and inconsistent in how it defines and treats "income," it has grown over the years to become almost impossible for ordinary citizens to decipher. Yet responsible members of Congress hesitate to support reform and simplification because of the enormous lobbying power that will be applied by special interests. An example is the perversion of our tax system through "special orders" written into the tax code by Congressmen acting as stealth panderers for America's largest corporations. Shrewdly written so that neither corporate beneficiaries nor congressional sponsor/shepherds are revealed, these very specific tax breaks transfer millions of dollars of the corporate tax load onto the shoulders of America's small businessmen and public with hardly a mention in the public media according to Pulitzer Prize-winning reporters Donald L. Barlett and James B. Steele of *The Philadephia Inquirer.* The two spent over a year digging out which members of Congress had sponsored each of the 1986 Tax Reform Act's thousands of special orders relieving American companies from paying millions of dollars in taxes.[b]

When some industries have difficulty competing in the free market, government is pressured to provide a subsidy. For example:

> The ethanol industry is dominated by ADM (Archer-Daniels-Midland Inc.) whose three main businesses — alcohol-based ethanol, corn sweeteners and soybean products — all depend heavily on government subsidies [of some $700 million per year]. Its TV commercials on Sunday political talk shows aren't directed at consumers so much as they are at the Members of Congress who watch them.[20]

A classic treatise of the post-Depression 1930s, *The Corporation and Private Property,* written by economist Gardiner C. Means and attorney Adolf A. Berle, characterized the struggle in government to maintain a balance between public and corporate interests:

> The rise of the modern corporation has brought a concentration of economic power which can compete on equal terms with the modern state. The state seeks in some aspects to regulate the corporation, while the corporation, steadily becoming more powerful... where its own interests are concerned... attempts to dominate the state.[21]

The power of corporate money distorts if not controls almost every federal and state legislative process and regulatory agency. Their demands dominate the nation's social, fiscal, and tax policies. Their requirements dominate the nation's foreign policy, which wars we fight, which tyrants we will embrace and which revolutions we will oppose. Once every two years the public has an opportunity to voice its pleasure

---

[b] The results of their research, "The Great Tax Giveaway," published as a special section of *The Philadelphia Inquirer* in 1988, won a second Pulitzer Prize.

or displeasure with government through the elections. But the mother's milk of politics – campaign money – flows most freely from corporate cows. The overwhelming presence of special interest money diminishes citizen participation in politics because "about 80% of Americans think that money matters more than the citizens in determining the outcome of campaigns." [22] Writes the Public Interest Research Group in "The Wealth Primary: The role of big money in the 2002 Congressional Primaries":

> The problem with money in politics is that large contributions – which only a fraction of the American public can afford to make – unduly influence who can run for office and who wins elections in the United States. Money is a critical factor in election outcomes.
>
> Nowhere is the influence of big money on elections more apparent than in the congressional primary elections throughout the United States. Our analysis of Federal Election Commission (FEC) campaign finance data for the 2002 election cycle indicates that money played a key role in determining election outcomes and that the majority of campaign contributions came from a small number of large donors (31% of whom reside out-of-state).
>
> According to FEC data, major party congressional candidates who raised the most money won 90% of their primary races in 2002. Winning candidates out-raised their opponents by a margin of more than 4-to-1. [23]

In addition to pouring money into political campaigns, Corporate America controls the microphones, cameras, transmitters, newsrooms, editorial boards, and printing presses of the nation.

Congress: money talks

Corporate tax breaks, subsidies, protection from competition, and relief from legal responsibilities do not spontaneously arise in the halls of legislatures and the Congress. They are created in the accounting and legal offices of big businesses, then promoted to legislators and the public using the power of the corporate purse. The average citizen or small businessperson who disagrees with these policies can express opposition only at the ballot box. He/she can neither afford lobbyists, frequent visits to the nation's capital nor campaign contributions of a size that provides them with easy access to and willing ears in Congress.

"Absolutely. When I'm elected, all you'll have to do is whistle."

Consider for a moment the CEO being told by his accounting firm or chief financial officer that a small change in a tax law would increase his company's after-tax net by a hundred million dollars. Putting aside for the moment what that might to do for his personal bonus or stock-option holdings, the CEO would be remiss in the extreme if he did not direct his Washington-based lobbying firm to get that change made, even if it cost the entire first-year's gain of $100 million.

A hundred million dollars, or even half that, properly placed in political hands, expended for supporting economic studies, in advertising, public relations, and in fomenting or faking "grass roots" support has an enormous impact, on the body politic. Special legislation, subsidies, and government support that small business people can only dream about are easily accomplished by big businesses with millions to spend.

Power exerted by our largest corporations over government at all levels was explored and detailed by writer-researchers Dan Clawson, Alan Neustadtl, and Denise Scott in *Money Talks:*

> This definition of power as the ability to make someone do something against his or her will is what Steven Lukes calls a one-dimensional view of power. A two-

dimensional view recognizes the existence of nondecisions: a potential issue never gets articulated or, if articulated by someone somewhere, never receives serious consideration. Wartenberg argues instead for a field theory of power that analyzes social power as similar to a magnetic field. A magnetic field alters the motion of objects susceptible to magnetism. Similarly, the mere presence of a powerful social agent alters social space for others and causes them to orient to the powerful agent. One of the executives we interviewed took it for granted that 'if we go see the congressman who represents [a city where the company has a major plant], where 10,000 of our employees are also his constituents, we don't need a PAC to go see him.[24,c]

Giants stalking the earth

"Corporations are now bigger than countries and governments," wrote Charles Gray in the June 1999, *Multinational Monitor.* "The giant corporations have greater economic power than all but a few of the world's governments. Each of the top three, Exxon-Mobil, General Motors and Ford – has more annual revenue than all but 7 of the 191 national governments of the world. Taken together, the combined revenues of the top 14 corporations," writes Gray, "surpass the total revenue of the United States government."[25]

It's astonishing to consider that the CEOs of these and the rest of the *Fortune* 500 giants dominating our economic futures are answerable to no one but themselves. Their stockholders have no means to vote them into or out of office. The boards to whom they are ostensibly responsible consist of friends, business associates, and fellow corporate animals with little inclination to use what powers they have. Government is the only arbiter strong enough to impose discipline. But corporations and their associations, lobbyists, think-tanks, and media dominate the halls of government as well.

---

[c] References are made to philosopher/sociologist/writer Steven Luke's *Power, a Radical View*, McMillan (UK) Humanities, 1974, and Thomas E. Wartenberg's *The Forms of Power: From Domination to Transformation*, Temple U. Press, 1990.

It's worth repeating: CEOs are answerable to no one but themselves and the mysterious "market." Stockholders cannot vote them out. The public cannot touch them. The government cannot remove them except through rarely successful and unevenly administered criminal prosecution.[d] Yet these CEOs direct enterprises powerful and rich enough to dominate economic, foreign, and domestic policies from the global down to the family level.

Who is to blame?

No single factor or organization can be deemed responsible for the present state of affairs. Influence of the Rich and Powerful has waxed and waned over our country's 300 years of post-Pilgrim occupation. It waxed, for example, during the great Robber Baron era of the late 1800's, and waned with the emergence of labor unions and the strong regulatory controls arising out of the Great Depression. Through the industrial build-up caused by World War II and the impact of returning veterans, the GI Bill education program, and the early period of the Cold War, the middle-class dominated local and national political agendas. Beginning in the 1970s the corporate upper class took charge and had called the shots right up until the bubble burst in 2002. Will that be the apogee of this cycle? Has corporate lying, cheating, and stealing aroused sufficient anger to make us willing to look beyond punishment of the malefactors and "tough" regulation to the core issues themselves?

"In my lifetime, American business has never been under such scrutiny, and to be blunt, much of it deserved," said Goldman Sachs' CEO Hank Paulson. "Phony earnings, inflated revenues, conflicted Wall Street analysts, directors asleep at the switch – this isn't just a few bad apples

---

[d] Spurred on by angry investors and a dramatic loss of consumer confidence in the market, the SEC and courts pressed securities and accounting fraud against a number of high-profile defendants. ImClone CEO Waksal was given a 7 year term for securities fraud and perjury, the ex-CEO of Rite Aid pleaded guilty to massive accounting fraud and six former and current Xerox executives were ordered to pay $22 million in fines. At the same time the SEC was considering forcing defendants to pay all financial penalties out of their own pockets instead of being able to use insurance to cover fines. However, reported the paper, "The SEC, which brought about 600 enforcement cases in 2002, lacks the resources to litigate every case and tries to settle most of them." The Wall Street Journal, June 16, 2003, "SEC Considers Sanctions, Boards" by Deborah Solomon.

we're talking about here," writes Nocera, "This, my friends, is a systemic breakdown. And that has created a crisis of investor confidence the likes of which hasn't been seen since – well, since the Great Depression." [26] There is, of course, no single "mistake" or act leading to the current state of affairs. The Marshall Court decision certainly opened the door to corporate power, but its reasoning – that a corporation is endowed with human rights — has been enlarged by a number of courts and congresses since. One often-overlooked factor is the argument between Jefferson and Marshall on the question of "national" corporations – federal charters of incorporation rather than state – that centered around the formation of a federally chartered bank. Marshall favored federal charters; Jefferson favored states', an opinion he might have reconsidered if he had foreseen the race of state standards to the lowest common denominator that would follow.

But none of these early decisions would have resulted in the current state of affairs were it not for the acquiescence of the body politic – we the people – us.

Our first mistake was to look upon the growth of American businesses into Big Businesses like proud parents or neighbors. "Can you imagine the kid getting that big, that strong?" It wasn't just a steel company. It was U.S. Steel, biggest steel producer in the world! Bigger is better! More is best! We're Number One! Only cynics cheered when Honda, then Toyota, began importing and selling cars more reliable, less costly, and just as comfortable (if not more so) as tail-finned Cadillacs. The fruits of real free enterprise, real competition in quality, innovation, and price became apparent to all.

Another mistake was to forget our own Industrial Revolution, the battles of workers to organize and unionize against the Robber Baron industrialists of the late 1800s and early 1900s. With the 40-hour week won and workers earning a living wage, families no longer needed to send their ten- and twelve- year-olds into the mills to stave off eviction and starvation. The third generation of union-organized labor no longer remembered workers being gunned down on the picket line by mill owners' goons, or how their grandmothers had perished in the flames of rag-trade sweat shops. Now these memories have faded and Americans are convinced that they no longer needed unions to get good wages, safe working conditions, and a guaranteed retirement.

Great Depression memories have faded. Middle-class Americans now believe in "the market" and their ability to share in the growth of industry and innovation. Unfazed by regular bouts of fraud and deception, we still believe the hype of Wall Street that "a piece of America" is the way to the good life, the second home, and a secure retirement.

With years of evidence to the contrary, we still bestow on corporate leaders the mantle of "Captains of Enterprise" guiding massive ships of commerce through the shoals of government interference and foreign competition, providing cargoes of household conveniences, good jobs, comfortable retirement, and good works to our land.

But, as we learned in the market meltdown of 2002, our champions have feet of clay. Given the opportunity to take advantage, cheat, lie, and steal, they will. We've succumbed to the cynical calumny that necessity alone provides the motivation for the lower classes to get off their lazy butts and work and it's corollary; that greed is all that motivates the upper class to be entrepreneurial.

We have allowed those who game the system to define the government as "them" rather than "us." We are taught to see government not as the protector of the little guy against the big wheels, but as a bureaucracy stealing substantial portions from each pay check, wasting it on billion-dollar boondoggles, and sending it off to ungrateful welfare queens and foreigners. Years of anti-government propaganda have convinced us that it is government, not General Motors or Microsoft, that stifles our entrepreneurial creativity, snoops into our private affairs, and kills our incentive.

Big Business sees government as an easily manipulated assistant in stifling domestic and foreign competitors, funding marketing adventures, and cleaning up their environmental mess. Government will replace employee retirement funds after they've been misappropriated for corporate use. Government will force products through trade barriers and into foreign markets. Government will pay the social costs when U.S. plants are closed and the jobs moved overseas.

Yet, to use comedian Rodney Dangerfield's favorite phrase, government "don't get no respect."

> *The liberty of a democracy is not safe if the people tolerate the growth of private power to a point where it becomes stronger than the democratic state itself. That in its essence is fascism: ownership of government by an individual, by a group or any controlling private power.*
> Franklin D. Roosevelt [27]

John David Rose

"It's not cheating. It's accounting!"

1 Speech given at Sacramento (California) Host Breakfast, 9/4/70, from A Time for Choosing, Regnery Gateway, Chicago, 1983.

2 In "What's News" column, *The Wall Street Journal*, September 19, 2002.

3 "Feed the Hungry," by Bill Heavey, *Field and Stream*, October 2002.

4 Institute on Taxation and Economic Policy, "Study Finds Resurgence in Corporate Tax Avoidance," October 19, 2000.

5 "Study: Companies pay less in taxes," by Gary Strauss, *USA Today*, October 20, 2000.

6 Op cit. Institute on Taxation and Economic Policy, October 19, 2000.

7 "The Wealth Primary; The Role of Big Money in the 2002 Congressional Primaries," by U.S. Public Interest Research Group Education Fund, October 2002.

8 Internal Revenue Service Data Book 2001, Table 7 – Internal Revenue Gross Collections, by Type of Tax, Fiscal Years 1972-2001.

9 "Converging Forces Afflict Farms," by Neil E. Harl, *The New York Times*, "Money&Business," April 29, 2001.

10 "Turning the Tables on Pennsylvania Agri-Corporations," an interview with Thomas Linzey of the Community Environmental Legal Defense Fund, published in *By What Authority*, a publication of the Program on Corporations, Law & Democracy, Vol 3, #2, Spring 2001.

11 National Labor Committee Web site <nlc@nlcnet.org>.

12 "Robert Kennedy, Jr.: Environmental Horrors Are Stalking America," by Robin Lawless, *The Word*, Hunter College of New York, January 18, 1999.

13 "Welfare for the Rich," by Ralph Nader, *New York Times* Op-Ed, May 15, 1999.

14 *People of Plenty: Economic Abundance and the American Character*, Ch. 6, by David M. Potter, University of Chicago Press, 1954.

15 Ibid.

16 "The Regulators: Did Washington Help Set the Stage For Economic Woe?" by Jacob M. Schlesinger, *The Wall Street Journal*, October 17, 2002.

17 Ibid.

18 Ibid.

19 Borsos, John, "The Judge Who Stood Up to G.M.," *The Nation*, 4/12/93.

20 Editorial "They're Interested," *Wall Street Journal*, 3/20/93.

21 Berle, Adolf A. and Means, Gardiner C., The Corporation and Private Property, *Annals of America*, Vol XV, pg139.

22 "The Vanishing Voter: Why Does This Describe Half Of The U.S. Electorate?", an interview with Professor Thomas Patterson, TomPaine. com. feature.cfm/ ID/6567.

23 "The Wealth Primary; The Role of Big Money in the 2002 Congressional Primaries," U.S. PIRG Education Fund, October 2002.

John David Rose

[24] *Money Talks*, by Dan Clawson, Alan Neustadtl, and Denise Scott, Basic Books, NYC, © 1992.

[25] "Corporate Goliaths, Sizing Up Corporations and Governments," by Charles Gray, *Multinational Monitor*, June 1999, Volume 20, Number 6.

[26] "System Failure," by Joseph Nocera, Fortune, June 24, 2002.

[27] Quoted in "Challenging Corporate Power," interview by David Barsamian of Richard Grossman, co-director of the Program on Corporations, Law and Democracy, August 23, 1998.

CHAPTER THIRTEEN
WHAT'S TO BE DONE?

*"Fascism should more properly called corporatism, since
it is the merger of state and corporate power."*
Benito Mussolini

What's To Be Done?

Can we stop or even re-direct the corporate steamroller? Is it time for
The Revolution? Are 250 million abused middle and lower classes ready
to march against the 15,000 or so Americans who own or control most of
the nation's wealth and productive resources?

The idea is not as far-fetched as it might seem. Following a *New
York Times Magazine* article "The End of Middle-Class America" by Paul
Krugman (October 20, 2002), hundreds of readers wrote to the "Letters"
section. Samples include:

> "…an alert to the stagnating middle class and to the upper
> class as well. The ultrarich and the politicians who serve
> their interests have ridden high on obfuscation and attacks
> (like castigating critics for advocating class warfare) while
> engendering a society with disparities of wealth that are
> historically unsustainable." [1]

"Krugman's concerns about the inequity of wealth in the United States
are right on target. Corporate and political exploitation of the middle and
working classes has not escaped the notice of the 'rabble.'" [2]

> "The phenomenon of the rich getting richer and the poor
> getting poorer is as old as ancient Rome. What is different
> in our day is that the gains of the superrich come not
> from exploiting the poor but from fleecing middle-class
> stockholders and buying tax privileges." [3]

> "A mystery remains why are (sic) the policies that lead
> to the outcomes Krugman describes are so popular even
> among the 99 percent who are not their beneficiaries? Why
> are people who are being crushed by this new overclass so
> eager to defend the policies that led to its creation?" [4]

As the last letter writer observed, how can the middle class be worked into a revolutionary frenzy when it doesn't realize how badly it's being taken?

Business people are more aware of the losses, actual and perceived, caused by each fraud-spawned economic crisis. "Enough is enough," was the headline in 96 point type of a Business Roundtable advertisement in the July 8, 2002, *Wall Street Journal*. "When even one CEO betrays investors, it's one too many." This was an curious lead-in to a text expressing anger at "corporate misdoing in a number of major public firms," considering that over 1,000 large corporations, including many members of the Business Roundtable, had been forced to "re-state their earnings."

Historically revolutions have been mounted by the poor and landless against land owners. The huge market losses of 2001-2002, however, had a significant impact on the upper class. As Kathleen O'Brian pointed out in a *New York Times* "Money & Business" sidebar:

> "The very rich – the top 1 percent in terms of net worth – have almost one-third of assets in stocks and mutual funds, and therefore have a larger share of their wealth tied to the market."[5]

The heavily-invested as well as corporate leaders may express concern over corporate crime, but their concern will not result in remedial action. They have too much stake in the status quo, no matter how flawed. When and if a new American Revolution takes place it will have to be initiated and led by the middle class who are faithful to the concept of capitalism, but frustrated with systematic dishonesty.

Before we consider draconian measures to forestall such an unfortunate occurrence, let's consider what has been and is currently being proposed to improve corporate governance.

Improving the board

More responsive corporate governance starts with the structure of the Board of Directors. The business scandals of past and present clearly mandate change in the way boards are constituted and selected. Shame and chagrin are apparently insufficient motivation to avoid repetition of the kinds of corporate disasters represented in 2002 by Enron, WorldCom, Rite Aid, and their ilk. The history of American capitalism, however, is one cycle of fraud following another. There's a brief respite when public outrage and government reaction peaks. Then forgetfulness sets in, investors re-enter the market, and a short period of growth is enjoyed before the next paroxysm of corporate deceit occurs.

For those who doubt this grim characterization, a brief review:

"The Great Panic of 1791" was caused by Alexander Hamilton's friend William Duer who was a member of the Continental Congress, and a co-founder with Hamilton of New York Bank. In a complex insider-trading double-cross, Duer caused his bank to fail and took many others with it.

Between 1793 and 1933, the Federal Reserve notes twenty "runs" on banks before stiff banking regulations were enacted by Congress and the Federal Reserve was created as "The bank of last resort." [a] Each run robbed millions of Americans of their savings, stopped industries cold, and threw millions out of work.

Less than 50 years passed before the Panic of 1837 which, again, cost small savers and businesses their cash and capital, millions their jobs, and the nation its confidence. In 1873, Jay Cook & Co., then the largest bank in the U.S., closed its doors and caused a stock market crash. Twenty years later the nation again took a huge economic hit in the Panic of 1893, when failure of the Reading Railroad caused the failure of hundreds of banks and businesses. Just as in 2000, the stock market plunged, European investors pulled their funds out of the country and, once again, small business and working people lost their livelihoods and savings.

Writes historian Lee I. Niedringhaus:

> It was as though all the excesses and avarice of the Gilded Age had been ignited and catapulted the country into a financial inferno. The Panic of 1893 and its aftermath shifted the psyche of the American public toward a broader acceptance of reform and regulation, deftly discredited the business doctrine of 'survival of the fittest,' and brought in the earnestness of the Progressive Era. [6]

Despite reform, regulation, and "earnestness," just 36 years later the nation suffered The Crash of '29, followed by the Great Depression. Again, Congress enacted a spate of banking regulations and formed the SEC. The

---

[a] Bank runs in the U.S.: 1793,1797, 1810, 1815, 1819, 1825, 1833, 1837, 1839, 1847, 1857, 1884, 1890, 1893, 1907, 1929, 1930, 1931, 1933. Source: "Learning the Lessons of History: The Federal Reserve and the Payments System by Adam M. Zaretsky, Regional Economist, July 1996.

lesson was quickly forgotten. Banking institutions lobbied successfully to have regulations eased and restrictions against their entry into stock brokerage activities removed. In 1982 the savings and loan industry pushed through the Garn-St. Germain Depository Act which President Reagan hailed in his bill-signing message:

> This bill ... provides a long-term solution for troubled thrift institutions. It's pro consumer, granting small savers greater access to loans, a higher return on their savings. It means help for housing, more jobs, and new growth for the economy. All in all, I think we hit the jackpot. [7]

Instead of the jackpot, deregulation of the thrifts:

> produced the greatest collapse of U.S. financial institutions since the Great Depression. Over the 1986-1995 period, 1,043 thrifts with total assets of over $500 billion failed. The large number of failures overwhelmed the resources of the FSLIC, so U.S. taxpayers were required to back up the commitment extended to insured depositors of the failed institutions. [8]

Was the collapse of the thrifts caused by ineffectual and careless boards? Most certainly. After research based on more than 100 interviews with thrift institution leaders and government officials, University of California criminologists Kitty Calavita and Henry N. Pontell with Robert H. Tillman of St. John's University, New York, concluded:

> Many experts tend to chalk the savings and loan crisis up to business risks gone awry or adverse economic conditions. But our research shows that deliberate insider fraud was at the center of the debacle – and that systematic political collusion was a critical ingredient in this unprecedented series of frauds. [9]

Political leaders learned nothing from the 1990's savings and loan deregulation disaster. In 1999, President William Jefferson Clinton signed the Financial Services Act, finally removing the regulatory barriers between banking and stock brokering put in place after the Crash of '29. Within months, payola and fraud began to infect reputable firms such as

CitiCorp, J.P. Morgan Chase, Solomon Barney, Merrill Lynch, Goldman Sachs, Morgan Stanley, even Credit Suisse. The financial cataclysm of Enron, WorldCom, and Global Crossing *et al* can be traced directly back to the passage of the '99 deregulating act.

The point of this recitation of bank failures, market panics, and self-inflicted economic disasters is that every one of the corporations creating or participating in these calamities had a board of directors supposedly monitoring their operations and ethics. The history of our greatest corporate failures is a continuing soap-opera series of boards of directors failing to keep their executives honest. For all their business acumen and personal rectitude, the "best minds" of the corporate world participated in or closed their eyes to actions that resulted not just in fraud or failure but enormous suffering for the "little people" who entrusted them with their savings. In addition they caused additional millions of families to suffer, families who had no direct connection to the problem firms yet suffered the loss of their livelihoods, their homes and sometimes their lives.

Can boards be made responsive and responsible?

In spite of the tiresome regularity of corporate moral failures, each epidemic of fraud stimulates a flurry of activity but no reform of the system that creates the fraud. "GE to Announce Set of New Policies To Shore Up Board," [10] and "Companies Add Ethics Training; Will It Work?" [11] were two of many similar business media stories in the aftermath of the 2002 meltdown. Each crisis generates assurances that corporate boards have learned their lesson.

The most popular cure today for ethically challenged companies is the "outside" director. It's a placebo, however, not a remedy, write Lorsch and MacIver:

> Outside directors, however, are seldom cohesive. These talented, successful individuals meet infrequently and relatively briefly at tightly structured meetings with a full agenda. Busy themselves, they don't object to the boardroom norm discouraging extra meeting contact....
>
> But the most obvious impediment to outside directors exercising their power is that the acknowledged and formal leader in 80% of U.S. boardrooms is the CEO, whose power is greater, primarily because of his knowledge of and expertise in company matters. [12]

Another remedy is to ban the practice of appointing CEOs as chairman. Shareholder activists have long argued against combining the two positions.

> The outside chairman concept "is really now being seriously discussed in boardrooms instead of being dismissed out of hand," says Ira Millstein,… co-chairman of [a blue-ribbon commission of the National Association of Corporate Directors].
>
> On the other hand, external candidates for the CEO spot… often want the chairman's seat as well. Directors at Tyco International, Ltd., the troubled Bermuda-based conglomerate, dropped tentative plans to split the top two roles so they could snare Motorola Inc. executive Edward Breen. Mr. Breen preferred to be both chairman and chief executive… "to get an enormous amount of things done as effectively as possible". [13]

Meeting outside the presence of the CEO has also been suggested as a way to encourage board members to be more candid in addressing real or perceived problems.

> Seventy-three percent of the 908 *Fortune* 1000 directors who responded to a survey say they want CEO-free meetings. But if only four in 10 companies are holding them, many of these directors either aren't insisting on the meetings, or CEOs aren't permitting them. [14i]

In the military, annual visits by the Adjutant General's staff are specifically designed to provide opportunities for enlisted personnel and non-commissioned officers to air their concerns and gripes without the presence of the unit commander. Perhaps corporate charters should include the requirement that corporate boards conduct similar confidential gripe and whistle-blower sessions.

Employee representation on the board of directors is normal for German corporations thanks to a 1950's law creating "codetermination", with labor controlling from one-third to one-half the seats on the board. [15] In the United States, board positions for employees sometimes accompany Employee Stock Ownership (ESOP) plans most often put in place by owners of small, closely held corporations. [b] Owners use the ESOP to convert a portion of their ownership position into cash without the discounting that may occur in unrelated third party sales. The National Center for Employee Ownership (NCEO) estimated that in 2000 there were over 11,500 employee-owned firms in the U.S., covering more than 8.5 million employees and with assets of over $650 billion.

Labor representation on the boards of large publicly-held U.S. corporations is almost non-existent largely because of legal barriers as well as the tradition of an adversarial relationship between management and labor. The National Labor Relations Act does not allow union representation of employees with management responsibilities. Board members, by definition, have management responsibilities. In addition, laws of corporate governance generally "impose a duty on all corporate supervisory board members to supervise management on behalf of the corporation in general and in the interests of shareholders in particular." [16] Should a board face a decision that separates the welfare of the employees from that of the shareholders, the ability of an employee-member to put the interests of shareholders first would be in question.

Are stakeholders represented?

Various avenues have been tried to create a balance of board representation among stakeholders — shareholders, employees, community/state. As described in Chapter 2, colonial and early state constitutions required a state official to serve on the board. Some European countries require labor representation on boards. Although the presence of such "outsiders" would not guarantee the end of deception and fraud, the presence of any board member coming from outside management's circle of peers would make it more difficult.

The problem of how to select and/or elect outside members to a board (especially in the absence of a unionized work force) brings into focus the complete fiction of shareholder ownership. Shareholders neither nominate board candidates, nor do they have a choice from among different slates. Shareholders cannot fire a board member for malfeasance in office, much less high crimes and misdemeanors. Only under the most unusual of circumstances – an unfriendly takeover or a lawsuit by disgruntled major shareholders – are investors privy to board deliberations.

---

[b] A study by th U.S. General Accounting Office in 1986 found that around 4% of ESOP firms had worker representatives on the board. Noted in *Doing Well by Doing Good*, by Ted Baker, Economic Policy Institute, 1999, Ch. 3, page 40.

An alternative to the standard one-share one-vote rule is "scaled voting," a formula for which was described in the original United Parcel Service Charter of Incorporation:

> A beneficial owner of more than 10% of the voting power of UPS stock is entitled to cast only 1/100th of a vote for each share in excess of the ten percent held, effectively limiting that person to no more than 10% of the Company's total voting power. [17]

In addition to the scaled voting formula, UPS required a "supermajority" — 80% of the votes cast — to approve certain actions such as the sale of the company or changes in the charter.

In a company with 100,000 shares outstanding, the holder of 10,000 shares, or 10%, would have 10,000 votes, and the owner of 25,000 or 25%, would have 10,150 votes (10,000 plus 1/100th of 15,000). But it would take at least 80,000 votes, the agreement of at least seven to eight shareholders, before some actions could be taken by the board.

The question is one of equity. Which is more "fair," dollar for dollar representation of capital, one-share equals one- vote, or equality of persons — one-shareholder one-vote? Scaled voting attempts to achieve a balance between the two.

Mutual companies, such as Northwestern Mutual Life Insurance, give each policyholder one vote for each insurance policy or annuity contract, regardless of the dollar amount of the policies and contracts. The owner of a $10,000 policy has exactly the same voting power as the owner of a $1 million policy. This gives the appearance, at least, that policyholders of the company have a voice in the selection of the board. But the company presents only one candidate, its own nominee, for each open position.

When stock ownership is spread over tens of thousands of individuals, the concept that stockholders "own" the company is pure fantasy. Even more so when large blocks of the stock are managed by funds. Scaled voting provides an opportunity for shareholders to be an effective voice in corporate decision-making.

Remedies — Regulations

Soon after corporate fraud revelations peaked in mid-2002, a Harris Poll showed 82% of the American people supported "tough new laws" against corporate fraud. Congress, in high dudgeon and full reformer cry, rushed to enact a bill to punish miscreant executives. But then, as *New York Times* writer Louis Uchitelle points out, reform passion quickly cooled. Quoting liberal Democratic Senator Carl Levin of Michigan: "I don't think anyone here lusts to regulate."[18] Uchitelle then continues:

> Similar reluctance showed up in interviews last week with mainstream economists.
>
> For all the mayhem of recent weeks, most mainstream economists say they still hold to the theory that unfettered competition, achieved through deregulation, tends to lower prices and promote efficiency and innovation.
>
> There are dissenting voices, however, among some economists slightly to the left of the mainstream. James K. Galbraith of the University of Texas at Austin argues for balance between regulation and deregulation in an economy that relies for prosperity as much on the public sector as the private sector.
>
> *...Robert Kuttner, co-editor of the American Prospect magazine contends that mainstream economists are caught in a bind.*
>
> 'You have a whole generation of economists who have devoted their careers to supporting deregulation,' he said, 'and now they are twisting themselves into intellectual pretzels to deny that they are recanting on deregulation.'[19]

The debate over re-regulation of business waxed furious in the business press. Wrote David Wessel, "Capital" columnist for *The Wall Street Journal:*

> A modern capitalist economy requires more than intricate rules to thwart accounting deception and more than carefully crafted compensation schemes to keep executives on the right path.
>
> One way to rebuild trust is capitalist punishment – jailing, fining or ostracizing wrongdoers.
>
> Another way is to rewrite the rule book, so obviously inadequate to the cleverness and complexity of modern business practices.
>
> The key to a prosperous economy, we are reminded daily, is trust but verify.[20]

"How Much Reform of Business?" was the question asked in a another *Wall Street Journal* article, this time on the front page. The article was accompanied by a chart outlining "provisions in bills expected to become law," some of which were: "Create government board to oversee corporate audits, discipline auditors;" "Require CEOs, CFOs to certify accuracy of financial reports;" "Require shareholder approval of option plans." [c]

The Wall Street Journal article, however, expressed confidence that major re-regulation or reform of business would not take place.

> First, the current crisis of confidence in business and markets would have to turn into a broader economic decline. When Franklin Roosevelt embarked on the New Deal, one in four Americans was out of work, four times today's unemployment rate. The spread of stock ownership means Main Street is feeling Wall Street's pain, but so far, that pain has produced public anger – not desperation. [21]

What the entire de- and re-regulation debate ignores is the total lack of oversight on corporate officers and boards. Because stockholders – the purported owners of the enterprise — have no voice or power, CEOs and their self-appointed boards are Supreme Rulers of the empires under their command. In place of an effective voice, shareholders are urged simply to have faith in the character of the people managing these huge economic powers.

Some executives, of course, attempt to play by the rules, so long as they do not face competitors who are profiting by bending and breaking them. When that happens – and it will always happen — the "good" executive has little choice but to follow the rule-breakers into the ethical cesspool.

We're left with the nagging concern that just as the business regulations of the past have been lobbied into ineffectuality, so too will be any regulations arising from this most current spasm of corporate crime.

---

[c] The first two items were included in the Sarbanes-Oxley bill passed by Congress in October 2002.

Remedies — Self Regulation

In his paper, "The Moral Economy," presented to a Boston Theological Institute Ethics Colloquium, author and Sociology Professor Severyn T. Bruyn [d] reviews the "civil society" envisioned by 18th Century philosophers Adam Smith and David Hume. He then briefly explores 19th Century American attitudes toward corporations and their sanctions against "venal" corporate conduct before addressing contemporary governance via (his term) "Mutual Governance."

> As moral standards seemed to decline with the rise of big corporations, a new system of relative "moral" activity arose among associations of competitors. Civil (mutually-governed) associations developed in the field of business, professions, and labor organization in the context of a competitive market. Nonprofit associations were created so that people in their own sector of interest could protect themselves from their opponents and advance their cause....
>
> In the midst of burgeoning federal legislation to create a measure of morality (justice) in free markets, a private "mutual system" of nonprofit unions, trade and professional associates began to develop codes of conduct. These associations established ethical principles and standards for their members....
>
> None of these self-governing, moral and civic-like systems worked perfectly, but all of them were based in a system [of] 'mutual governance'... civil forms of self regulation. [22]

Mutual governance among competing producers of similar products has resulted in "industry standards" for such things as screws and other fasteners, light bulb sockets, shoe sizes, etc., without the intervention of a government agency. Movie ratings and advertising standards are also examples of mutual governance.

---

[d] Professor, Dept. of Sociology, Boston College, 1966-Present, Director, Graduate Program in Social Economy and Social Policy, 1977-1986, author or numerous articles and books, including *A Civil Economy: Transforming the Market in the 21st Century* (U. of Michigan Press, 2000), *A Future for the American Economy: A Social Market*, (Stanford University Press, 1991, and *Beyond the Market and the State* with co-editor James Meehan, (Temple University Press, 1987).

In matters of business ethics, Bruyn suggests that non-profit organizations and "households" — the court of public opinion — offer some balance to the for-profit sector of society. He cites John Kenneth Galbraith's concept of "countervailing powers" in the market, such as airlines competing with automobiles and railroads and thus preventing a corporate monopoly in the transportation industry. Nonprofit public-interest groups act as "public witnesses" demanding social justice and morality in the marketplace.

Bruyn closes by citing rays of hope, islands of countervailing power, for a Civil Society, such as employee ownership plans (ESOPs), social investment funds, and The Interfaith Center for Corporate Responsibility. Yet he notes that these are merely "seeds for a civil-society economy." [23]

Can these seeds germinate and flower in a society where the public information media is controlled by a handful of media giants affirming the status quo? Is there an antidote to corporate immorality when corporate interests create faux grass-roots organizations to drain power from real public interest organizations? What countervailing power can labor unions provide against the wealth and political power of Fortune's 1,000 when they represent less than 10% of working people and even less of the electorate? And what countervailing power exists when buy-outs, mergers and consolidation remove all but a few of the largest competitors from the field?

Remedies — Moral Persuasion

In *The Wealth of Nations*, Adam Smith argued that the moral basis of both enterprise and individual life was "mutual relations," that is, a shared sympathy and mutual appreciation among trading and social partners which formed the principles of his "civil society."

In the discussions following the moral meltdown of 2002, arguments generally represented one of two persuasions: those who felt that government regulation was the answer to keeping corporations operating ethically and those who believed that the key was selecting executives and board members with high moral standards and ethics.

> With all the recent corporate scandals, there's a temptation to call for new regulations and laws that will ensure no such malfeasance occurs again.... But the scandals are not so much a failure of laws and regulations as they are a failure of behavior. [24]

So argues columnist Jeffrey L. Seglin in *The New York Times Business* section:

> It's impossible to contemplate a law or regulation that would keep every bad move in check....
>
> If there's a lesson to be learned from the high-profile scandals, it's that corporate behavior stems directly from the example set by the leaders at the top of organizations. The antidotes to corporate malfeasance then are not new laws and regulations, but putting corporate leaders in place who have shown they are capable of doing the right thing and then holding them accountable. [25]

Hold corporate leaders accountable how? And who can hold them accountable? Not the stockholders, for they have only one means of communication with corporate leaders: sell the stock. Then they're no longer an interested party. Or keep the stock and fire off a totally useless letter to the board.

Time after time those writing about corporate moral failures put the burden for action on the stockholders. "Ultimately, it's going to take investors being highly vocal and critical of directors who have approved these deals and working to get them replaced on boards," says Ann Yerger, director of research at the Council of Institutional Investors. [26]

She must be referring to institutional investors. They have an advantage over individual shareholders when it comes to communicating with CEOs and boards of directors. But even their judgment of a CEO or board member's character is based on incomplete data. Fund managers might express dissatisfaction to an executive of a corporation in whose stock they hold a strong position, but that is the extent of their power. Their interest is – and must be – limited to financial results, not whether or not the company is operating ethically. Is the company making money? Is investor value increasing? If yes, hold the stock. If not, dump it.

Selecting people of good character and strong ethics to lead a corporation does not alter the fundamental *raison d'etre* of corporate existence – profit. No other objective comes close. Nor can corporate leaders of the highest moral character reverse the necessity to compete in the marketplace against all comers, ethical and not.

New directions in corporate governance

Numerous organizations have sprung up over the years to analyze the issues and promote means of correcting corruption and regaining democratic control.[e] As Jonathan Rowe described the problem:

> The issue here is not the hoary ideological debate between the government and the market. Rather, it concerns the kind of entities that will comprise the market. In simple terms, how can we reconnect the corporation to the social and community concerns it was originally intended to serve?[27]

Citizen Works, under the direction of Ralph Nader, has developed "The Model Uniform Code for Corporate Responsibility" which it promotes to state legislatures as an addition to business corporation acts and charters. Its thrust is to expand the responsibility of boards of directors from a single focus on profiting shareholders to the broader welfare of the community – the "public good" — as demanded in early state charters of incorporation. The model code not only assigns liability to officers and directors who approved of actions resulting in damages but also to "every person who, by or through stock ownership, agency or otherwise... controls..." the culpable corporation's officers and directors. This, to a certain extent, would "pierce the veil" of the corporate shield.[28]

Among the leading activist organizations is POCLAD, The Program on Corporations, Law & Democracy, headed by Richard Grossman. The organization has published a number of well-researched tracts, articles, and books, including *"Asserting Democratic Control Over Corporations: A Call to Lawyers,"*[29] *"Minorities, the Poor & Ending Corporate Rule,"*[30] and *"Taking Care of Business: Citizenship and the Charter of Incorporation."*[31] The organization stimulates, organizes and promotes citizen activism "contesting the authority of corporations to govern."[32]

Using reports of Enron's misdeeds as an opportunity to call upon state governments for remedial action, a POCLAD press release challenged "all attorneys general in every state where Enron Corporation did or does business to seize all Enron's assets."[33]

---

[e] A by no means complete list of organizations concerned with corporate power is included in the Appendix.

One of the most aggressive disciplinary actions urged by anti-corporate-power proponents is revocation of a malefactor corporation's charter. In the 1800's, states routinely revoked charters, including an action in 1894 that revoked the charter of the Standard Oil Trust of New York. The revocation option was put to a more recent test in Vermont. In 1996, "Officials in Vermont Move To Revoke Utility's License" was the headline of a *New York Times* news item:

> For 61 years, Citizens Utilities has sold electricity in Vermont. But if state regulators get their way, the company will not be doing so much longer.
>
> "Never before have Vermont officials said an electric company's behavior was so egregious that it should no longer be allowed to do business in the state. [34,f]

The Internet has empowered the anti-corporate movement by providing a tool for recruiting like-minded individuals and groups and by functioning as a channel for non-monitored, mainstream-media censorship-free communication. Regular newsletters such as "Focus On The Corporation" [g] by Russell Mokhiber, editor of the Washington, D.C.-based *Corporate Crime Reporter,* and Robert Weissman, editor of the Washington, D.C.-based *Multinational Monitor*, are forwarded weekly by E-mail to subscribers. Co-authors of *Corporate Predators: The Hunt for MegaProfits and the Attack on Democracy* (Monroe, Maine: Common Courage Press, 1999). The authors of the column offer a regular fare of well-documented screeds against both national and global corporate villains.

Other notable and active (as of 2002) Internet sites include "CorpWatch: Holding Corporations Accountable," "PIN: Public Information Network," "Mystic Cottage," and "www.ratical.org,"(sic) which ranges widely (and wildly) over most ultra-liberal concerns. In past years, much of the anti-corporate activist activity was devoted to researching and revealing corporate restrictions in early state constitutions and law. More recently the focus has shifted to globalization.

---

[f] On June 16, 1997, the Vermont Public Service Board issued Final Order 5841/5859 placing Citizens Utilities on probation for five years, ordered a rate reduction of 16.35%, and imposed a fine of $60,000.

[g] A list of similar Internet-based organizations and their Internet addresses is included in the Appendix.

Corporate power limits sought by activist organizations today revisit those of corporate charters issued in the 1800's, including:

- limiting the life-span of a corporation;
- limiting real estate holdings to those actually required for productive facilities;
- prohibiting ownership of stock in other corporations;
- appointment of a state official to a corporation's board;
- prohibiting corporations from operating under pseudonyms;
- prohibiting conglomerates; charter allows one activity/ business only.

Other restraints suggested arise from court decisions and modern corporate practices:

- prohibiting financial contributions to, participation in, or use of corporate assets in political campaigns;
- forbidding subsidies or the transfer of public credit, monies, or resources to private, for-profit corporate entities;
- requiring corporate headquarters to be established only in the state issuing the charter;
- restricting the sale of stock to residents of the state chartering the corporation.

Several of the more dramatic remedies were suggested by Jerry Mander in his "Corporations as Machines" essay published within *Buying America Back*. [35] These include:

- Eliminate the corporate "veil" by which managers and directors are protected from liability for corporate acts which cause harm.
- Eliminate the stock market.
- Require that the highest salary paid to any officer be no greater than three times the lowest salary paid to any corporate employee.

Perhaps the most far-reaching restraint of all is for legislatures and Congress to re-define the corporation for what it really is – not a citizen, not a person, but an organization created by humans for a single purpose. How corporations could ever be considered otherwise, to have "freedom of speech" and other protected rights, is a lunatic perversion of the intent of the Constitution and its writers. A corporation is no more a person than a piece of paper, no more entitled to "human rights" than a computer or an automobile.

Corporate "personhood" is the particular target of the Women's International League for Peace and Freedom's campaign to "Challenge Corporate Power." Writes spokesperson Molly Morgan:

> Slavery is the legal fiction that a person is property. Corporate personhood is the legal fiction that property is a person. Like abolishing slavery, the work of eradicating corporate personhood takes us to the deepest questions of what it means to be human....
>
> We think the campaign to end corporate personhood is like applying a massive crowbar at the most pivotal point against a stuck door holding back democracy.... By focusing on the crucial block – corporate personhood – and applying enough force to pry the door open, the whole concept of what's politically and humanly possible shifts in profound and exciting ways. [36]

A state legislature revisiting corporate personhood or contemplating enacting any of the provisions listed above would unleash a firestorm of objections from corporate interests. Legislators proposing and supporting such action would be pilloried by industry, small business, chambers of commerce, economic development groups, and the media.

Will reform take place?

Despite the anger over corporate fraud generated by the Enron-triggered market meltdown, there has arisen no groundswell of support for major changes in state or federal corporate control. Instead the emphasis has been on improving the character of chief executives, improving enforcement capabilities of the Securities and Exchange Commission or, as a last resort, enacting a few new regulations.

Less than six months after the worst revelations of corporate misdeeds, even the mildest of possible reforms was being put on the back burner. "The Zeal for Reform Fades," was the title of Dave Kansas' *Wall Street Journal Online* column, "And That's Not a Good Thing."

> This past summer, cleaning up Wall Street was the issue du jour. To see how the world has shifted since then, check out these two headlines:
> - Merrill Lynch pays $100 million fine after e-mails reveal deep conflicts among research analysts (May 2002).

- Five Wall Street firms fined $8.25 million for destroying e-mail records. (Dec. 2002)

An $8.25 million fine divided among five firms for destroying e-mails compared with a $100 million fine paid by one firm that kept its e-mails.... It's a contrast that has Wall Streeters (excluding the folks at Merrill Lynch) snickering in amusement and individual investors looking on with resigned disdain. It illustrates starkly how things have – and haven't – changed on the Street.

Changing such a mindset requires real champions of reform as much as actual changes. For individuals to regain confidence [in the market] they need Giuliani-esque leadership: fair, firm, proper enforcement of the rules and a sense of reassurance that someone is looking out for their interests, keeping the bad guys at bay. [37]

Fading enthusiasm for reform described by Dave Kansas was reinforced in the paper edition of *The Wall Street Journal.*

Wall Street firms are pressing securities regulators to reduce the level of fines they will pay as part of an agreement to settle allegations that they misled small investors with faulty stock research – and they could very well get their way. [38]

When government steps out of bounds, there is a remedy: the vote. As slow, unrepresentative, and ineffectual as it may be, at least it's *possible* to get a hearing and perhaps relief. A call to a sympathetic Congressman or Senator may get some action from a government agency or department, or put a stop to improper government action. When enough voters become energized, laws are changed and regulatory agencies brought into line with public thinking.

There is no such route of appeal when big business cheats. With millions at stake, democracy is road kill.

[1] Letters to the Editor, *New York Times Magazine*, October 27, 2002.

[2] Ibid.

[3] Ibid.

[4] Ibid.

[5] "The Rich Have More, and More to Lose," by Kathleen O'Brien, *The New York Times*, July 28, 2002.

[6] "The Panic of 1893" by Lee I. Niedringhaus, The Museum of Financial History, <www.financialhistory.org/fh/1998/61-1.htm>.

[7] "Remarks on Signing the Garn-St Germain Depository Institutions Act of 1982"; President Ronald Reagan, October 15, 1982.

[8] "The Cost of the Savings and Loan Crisis: Truth and Consequences," by Timothy Curry and Lynn Shibut, FDIC Banking Review, undated.

[9] *Big Money Crime: Fraud and Politics in the Savings and Loan Crisis*, by Kitty Calavita, Henry N. Pontell and Robert H. Tillman, University of California Press, 1997.

[10] "GE to Announce Set of New Polcies To Shore Up Board," by Rachel Emma Silverman, *The Wall Street Journal*, November 6, 2002.

[11] "Companies Add Ethics Training; Will It Work?," by Richard B. Schmitt, *Wall Street Journal*, November 4, 2002.

[12] *Pawns Or Potentates, The Reality of America's Corporate Boards*, by Jay W. Lorsch with Elizabeth MacIver, Harvard Business School Press, 1989, page 170.

[13] "Splitting Posts Of Chairman, CEO Catches On," by Joann S. Lublin, *The Wall Street Journal*, November 11, 2002.

[14] "Boards want CEO-free meetings," by Del Jones, *USA Today*, October 17, 2002.

[15] *Doing Well by Doing Good*, by Ted Baker, Economic Policy Institute, 1999, Ch. 3, page 39.

[16] *Harper* 1988, 18, as quoted in *Doing Well by Doing Good* by Ted Baker.

[17] Taken from redacted text of filing in the Court of Chancery of the State of Delaware in and for New Castle County, the Linda Dee Starkman, Trust v. United Parcel Service of America, October 12, 1999.

[18] "Broken System? Tweak It, They Say," by Louis Echitelle, *The New York Times*, Money & Business, July 28, 2002.

[19] Ibid.

[20] "Invisible Hand Works Because of Invisible Handshake," by David Wessel, *The Wall Street Journal*, July 11, 2002.

[21] "Rising Anxiety, What Could Bring 1930s-Style Reform of U.S. Businesses?" by Gerald F. Seib and John Harwood, *The Wall Street Journal*, July 24, 2002.

[22] "The Moral Economy," by Severyn T. Bruyn, published by the Boston Theological Institute in its "Faculty Colloquia – Ethics Colloguium," Undated.

[23] Ibid.

[24] "Will More Rules Yield Better Corporate Behavior?" by Jeffrey L. Seglin, *The New York Times*, Business, November 17, 2002.

[25] Ibid.

[26] Quoted in "Investors Have to Lead The Charge to Keep Big Bosses in Line," by Carol Hymowitz, *The Wall Street Journal* Marketplace section, September 17, 2002.

[27] "Reinventing the Corporation," by Jonathan Rowe, *The Washington Monthly*, April 1966.

[28] From Citizen Works "Campaign for Corporate Reform" Web site, Citizen Works. PO Box 18478, Washington, DC 20036.

[29] National Lawyers Guild Practitioner, Vol. 52, number 4, Fall 1995.

[30] Poverty & Race, September/October 1995, Col. 4, number 5, p. 1," and "Taking Care of Business: Citizenship and the Charter of Incorporation, *Earth Island Journal*, Spring 1993, p. 34.

[31] Ibid.

[32] Taken from POCLAD press release letterhead.

[33] POCLAD press release dated February 45, 2002: "State Officials Should Seize Enron's Assets."

[34] "Officials in Vermont Move To Revoke Utility's License," *The New York Times*, August 16, 1996.

[35] *Buying America Back*, edited by Jonathan Greenberg and William Kistler, Council Oak Books, Tulsa, OK, 1992.

[36] Op Cit. "Abolish Corporate Personhood," by Molly Morgan

[37] "The Zeal for Reform Fades, And That's Not a Good Thing," by Dave Kansas, *The Wall Street Journal* Online, December 10, 2002.

[38] "Securities Firms Ask Regulators To Lower Fines," by Charles Gasparino, *The Wall Street Journal*, December 10, 2002.

CHAPTER FOURTEEN
LIMITING CORPORATE POWER

The sovereign has ... the duty of protecting, so far as possible, every member of society from the injustice or oppression of every other member of it. [a]

Adam Smith

Seven Limits – Seven Proposals

The epidemic of corporate scandal that first came to public attention in 2000 with Enron was, three years later, still very much on the minds of the investing public. Witness this lead-in to a July 7, 2003, *Fortune* magazine article: "In the Lucent scandal, the ex-boss will walk. The woman who accused him is now an SEC target. And guess who's paying the penalty? Owners like you." [1]

Reporter Carol J. Loomis describes a pattern of fraud that cost the 5.3 million shareholders of Lucent stock $242.4 billion dollars in lost market value in less than three years, "and so far no individuals but its shareholders are taking the rap." [2]

"That is the maddeningly unfair aspect of today's corporate scandals," Loomis writes. "Inanimate, Delaware-incorporated creatures like Lucent don't commit crimes. People do. Sometimes they leave their fingerprints all over the scene.... And sometimes they just instill a 'tone at the top' that can encourage employees to go too far.... This outcome is not fair when it falls on a single person, much less on more than the combined populations of Los Angeles and Detroit. But it is the miserable way the system works." [3]

The essential problem addressed by 18th Century economic philosopher Adam Smith is as relevant today as it was when written. How can we employ the power of capitalism yet protect society from "the miserable way

---

[a] The full quote from *The Wealth of Nations*, Book IV, Chapter IX: "According to the system of natural liberty, the sovereign has only three duties to attend to ... first, the duty of protecting the society from the violence and invasion of other independent societies; secondly, the duty of protecting, so far as possible, every member of society from the injustice or oppression of every other member of it, or the duty of establishing an exact administration of justice, and thirdly, the duty of erecting and maintaining certain public works and certain public institutions which it can never be for the interest of any individual, or small number of individuals, to erect and maintain...."

the system works?" Huge and almost untouchable corporate organizations wield enormous power over our economy, courts and nation. Weren't they supposed to be our servants? Whose liberty should take precedence, those of legal fictions or those of human beings?

The theft by fraud of seven trillion dollars from business people and investors over less than three years, 2000 to 2003, should be a clear signal that the current system of corporate governance is not working. Loomis's view was confirmed in an adjacent *Fortune* report on HealthSouth's fraudulent overstatement of earnings by $2.5 billion. Reporter John Helyar concluded, "The corporate culture created the fraud, and the fraud created the corporate culture." [4]

The preceding chapters have amply illustrated that attempts to change the corporate culture through government regulation and the courts are generally ineffective. From *The Wall Street Journal:*

> Wall Street firms are getting ready to pay out billions of dollars to resolve alleged stock-research abuses. But the pain will be much easier to take, thanks to U.S. taxpayers.
>
> The reason: Most of the payments likely will be tax deductible for the companies.
>
> As securities firms and regulators work out the final details for the $1.5 billion global settlement announced last year – and set aside millions more to settle lawsuits from investors – people close to the global-settlement negotiations say that only about $450 million of the $2.5 billion total is likely to be characterized as "penalties" or "fines," which aren't tax deductible. The rest, totaling more than $1 billion will likely go toward investor restitution ... meaning that it will be deemed tax deductible since federal tax laws generally view such expenses as part of the cost of doing business. [5]

Government prosecutors of corporate crime face a monumental task in obtaining convictions, even after a company admits to criminal activity as did Rite Aid when caught in a $1.6 billion inflated-earnings fraud.

> Rite Aid has already admitted its books were cooked, so the government has to prove only that the defendants were the willing chefs.... The governments case will be complicated: 35 charges against each defendant involving

everything from allegedly falsified board minutes to Mr. Grass's purported use of Rite Aid funds in a personal real estate venture. If the defense can establish reasonable doubt about some of the charges, it could cast a shadow over the rest.[6]

Stockholder complaints over skyrocketing executive compensation with stock options created some action by the government agency charged with stock option oversight. In 2002, the SEC began considering requiring companies to deduct the value of stock options from earnings. A heated battle erupted with stockholder activist organizations, including many investor fund managers, calling for the action, and companies, especially in the high-tech field, vigorously opposed. The SEC backed down to a safer position, fuller disclosure:

> The Securities and Exchange Commission voted unanimously to require companies to disclose more clearly a number of details that will help investors keep tabs on how stock options are doled out and how those options could affect earnings.
> For the first time, companies also must disclose stock option plans they have set up without shareholder approval.[7]

Corrective action was finally imposed, not by the SEC, but by the New York Stock Exchange and the Nasdaq. As reported by *The New York Times* July 2, 2003: "Companies trading on the biggest United States stock markets must obtain shareholder approval before granting stock options and other equity compensation under rules cleared yesterday by the Securities and Exchange Commission."[8]

Stockholder complaints were also being heard at annual meetings, though with little effect according to *Fortune* magazine:

> Spurred by a depressed stock market, corporate scandals, and disgust at greedy CEOs, investors have managed to pass a record number of proxy resolutions: more than 125 as of May 30, with the 2003 total likely to climb past 150. That's 50% more than in 2002, itself a record year. While... the vast majority of shareholder resolutions failed, as they do every year – investors are making management take notice.[9] (Emphasis added.)

However, "professional money managers," noted Gretchen Morgenson in *The New York Times* Money & Business section, "remain deeply skeptical ... that corporate governance reforms put in place since Enron's collapse [will] prevent such scandals from recurring." [10]

The problem government faces in regulating Big Business was the focus of a *Wall Street Journal* Politics & Policy feature, "Are Firms Too Big to Debar?" by Anne Marie Squeo.

> The government awards contracts worth hundreds of billions of dollars annually to thousands of companies providing everything from telephone service to toilet paper. Under the Federal Acquisition Regulations, officials are required, among other things, to grant contacts only to "responsible sources" with a "satisfactory record of integrity and business ethics."
>
> A May 2002 study by the project on Government Oversight, a nonprofit watchdog group, found 43 of the government's top contractors paid about $3.4 billion in fines and settlements since 1990, ... but only one was banned from government work: General Electric Co., the worst offender, which had 63 alleged or actual violations and paid the government nearly $983 million.... And the ban... affected only GE's aircraft-engine division for five days. [11]

It's obvious that corporate governance cannot be made scoundrel proof. The human and systemic failings that created theft, fraud, and scandals in the past will continue to plague capitalism in the future unless we make significant revisions to how we charter and regulate our corporate entities. The choice is clear, either we resign ourselves as investors to being defrauded and cheated in regular cycles of fraud, or we make the effort to bring these corporate creatures back under stakeholder control.

Reasserting control

Our nation's founders struggled to create a government that could overcome the weight of wealth and power to make the business game fair for big and small, rich and poor alike. Students of Locke, Mills, and Adams (more philosophers than economists) they attempted to construct a republic that would be sustainable, that would not be expropriated by the most rapacious and avaricious. As expressed by Charles de Montesquieu in his *The Spirit of Laws* (1748): "In the state of nature… all men are born equal, but they cannot continue in this equality. Society makes them lose it, and they recover it only by the protection of the law."

Hundreds of years of experience with capitalism has made it abundantly clear that patterns of monopolization and collusive and dishonest behavior repeat themselves, over and over, year after year, decade after decade. Guidance from the pulpit and from the courts have failed to restrain bad behavior on the streets or in executive suites. Industry "self-regulation" is a fiction and mockery of the word. Jeffrey L. Seglin, author of *The Right Thing: Conscience, Profit and Personal Responsibility in Today's Business* quotes Harvard Divinity School professor Ronald F. Thiemann: "Retributive justice and the fear it engenders can, in the most serious cases, provide a kind of wake-up call. But it cannot on its own engender ethical behavior." [12] We can ignore all the sincere declarations of probity, integrity and rectitude emanating from Chambers of Commerce, the Business Roundtable and other advocates of business. Nothing has been found that keeps our merchant mankind on the straight and narrow path for long.

It's time for capitalists to acknowledge up front that society and all its laws cannot rein in mankind's innate greed and lust. Mankind cannot be reconstructed. Therefore, we must reconstruct the corporate entity. We must install (or re-install) controls over corporations that minimize the damage bad operators can cause.

The best cure for corporatism is man's inventiveness and unquenchable entrepreneurial spirit allowed to flower and compete with established firms on a playing field kept level by (who/what else?) a strong and uncorrupted government.

Seven "Founder-tested" Limitations
The following are offered as corporate-power-limiting options which, applied singly or in combination, will lead to the rescue of capitalism from corporatism. The goal is to open up the discussion by considering what each might accomplish, as well as to challenge the myths of the status quo. Knee-jerk defenders of Big Business will charge that any limitation of corporate "freedom" is a step on the slippery slope to socialism or worse. Yet all of them were once a part of every corporate charter granted by our forefathers. Corporations not only survived limitations such as these, but investors, businesses and the nation prospered.

Limit 1: Limit the corporate life-span

"Common wisdom" holds that we are governed by a balance of power among conflicting interest groups attempting to direct government. Many political scientists hold to this theory – pluralism – as producing the most good for the most people. An opposing view is the "Elite Theory," the belief that wealth equals power. The economic elite consists of the same people as the political elite. The agenda of the wealthy and powerful is forced downward on the masses through their influence over government. "Although few political scientists who believe the elite theory consider it good for democracy, they consider it to be an accurate view of reality." [13]

The great fortunes created in the Robber Baron era – Carnegie, Cooke, Morgan, Rockefeller and others – dominated political politics in the nation's and state capitals for many generations. But death dissipates wealth among heirs and beneficiaries. The largest fortunes may influence government for decades.

Corporations do not die as men die. They may continue to grow and accumulate wealth and power for multiple decades, even centuries. Production, distribution and marketing facilities spread across the globe employ tens of thousands. Hundreds of communities and numbers of states rely upon the taxes they pay. Significant land, water and natural resources come under their control

The result of this life-span-without-limits is political, economic and social power that shapes nations. Two-thirds of the world's 100 richest economic units — governments and corporations — are corporations. [14] The world's second largest corporation, Exxon-Mobil, was "born" in 1882 as an outgrowth of the Standard Oil Trust. Third largest, General Motors, was founded in 1897 as Olds Motor Vehicle Company. Fourth largest, Ford Motors, is, at age 95, the youngest of the world's largest industrial firms. General Electric, the world's fifth largest corporation, was founded by Thomas Edison in 1890. The largest U.S. Corporation with over a million employees is Wal-Mart, is also the youngest of the largest U.S. Corporations, founded in 1962.

The world's largest firms span the globe with their products and production plants. Their financial maneuverings shake nations' economies; their raw material demands shape foreign and domestic policies in large and small countries of the world, and their employment practices set wages and standards for all other fields of employment. Through their outsourcing they can raise the standards of living in chosen communities, states, and nations or create economic disaster zones when they shutter or move facilities. In sum, their sheer size – numbers of plants and employees, ownership of natural resources, impact on foreign and domestic trade accounts — gives them the power to move and direct the fate of nations. Our largest corporations are the tail that wags the world dog.

What would happen if corporations were limited to the life spans contemplated by our founders – 20 to 40 years? Would the nation's economy crash? Would we be at the mercy of foreign firms? Would we lose our lifestyle, our conveniences, our employment prospects, our pensions?

The most probable result of large corporations forced to "die" after a charter-defined number of years would be renewed economic vitality for the nation, more opportunity for inventors and entrepreneurs, and even more scope for financiers and speculators.

It's not as if corporate "death" is unknown. Today corporations die through sale, merger, or bankruptcy. Of the '400' companies listed in Standard & Poor's in 1977, 157 had disappeared 10 years later. In fact, it is the rare corporation that lives beyond 30 years. In most capitalist countries, an insolvent corporation is liquidated – assets sold, debtors paid off and accounts closed. The stockholders then share whatever is left. Somewhat peculiar to the U.S., bankrupt companies may be resurrected and reorganized to live again. Reorganization, however, frequently provides an unfair disposition of corporate assets. Holders of common stock do not retain any of their investment. Pension funds for employees evaporate. Yet owners of classes of stock considered priority instruments of debt may not only recover their initial capital but may retain ownership in the reorganized firm.

Reorganization is also unfair to competitors. Relieved of its debt, a reorganized firm has an immediate advantage over competitors still burdened with loans and accounts payable.

Big businesses "die" all the time. Notable business failures in the 1970s were the bankruptcies of Penn Central Transportation Corporation (railroad) and the W.T. Grant Company, a leading retailer. During the 1980s and early 1990s record numbers of bankruptcies of all types were filed including well known companies such as LTV, Eastern Airlines, Texaco, Continental Airlines, Allied Stores, Federated Department Stores, Greyhound, R.H. Macy, and Pan American. Several large bankruptcies such as Maxwell Communication and Olympia & York involved the insolvency rules of several different countries. Yet the country and economy hardly noticed. Vacancies left by these "deaths" were quickly filled by new firms and competitors.

The forced break up of AT&T in 1984 demonstrated that even the largest of corporations can disappear, and younger, more aggressive ones take their place without major disruptions in service and with hardly noticeable economic impact. A decade later, in 1995, the shrunken but still huge AT&T began divesting itself of some of its subsidiaries, but this time voluntarily. Noted the "Outlook" column in the *Wall Street Journal*: "AT&T's Latest Moves Vindicate Trustbusters":

> By agreeing to break itself apart again – indeed celebrating it as a bold strategy – AT&T vindicated the Justice Department's position in 1982 that competition is best served through divestiture, not megafirms. "For AT&T's businesses to take advantage of incredible growth opportunities, they have to separate into smaller and more focused businesses," says AT&T's chairman, Robert Allen. [15]

A corporation's "natural" death imposed by its charter would be a far less traumatic event than bankruptcy. Stakeholders would know in advance that the enterprise would be winding down. Suppliers and employees would be paid and pension funds protected. Stockholders would recover their capital either in cash or, in the case of a sale of a trademark or patents financed with stock, in shares in the purchasing enterprise.

Rather than be troubled over the disappearance of our current corporate giants — General Motors, General Electric, Boeing, Mobil-Exxon, etc. – we should think of the potential gains. Capitalists will continue to seek opportunities to invest. Entrepreneurs will be just as anxious to test their operating and marketing skills. Inventors will have more potential business partners to attract to their ideas. As megafirms reach the end of their lives, buyers with new ideas will line up to purchase their assets, their production facilities, even their brands. New combinations of capital will form new firms to rush into openings in the marketplace. The result of this will be a revitalization of the American Dream of opportunity. The ideal of a truly competitive marketplace would be closer to reality.

Founder-CEOs of new firms will be more likely to remain in control to the end of a firm's life. Certainly boards of directors will be less inclined to pay superstar salaries and perks to manager-CEOs hired to see a ship of enterprise to its final port. Incentive for price fixing and collusion among competitors will be reduced. Innovation and competition will be stimulated.

Giving the corporate creature a defined set of years of "life" brings it into line with natural law. Mother Nature demonstrates how this is done in fields and forests where the cycle of birth to death is continuous. Death or disaster for one produces opportunity for others. Removing the dominant giants in an industry is like a fire opening up an old-growth forest. Just as sunlight stimulates seedlings struggling out of the earth, subjecting the world of corporate enterprise to the normal cycle of life opens up opportunities for new firms, new ideas, new products, and new ways of doing things.

Limit 2: Limit corporate land holdings

The earth, and all things therein, are the general property of all mankind, from the immediate gift of the Creator.
William Blackstone[b]

The increase in the value of land, arising as it does from the efforts of an entire community, should belong to the community and not to the individual who might hold title.

John Stuart Mill

Equity does not permit property in land. The world is God's bequest to mankind. All men are joint heirs to it.
Herbert Spencer[c]

The earth is given as a common stock for men to labor and live on.

Thomas Jefferson

The land, the earth God gave to man for his home, sustenance, and support, should never be the possession of any man, corporation, society, or unfriendly government, any more than the air or water, if as much.

Abraham Lincoln

The founders of our nation appreciated the precious and finite quantity of land far more than modern Americans. Land was their wealth, their living, their future. It produced bread and meat for their tables, fabrics

---

[b] Sir William Blackstone (1723-1780). English jurist; professor of common law at Oxford; author of Commentaries on The Laws of England.
[c] Herbert Spencer (1820-1903). British philosopher and sociologist.

for their clothing, produce for trade. To the pioneers, usable land was the breast of Mother Nature sustaining them. But in urbanized America, modern Americans rarely make the link between grassland and the meat on their table, and cotton fields and the shirt on their back. Land is lumped in with other "property" such as automobiles and houses.

Yet land is the ultimate wealth of a nation, and the ultimate source of liberty. A person with only a few acres of fertile land can feed his family and raise enough surplus to trade for what he cannot produce himself. Far greater than legal freedom of speech or travel across borders, the ability to feed, clothe, and house oneself is real liberty. The owner of a few farmable acres can tell an employer to, as the song made famous by Johnny Paycheck goes, "Take this job and shove it." [d] It is liberty not enjoyed by even those taking home six figure salaries. A Rolls Royce may cost the price of 10 acres and a mule, but it can't keep the kids in turnips and overalls for long. Land keeps on producing; stocks, bonds, homes, and autos can be exchanged only once.

Given its importance, the constitutions of many states placed strict limits on, and even prohibited, land ownership by corporations. Corporations could lease or rent land for production facilities, and pay royalties or extraction fees for mining or timbering it, but ownership was reserved for humans. Writes Dr. Robert V. Andelson of the American Institute for Economic Research:

> Land monopoly is the great monkey-wrench which is caught in the works of the free enterprise system, and which prevents the proper meshing of its gears; it is the hidden cancer that is eating the heart of Capitalism. [16]

---

[d] TAKE THIS JOB AND SHOVE IT By David Allan Coe, © 1977 Warner-Tamerlane Publishing Corp. (BMI). All Rights Reserved. Used By Permission. WARNER BROS. PUBLICATIONS U.S. INC., MIAMI, FL 33014

They'll have you in this factory
From now on for fifty years.
All this time I see my woman
Drowning in her tears.
I see a lot of people who
Got to have a piece of me.
I'd give the shirt right off my back
If I had the nerve to say

Take this job and shove it
I ain't working here no more.
I will not get all the pieces
I've been working for.
Paper cups, minimum wage
Just walk on out the door.
Take this job and shove it
I ain't working here no more.

Today concern over corporate monopolization of land rises more often from offensive odors wafting downwind from industrial livestock farms than from philosophical claims for "all mankind." Whatever the cause, however, there is a reawakening of interest in land use being controlled by human rather than by corporate interests.

> In Pennsylvania, nine townships have passed laws banning the corporate ownership of farms. The issue was big corporate hog farms coming in. And so people decided that they weren't going to do regulations about hog manure, and how many hogs per square feet, which activists are doing in North Carolina and many other states. They're saying, 'In our jurisdiction, no corporations can own farms.'[17]

The municipalities have been taken to court by agribusiness corporations on the basis that they cannot be treated differently from human property owners, the same argument addressed by the Supreme Court in 1886 in *Santa Clara County v. Southern Pacific Railroad Co.*

In the 1970's other jurisdictions – Iowa, Minnesota, Missouri, North Dakota, Oklahoma, South Dakota, Nebraska, and Wisconsin — adopted restrictions on corporate ownership of farms. Restrictions generally do not limit farm size or the employment of hired labor, but limit ownership to family corporations.

Efficiency and productivity are cited by proponents of corporate farms, but without proof. Agricultural counties (defined as 75% of land in farms, 50% of gross receipts from goods and services from farm sales) with anti-corporate farming laws generate lower rates of poverty, lower unemployment, and greater cash returns from farming. [18]

Corporate land ownership is a critical issue when you consider the potential of infinite life. Over time it would be possible for a corporation to acquire every acre of productive land in a county, a state, or even a nation. How better to guarantee profitability into an infinite future than ownership of an essential-to-life resource? It's not out of the realm of possibility. Utility companies are currently engaged in buying control of sources of potable and irrigation water in water-poor regions of the United States. It's as much a sure-fire profit opportunity as controlling breathable air. All essential-to-life resources can be monopolized given enough money and time.

Limit 3: Appoint government official to the board

Nothing could generate more angst in the executive suite than a government official sitting as a voting member on the board of directors. Yet nothing would be more effective in putting an end to corporate morality issues of the Enron, WorldCom, Merrill Lynch, CitiGroup genre.

Board reform was very much on the minds of investors as the 2000 scandals began to fade from public consciousness. A *Wall Street Journal* feature, "Boardrooms Under Renovation; Independence of Directors is Elusive Goal" addressed the problems corporations faced in replacing the "old-boy" board-member network:

> It is far from certain however, how much better public companies govern themselves than they did before the reform.... Critics say the new regulations have buried directors in extra paperwork while failing to address the issues close to the heart of the average investor: overgenerous executive pay, little evaluation of directors' own performance on the board and a feeling among shareholders that they are left out of the director-selection process. And there still isn't an easy way for corporate whistleblowers to communicate directly with board members. [19]

A significant portion of the "independent director" question would be met if corporate charters required (as they did in our Founders' time) that an elected government official sit on the board. A state legislator, for example, would provide assurance that stockholder and public interests were represented in determining corporate policies. Government representation would, no doubt, have a chilling effect on "aggressive" financial and competitive moves that might skate close to legal and ethical edges. There would be feedback both ways, of course, as the government representative became intimately aware of management issues. The potential for the government board member to become embedded in the corporate culture could be ameliorated through limited terms and regular rotation.

For the corporation, the positives include public relations cover for decisions unpopular with other stakeholders – plant closings, layoffs, etc.— and greater credibility with stockholders, employees, the public, and public agencies. A public official on the board is, of course, no guarantee that shenanigans would not take place, but having to stand for election regularly would be a strong restraint on chicanery.

Limit 4: Ban conglomerates

The founders limited corporations to one business activity. The company operating iron mines was not permitted to operate the foundry. Literature from the era is silent on the reason why conglomerates were banned but it may be presumed from their concern with concentrations of wealth and political power that a massing of businesses under one management was the issue.

Simply put, conglomerates are created when a company has either a surplus of funds burning a hole in its treasury, or sees an opportunity for synergy with its current endeavors. If stockholder wishes took priority, the treasury-fat company would share the surplus in the form of dividends. Executives, however, especially those whose compensation is based on the market value of the stock, generally opt for growth which can be achieved through acquisition of a competitor – leading to monopoly – or by going outside its field, frequently leading to financial disaster down the road.

Merger-mania appears to run in cycles keyed by an expanding economy and/or a run-up in the stock market that allows companies to leverage their stock in making acquisitions. For all their popularity, however, the results are not always positive. Merging companies frequently take a substantial hit in the price of their stock and have only a 40/60 chance of success. Conglomerates have had a checkered history of success as well. Writes the Centre For Economic Policy Research:

> Corporate conglomerates have received an increasingly bad press both in the business world and in academic research. They are deemed to be wasteful and inefficient in allocating resources. In the wake of a merger, conglomerates' shares trade at an average discount of 13-15%. However, merger and acquisition activity proceeds relentlessly, with around 40% succeeding. [20]

Companies merge and create conglomerates for purported "synergies, cost reductions, higher and more stable demand, exploitation of a greater range of opportunities" reports the paper cited above. And the costs to the merger partners? "Friction between divisions, distortion in the allocation of resources in internal capital markets, subsidizing less profitable divisions." [21]

In *Rich Media Poor Democracy; Communication Politics in Dubious Times,* Robert W. McChesney explains:

> The pressure to become a conglomerate is also due to
> something perhaps even more profound than the need for
> vertical integration. It was and is stimulated by the desire
> to increase market power. [22]

Thus the cost to the public of mergers and buy-outs may be even greater than that to investors: the power to restrain competition, to overprice, to demand discounts from suppliers – these are the sins of monopolization that fomented the Boston Tea Party.

Conglomeration of the nation's mass media, beginning with the passage of the Telecommunications Act of 1966, marked the beginning of the end of Jefferson's ideal of a "free press." The act removed barriers to mergers between print and electronic media and raised the percentage of national audience any one television network could have from 25 to 35%. This was followed in 1999 by a further relaxation of FCC rules that limited chain or network ownership to one TV station per market. FCC chairman at the time, William Kennard, expressed his misgivings about media monopolies to the Radio-Television News Director Association:

> One concern I have is concentration of ownership. What
> if four group owners owned every television station in
> every major market in ten years? Would this have an
> effect on the quality of news coverage for the country?
> Of course it would. [23]

Mr. Kennard's concern was realized. Writes Ben Bagdikian in his *The Media Monopoly, Sixth Edition:*

> In 1983, fifty corporations dominated most of every
> mass medium. In 1987 the fifty companies had shrunk to
> twenty-nine. In 1997 the biggest firms numbered ten.
>
> Corporations have multimillion-dollar budgets to
> dissect and attack news reports they dislike. But with
> each passing year they have yet another power: They are
> not only hostile to independent journalists. They are their
> employers. [24]

By 2003, four corporations controlled every commercial television station in over 90% of American markets and had succeeded in obtaining an FCC ruling lifting most market restraints.

The public's real concern over mergers and ownership concentration of the media is the quality and impartiality of their news and information sources. A FAIR (Fairness and Accuracy in Reporting) study of television network news coverage in 2001,[e] found that "92 percent of all news sources interviewed were white, 85 percent were male and, where party identification was available, 75 percent were Republican." [25]

Controlled by such a limited number of media conglomerates, controlled and directed by fewer than a handful of executives, our nation's media can no longer be considered "free." Thomas Jefferson wrote that freedom of the press was critical to maintenance of democracy: "The only security of all is in a free press. The force of public opinion cannot be resisted when permitted freely to be expressed." [26] Today the "force of public opinion" is much diminished, simply because of the difficulty of being heard above the corporatized clamor of a few very powerful media voices.

Limit 5: Prohibit corporations from operating under pseudonyms

Why would corporations want to operate under false names? And why should it not be prohibited? A Las Vegas, Nevada, public official had this to say:

> For years, frustrated homeowners have tried, to no avail, to find out who is truly behind that pesky county rezoning application calling for 500 apartments to be plopped down in their rural neighborhood. Instead, they often get an alphabet soup of vague corporate pseudonyms.
>
> Under a proposal... the county will require that the names of the owner of the property in question and the person acquiring the property through an escrow contingent on rezoning... be disclosed.
>
> "The more we put things out in the open, the more trust we'll receive from the public," [said the county commission chairman.] [27]

---

[e] An analysis of ABC World News Tonight, CBS Evening News, and NBC Nightly News, but not including the admittedly conservatively-biased Fox Network.

Logic implies that the only reason for a corporation to use a pseudonym would be to pursue some activity that it did not want competitors, the public, or authorities to know about because of potential damage to the public's interest or their own. In a Democracy, the publics' interest must take precedence.

Limit 6: Prohibit corporate contributions to political campaigns

Means and Berle wrote in the 1930's, "The rise of the modern corporation has brought a concentration of economic power which can compete on equal terms with the modern state...."[28] They could not have known that by the end of the 20th century corporations would not only compete with the modern state, they would virtually own it.

No substantive correction to corporate governance or effective remedy to corporate fraud and crime can occur as long as corporations dominate the political and legislative process. It is more than simple bribery of candidates, legislators, congress, or the courts. It is their control of the discussion through the media, sponsored "think tanks," lobbying, even universities. As bluntly described by Senator Henry Ashurst of Arizona:

> When I have to choose between the people and the special interests, I always stick to the special interests. They remember. The people forget."[29]

Thanks to their advantages over challengers – free mailings, travel, and the contributions of PACs (Political Action Committees) — 96.7% of incumbents were re-elected in 1996, 1998, and 2000. Recently enacted campaign finance reform may reduce the direct flow of corporate money into campaigns, but it will not reduce corporate domination of the media nor will it reduce Big Business's power to sway both the public and legislative bodies through direct lobbying and indirect public information and action programs. This lack of balance among competing interests – public, shareholders, corporate managers – has created a "corpocracy" that replaces government by the people with government by corporate interests.

Limit 7: Forbid subsidies to for-profit corporations

Early in America's history, corporations in which the state was a major shareholder funded, built, and operated much of the early commercial and transportation infrastructure – bridges, toll roads, ports, canals. Without an enormous subsidy from the federal government, the first transcontinental railroad would not have connected the east and west. Without subsidies from Tennessee, Nissan might have built its first American plant in Kentucky. Tax giveaways helped Kentucky land the Toyota plant over South Carolina. Public money that South Carolina spent on infrastructure and technical education, plus substantial sums in tax forgiveness, won BMW over Alabama. And Alabama's subsidies hooked Honda. And so it goes.

Corporate welfare "costs every working American the equivalent of two weeks pay every year," wrote *Time* magazine in its November 9, 1998, "Special Report." Even as corporations were making record profits in a healthy economy, "the Federal Government ... shelled out $125 billion in corporate welfare, equivalent to all the income tax paid by 60 million individuals and families." [30]

Time reported that states have also jumped into the corporate giveaway game in a big way. State and local politicians "dole out tens of billions of taxpayer dollars to businesses that are in fact eliminating rather than creating jobs." [31]

According to an analysis of South Carolina's industrial development success by *The State* newspaper:

> Nearly half of the 100 companies given South Carolina's most generous tax incentives paid workers less than the state's already low average salary.
> Among all 100 [subsidized] companies, 44 not only paid less than the state average wage, but also paid less than the average wage in the county where they are located. [32]

Their analysis also revealed that many of South Carolina's development deals became "substantial tax drains."

> In one of the state's least developed counties, a 400-job company... will cost the state $4.2 million over 15 years. That means each job will cost the state an average of $700 a year. [33]

The State newspaper's exposé on industrial recruitment's true costs included a report by Clemson University economists that concluded:

Incentives would cost so much in lost taxes that unless the state raises taxes or cuts services it will soon be in the red. The Clemson report projected the deficit would reach about $200 million in a decade.

Just days after the Clemson report was released [Governor] Beasley's spokesman dismissed the professors as nay-saying 'pointy-headed academics.'[34]

Four years later the State of South Carolina faced a $380 million deficit and drastic cuts in services.

New industry puts new demands on public utilities. New jobs bring new families and more children to be educated. The competition among states to give tax breaks and other incentives to new business simply shifts the burden of paying for these additional services to established industries, businesses, and residents.

Seven proposals

Concern with corporate power is not a phenomenon triggered by the frauds of Enron, World Com, et al. Past discoveries of corporate deception and swindles have stirred the interest and imaginations of legal and business scholars to propose a variety of solutions to the problems. A sample of those proposals follows.

Don't be put off by proposals that appear unworkable or "revolutionary." Often the first key to solving a problem is to step back from accepted wisdom and ask "what if?" What follows are opening salvoes in what will be an extended battle. Eventually each proposal that gains popular support will be fought out in legislative and legal arenas.

Proposal 1: National charters and state charters

Federal charters of incorporation — granted and regulated by Congress – may be the only way to end the destructive "race to the regulatory bottom" characterizing competition among the states. State charters are appropriate to startups, closely held/family firms, and corporations engaged in natural resource extraction – mining, natural gas, oil, forestry, and agriculture — but a federal charter creates a better balance of power between government and multinational firms..

A corporation would be required to apply for a national corporate charter upon attaining two or more of the following characteristics:

(1) major facilities located in three or more states; (2) a million or more shares outstanding held by 5,000 or more individual shareholders; (3)5% of its annual sales to the federal government; (4)10% of its annual sales as

foreign exports, (5)ownership or management of a production facility in a country other than the U.S. and its territories.

The criteria are based on characteristics that remove a corporation from under the authority of a single state – although at present, states rarely exercise what little authority they have.

Extractive, natural resource based corporations would remain under the control of the states in which their production facilities are located. The result would be a strengthening of states' rights for it would empower citizens of each state to determine the appropriate balance between environmental impact and employment and economic benefits of its extractive industries.

Corporations operating under a federal charter would enjoy – in charter authority terms at least – a single body of laws and a single standard of conduct to follow. It would if not quiet the perpetual state/federal regulation of commerce argument, at least offer the courts a possible resolution. In addition, federal charters would serve as "minimums" for state standards, although states should be free to go beyond the federal standard, much as California does in gas mileage and emission requirements for automobiles.

At present, Congress may not issue charters to private corporations. Any change would require an Act of Congress, possibly a change in the Constitution itself.

The above presumes, naively, that Limit 6 described above (prohibition of corporate political contributions) would have been imposed. Under current levels of lavish lobbying and campaign spending it would obviously be impossible to enact such legislation without the blessing of corporate America.

Proposal 2: Corporations required to maintain their headquarters in the state issuing their charter

Delaware officials boast of the fact that more than half of the *Fortune 500* – Detroit's General Motors Corporation and Atlanta's Coca Cola among them – have charters of incorporation granted by their state.

Writes Joseph N. DiStefano of *The Philadelphia Inquirer:*

> The speed, secrecy and state tax exemptions offered by Delaware, along with its business-friendly courts, have long enticed everyone from blue-chip corporations to international gangsters. The General Accounting Office cites Delaware as a haven for foreign money launderers. [35]

Corporate fees support more than 25% of Delaware's annual budget. Other states have been willing to prostitute corporate charter requirements even more to attract this source of revenue. In 1991, Nevada rewrote its corporate laws in an aggressive campaign to attract incorporators.

> According to Dun & Bradstreet's most recent figures, 16,888 new companies incorporated in Nevada in the first nine months of 1996, up 27% from the year-earlier period. [36]

It's expensive and difficult, indeed almost impossible, for a state attorney general to bring an action against a firm with production facilities and subsidiaries scattered across the nation and the globe. The states of Delaware or Nevada will not be quick to discipline or revoke corporate charters of firms committing their sins in Texas, New York, or Utah. Authorities in jurisdictions not directly affected by illegal or bad behavior have no incentive to act.

One of the canons of politics is, "The best government is the closest government," meaning government under the watchful eye of the citizens it governs. Requiring corporations to maintain their headquarters where their charters are granted offers a similar benefit. In restraining antisocial behavior, authority closest to the corporate citizen is more effective than remote authority.

The concept proved itself effective in the banking/broker scandals accompanying the Enron et al fraud of 2001-2. U.S. News & World Report wrote, "As [SEC Chairman] Harvey Pitt fumbles again, Eliot Spitzer and Wall Street run with the ball." [37] In its report, the magazine noted that while federal watchdogs sat on their hands, New York's Attorney General Eliot Spitzer moved aggressively against Wall Street icons such as Merrill Lynch and Salomon Smith Barney/CitiGroup for fraudulent analyst reports and payoffs to IPO clients.

The ability of New York's Attorney General to engage in lawsuits and enforce securities laws against major corporations is, however, unique. The brokerage industry and Wall Street are virtually synonymous; major firms must be located there. In almost every other industry, however, aggressive law enforcement or legislative pressure (or, for that matter, tax pressure) against a major corporate entity would risk that company picking up stakes and moving to a more relaxed jurisdiction.

A state charter of incorporation has authority, however little that may be, only over corporations with facilities and sales within that state.

"Foreign" corporations – incorporated in other jurisdictions – are almost totally outside their control. Control over national and multinational firms is more appropriately placed in the hands of federal authorities by the means of a federal charter.

The frauds committed by Enron point up the inability of state and local governments to control corporate citizens. Headquartered in Texas and incorporated in Oregon, Enron had 685 subsidiaries chartered in Delaware, as well as others created in Brazil, England, and the Cayman Islands. Which of the above jurisdictions, if any, would have the political will or even the finances to move against the company?

Proposal 3: Restrict the sale of stock to residents of the state chartering the corporation

If this law were in effect, the citizens of Delaware would be the sole stockholders of over 300,000 corporations.

Limiting the sale of stock to residents of the state issuing the corporate charter is not an unreasonable requirement for start-up, local, and extractive-industry corporations. By their very nature, start-ups raise their initial capital from friends, family, and close associates of the founders.[f] Local investors are frequently the primary source of capital for small, unlisted firms. With their money (not just stock options) at stake, they are more apt to be watchful stewards of the enterprise. CEOs are also more apt to pay attention to stockholders made up of neighbors who would not be bashful in giving management their opinions. As for extractive industries, limiting stock ownership to residents of the state where the natural resources are exploited makes sense on a number of levels. Environment quality versus economic development/jobs arguments will be more equitably resolved when the community has a stake in both.

National companies with federal charters of incorporation (as discussed above) would not be geographically restricted in selling stock. Although congressional oversight of our largest corporations is less than ideal under current campaign finance and lobbying conditions, at least congressional

---

[f] From *The Wall Street Journal*, 8/26/03, "Small Talk/Informal Funding: "For all the concern about venture-capital funds, in every country followed by the Global Entrepreneurship Monitor, with the exception of Israel, the amount of informal investment easily surpasses venture capital. And at the seed stage of a company, it is venture capital that is rare. When it comes to informal financing, by far the greatest percentage of investors provide funds to an enterprise that has close family members, followed by one with friends and neighbors, work colleagues, and strangers, and then more distant relatives."

"watchdogs" are elected and can be held accountable at the polls if they neglect their duties.

Proposal 4: Eliminate the corporate shield protecting managers and directors from liability for corporate acts

Unlike a sole proprietor or partnership, investors in a corporation risk only the money put into the enterprise; they have no other liability. Investors' other assets are untouchable behind the corporate veil – one of the key attractions of incorporation.

The shield from liability extends, however, to the parties responsible for corporate acts: executives and board members. They are the authority for and often the motivators of harmful, unlawful, or criminal acts. As discussed in Chapter 5, an inability to hold executives culpable is fabricated by a narrow interpretation of the law which often assigns fault to the fictional corporate "person" rather than responsible executives.

The Union Carbide Bhopal disaster of 1984 (described in Chapter 4) offers perspective on this issue. Was the disaster caused by a negligent employee, a negligent supervisor, or the plant manager? If so, the blame for the disaster rests on those whose inaction or wrong actions led to the gas's escape.

Was the disaster caused by a lack of maintenance of the plant and its equipment, and was maintenance insufficient because of supervisory inattention, or due to financial constraints imposed by corporate headquarters? Were financial constraints the result of policy decisions by top management? If so, then they are the responsible parties. Typically, lower level managers are held responsible no matter what executive decisions led to an accident. When executives are found to be at fault they are frequently not held liable thanks to the corporate shield.

We often speak of the "corporate culture" of firms such as IBM (in its heyday) or of Microsoft as a good thing. But what if through repeated crimes of a similar nature the corporate culture is to skirt environmental laws and hide the damage, suborn regulators and political figures, commit fraud upon the public, and collude with competitors to fix prices? General Electric, as previously pointed out, has been repeatedly convicted of collusion and price fixing while under the direction of a number of different boards and CEOs. Were the many repeated acts the result of GE's criminal culture? Or is GE simply incapable of finding ethical CEOs?

When courts find a corporation guilty of a criminal act the only punishment is a fine. This punishes the stockholders but not the perpetrators. Judges certainly can't throw a corporation into jail. They could, however, impose the death penalty – dissolution. If a corporation can be dissolved —

declared bankrupt — for financial mismanagement, why not for criminal acts?

Unethical and criminal behavior affects an entire industry and infects the business community in general. We can't lock a corporation up and throw away the key. But society can certainly close the book – revoke the charter — of an offending "legal fiction."

Proposal 5: Limit the highest salary paid to any corporate officer to a ratio of the lowest salary paid to any employee

Critics of excessive executive compensation fault the 1993 creation of Section 162(m) of the U.S. Tax Code limiting the ability of corporations to expense CEO salaries above $1 million. As described in Chapter 5, the attempt to restrain compensation unleashed the creativity of executives, attorneys, accountants and compensation consultants to subvert the law. If compensation limits had been described in terms of ratios rather than dollar amounts, however, the option-driven fraud might never have occurred.

Defenders of high compensation amounts assert that executive pay is linked to better outcomes. However, it is as difficult to find evidence of a CEOs impact on outcomes as it is easy to find otherwise. Common sense deems it highly improbable that there's a causative link between executive skills – leadership, market intuition, wisdom, etc. — and the size of the number written on a paycheck.

The second justification is that CEOs "work hard." No doubt CEOs frequently put in more than forty-hour weeks, put up with extensive travel and time away from home and family, and pace the floors at night sorting through weighty issues. How this effort compares with that of an office maid who comes in to work late at night via the subway to vacuum floors, clean ashtrays, empty wastebaskets, and pick up the mess left in the executive washroom is difficult to measure. One may be brain work, the other physical labor, but it is impossible to establish which demands more of the total resources of the work provider.

In the current decade – 1992 through 2002 – executive compensation has reached heights sufficient to establish dynasties. What, however, do multi-million-dollar inheritances for a CEO's heirs contribute to the strength of the company paying such sums?

There are enormous differences between business creator-founders and the CEOs that come after them. Non-founder CEOs are hired hands employed to manage the creations of others. A justifiable compensation percentage differential might be that of a plant manager to a work-crew supervisor. But to make one human's every breath worth tens of thousands of dollars to a company and the labor of another worth but $10 per hour cannot be rationalized.

Unless greed is a perquisite for executive selection, it's highly doubtful that business school enrollment would drop precipitously if CEO pay were $5 million a year versus the average (in 2002) of $28 million.

Financial potential is but one of the criteria people consider in making their career choices. By far the stronger motivator is personal satisfaction, making one's life "count for something." For some, perhaps, only big bucks motivate. For many more it's doing what the spirit demands. Why else would there be doctors, teachers, missionaries, actors, and artists?

Volker Dittmar writes, in his personal Web site publication, *Developer Topics – Topics for All Software Developers* – of the psychology of software development:

> There are two different kinds of driving forces [behind our behavior]: … a functional lust and the need to control the circumstances of our lives. Money is not the driving force behind all we do. Money is just a device for gaining control. [38]

A survey of construction workers in England found that a new challenge or a change was a bigger motivator (46%) than salary level (32%). "Flexible working hours and new challenges are the primary motivators for employees to either stay where they are or seek new horizons," said the head of human resources for the Coventry Building Society. [39]

A management psychology consulting firm, RHR International, found five prime motivators among top executives: *Money* (with the caveat that "People who work to get rich may be very difficult to motivate once they achieve the goal"), Power (noting that "these people are always willing to strive for more"), *Achievement* (achieving something significant), *Excitement* (competition, solving difficult problems), and *Legacy* (striving to make a mark in the world). [40]

The bottom line: businesses big and small are best managed by someone who is drawn to the product, service, trade or craft. The history of scandals for the past 200 years should make it obvious that business and capitalism itself are most poorly served by those in it just for the money.

Proposal 6: Eliminate the stock market

The above idea jumped off a page of *Buying America Back – Economic Choices for the 1990s,* a collection of essays edited by Jonathan Greenberg and William Kistler. [41] The sentence was contained among a list of suggestions to contain, control or curb corporate power in an essay, "Corporations as Machines," written by Jerry Mander. [42,g]

Talk about draconian! Mander gave only the following explanation for what may seem outrageous: "[Because it has] promoted the simplistic and impossible idea of unlimited economic growth. Parenthetically, the stock market also promotes the illusion of democratic participation in corporate decision making." [43]

Before relegating Mr. Mander's idea to the junk heap, it's instructive to consider what the stock market really is and what it is not.

Journalists normally refer to "investors" when writing about stock buyers and sellers. But only a very small fraction of those who own stock actually invest. They "trade." This has become more and more true as ownership of stock has spread down the economic scale. Today, stock is bought and sold primarily for its capital growth potential – increase in selling price – than for income. Buyers buy because they think their pick's price will go up. They sell when it reaches or (more often) when it doesn't reach their expectations.

Playing the stock market and playing the ponies – betting on horses – are similar wagers. The average race track bettor doesn't pay much attention to handicappers or pore over the Daily Racing Form before placing a bet. The average trader rarely considers the underlying value behind a stock – capital assets, licenses, patents, past and potential earnings.

Professionals do pay attention to the data before placing their bets. Fund managers pay analysts to delve deep into a company's numbers and history before deciding to buy a stock. But not even the best of analysts has a crystal ball. Just as at the track, buy and sell decisions in the stock market are made as much by "gut feel" as by research. Research simply provides a "cover-your-ass" excuse when things don't work out as predicted because, in the final analysis, who knows if the company is telling the truth?

---

[g] Mr. Mander's brief biography accompanying the essay described him as the author of *Four Arguments For the Elimination of Television*, a senior fellow of the Public Media Center in San Francisco, a director of the Berkeley based Elmwood Institute think tank, and recipient of the accolade: "the Ralph Nader of Advertising."

John David Rose

"I've been saving this baby for the stock market."

The accepted wisdom is that the liquidity of a company's stock – the ability to trade it easily for cash without actually selling a hard asset – increases the availability of capital. An active market in a stock makes it easier for the company to buy, trade, and sell its shares, but unless a company is selling its treasury stock, however, those who buy its shares on the stock market put not a penny into the company's treasury. They are buying from another shareholder. The stock purchase is not an investment. It's a bet, a gamble, and a guess based on wishful thinking.

In a fit of candor in his *Wall Street Journal* column, "Ahead of the Tape" Jesse Eisinger characterized the stock market as a "casino":

> The economy today (of the international flows) is primarily an economy of speculation with less than 5 percent of it having anything to do with goods and services.[44]

As Mander pointed out, investors fool themselves that they are part owners of a company when they buy its shares in the stock market. They're merely betting against other investors. The only difference between the stock exchange and a gambling casino is that a casino is more likely to run an honest game.

Could our economy survive or even prosper without a functional stock market? Of course, if we focus on the objective of a market in the first place. The objective is to give companies a forum in which they can trade ownership shares in the company for cash, and for those who trade their cash for shares an opportunity to trade them back into cash at any time. The current market of speculation and manipulation contributes nothing to capitalism or free enterprise.

Proposal 7: Subscriber Shares

One way to replace the stock exchanges, provide a source of capital for companies, give companies and stock-holders liquidity – the ability to sell their share of ownership — while reflecting corporate earnings and the values standing behind a share of stock is with what I call "Subscriber Ownership."

Subscriber ownership is a concept based on a type of restricted stock often issued to founders of a new enterprise. It is similar to debt instruments in that there is a guaranteed floor of resale value, yet it also reflects appreciation and earnings. Similar to certain classes of founders' stock, subscriber shares would be restricted as to when and to whom they can be sold.

Subscriber shares would be the only class of stock that a corporation could issue. The shares could only be sold by the corporation to investors and could only be sold by investors to the corporation. The issuing corporation "makes a market" in its own stock through (a) balance sheet value and (b) earnings per share. Stock is repurchased by the corporation at a price equal to the proportional share of current stockholders' equity plus 10 times the average of earnings over the preceding three years. Subscriber shares could not be sold within three years of issue date. After that period, the corporation guarantees that it will buy them back when proffered.

Subscriber shares can be offered to managers and employees on the same basis as to outside investors. Restrictions on resale remove any incentive managers might have to drive stock prices up through fraud and financial manipulations. Instead, managers and investors both profit from dividends and real appreciation in value.

Subscriber-ownership fulfills the essential requirements of investors: return on investment and appreciation of capital. At the same time, it removes incentives for fraud and financial manipulation.

What would investors lose if subscriber-ownership became the rule? They would lose the boom and bust of an insider-driven market. The nation would no longer suffer through constant cycles of fraud, scandal, and slap-on-the-hand enforcement of unenforceable business codes of conduct.

Focusing on just one of the techniques companies have used to boost earnings with phantom income, reporters Dennis K. Berman, Julia Angwin and Chip Cummings wrote in the Pulitzer Prize-winning *Wall Street Journal* article "Tricks of the Trade: As Market Bubble Neared End, Bogus Swaps Provided a Lift":

> When the business history of the past decade is written, perhaps nothing will sum up the outrageous financial scheming of the era as well as the frenzied swapping that marked its final years....
>
> But the swaps rage turned out to be no bargain for investors. The bad deals contributed to an epidemic of artificially inflated revenue. In many cases, swaps slipped through legal loopholes left in place by regulators who had failed to keep pace with the ever-changing deal-making of ever-changing industries. The unraveling of those back-scratching arrangements helped usher in the market collapse and led to the realization by investors

that the highest-flying industries of the boom era… were
built in part on a combustible mix of wishful thinking and
deceit. [45]

Wishful thinking and deceit – that sums up the stock market. Why
should it survive? Why shouldn't we come up with a better idea? As it is
today it is nothing but a floating crap game, a side show distraction to the
main event.

[1] "The Whistleblower and the CEO," by Carol J. Loomis, *Fortune* magazine, July 7, 2003.

[2] Ibid.

[3] Ibid.

[4] "The Insatiable King Richard," by John Helyar, *Fortune* magazine, July 7, 2003.

[5] "Wall Street's Settlement Will Be Less Taxing," by Gregory Zuckerman, *The Wall Street Journal*, February 13, 2003.

[6] "Rite Aid Case Gives First View of Wave of Fraud on Trial," by Mark Maremont, *The Wall Street Journal*, June 10, 2003.

[7] "SEC vote on options favors investors," by Mark Schwanhausser, *Mercury News*, SiliconValley. com, posted December 29, 2001.

[8] "S.E.C. Passes Rule Changes for Options," by Bloomberg News, *The New York Times*, July 1, 2003.

[9] "A big win for the little guys," by Marc Gunther, *Fortune* magazine, June 16, 2003, pg 21.

[10] "Wall St. Reform Falls Short, Survey Says," by Gretchen Morgenson, *The New York Times*, Money & Business section, August 31, 2003.

[11] "Are Firms Too Big to Debar?" by Anne Marie Squeo, *The Wall Street Journal*, June 10, 2003.

[12] "The Jail Threat is Real. So, Will Executives Behave?" by Jeffrey L. Seglin, *The New York Times*, Money & Business, July 20, 3003.

[13] Taken from web pages "Interest Group and Elite Theories," syllabus of Principles of Public Administration, Political Science 3420, Fall 2002, Professor Davis of the University of Toledo, Dept. of Political Science.

[14] "Corporate Goliaths," by Charles Gray, *Multinational Monitor*, Vol. 20, No. 6, June 1999.

[15] "AT&T's Latest Moves Vindicate Trustbusters," in "The Outlook" column, *The Wall Street Journal*, September 25, 1995.

[16] *Henry George and the Reconstruction of Capitalism*, by Dr, Robert V. Andelson, American Institute for Economic Research, Great Barrington, Massachusetts, 1994.

[17] Richard Grossman co-director of the Program on Corporations, Law, and Democracy, quoted in an interview by Ruth Conniff, published in The Progressive, March 2002.

[18] "Cornell Study: Anti-Corporate Farming Laws Promote Healthy Economies," excerpted from *Feedstuffs* Magazine, found in *Agribusiness Weekly*, Issue 32.

[19] "Boardrooms Under Renovation," by Carol Hymowitz and Joann S. Lublin, *The Wall Street Journal*, Marketplace, July 22, 2003.

[20] "Corporate Conglomerates: Costs, Benefits and Internal Capital Markets," unattributed paper published by Centre for Economic Policy Research, London, UK, undated.

[21] Ibid.

[22] *Rich Media Poor Democracy; Communication Politics in Dubious Times*, by Robert W. McChesney, University of Illinois Press, 1999.

[23] Quoted in FAIR (Fairness & Accuracy in Reporting) Action Alert, August 9. 1999.

[24] *The Media Monopoly*, Sixth Edition, by Ben H. Bagdikian, Beacon Press, 2000, p 45, pg 65.

[25] Quoted in "Corporate Influence in the Media: Media Conglomerates, Mergers, Concentration of Ownership," www.globalization.org, undated.

[26] Thomas Jefferson to Lafayette, 1923, quoted within *Thomas Jefferson on Politics and Government*, Compiled and Edited by Eyler Robert Coates, Sr., <http://etext.lib.virginia.edu/jefferson/quotations>.

[27] "County to require land use disclosure forms," *Las Vegas Mercury*, June 13, 2002.

[28] *"The Corporation and Private Property*," by Bearl, Adolf and Means, Gardiner C., Annals of America, Vol XV, pg. 139.

[29] Quoted in "Why Washington's Stalled" by Representative Timothy J. Penny, *The Wall Street Journal*, May 12, 1994.

[30] "What Corporate Welfare Costs You: Special Report," by Donald L. Barlett and James B. Steele, *Time* Magazine, November 9, 1998.

[31] Ibid.

[32] "Many Low-Wage Firms Get Tax Breaks; Incentives Lure Jobs, But Some Cost Taxpayers," by Douglas Pardue and John Welbes, *The State*, (Columbia, SC), July 26, 1998.

[33] Ibid.

[34] Ibid.

[35] "Delaware's laws helped Enron keep secrets," by Joseph N. DiStefano, *The Philadelphia Inquirer*, February 3, 2002.

[36] "Nevada's Aggressive Campaign Helps Lure New Corporations," by Tom Lowry, *USA Today*, March 5, 1997.

[37] "Lukewarm Reform," by Richard J. Newman and Matthew Benjamin, *U.S. News & World Report*, November 11, 2002.

[38] Developer Topics by Volker Dittmar, 12/18/1999, found at www.dittmar-online.net/devtopics/motivation.html.

[39] "Jobs: When a Pay Rise Isn't Enough," *Coventry Evening Telegraph*, May 29, 2003.

[40] "Motivate or Risk Losing Top Execs," published by Bell & Howell *Information and Learning*, Vol. 80, NO. 11; Pg 18; ISSN: 10928332, November 2001.

John David Rose

[41] B*uying America Back – Economic Choices for the 1990s*, edited by Jonathan Greenberg and William Kistler, Council Oak Publishing Company, Tulsa, Oklahoma, 1992.

[42] Ibid. Essay begins on page 293; quote is taken from page 311.

[43] Ibid.

[44] "Downside of Owning the Casino," in "Ahead of the Tape – Today's Market Forecast – by Jesse Eisinger, *The Wall Street Journal*, December 19, 2002.

[45] "Tricks of the Trade: As Market Bubble Neared End, Bogus Swaps Provided a Lift," by Dennis Ke. Berman, Julia Angwin and Chip Cummings, *The Wall Street Journal*, December 23, 2002.

CHAPTER FIFTEEN
COME THE REVOLUTION!

*"Every dictatorship which we now know flowed into power
like air into a vacuum because the central government, in the
face of real difficulty, declined to exercise authority."*
Thurmon W. Arnold, quoted in "A Question
of Power," by Arthur M. Schlesinger, Jr.,[a]
The American Prospect, April 23, 2001.

It's the system

The preceding chapters have described an appalling number of unethical, immoral, dishonest, illegal, criminal, even traitorous actions by some of the most respected names in corporate America. The examples were not selected for their shock value, although some are certainly worth outrage, but to illustrate the systemic deficiencies of corporations as they are currently chartered, structured, and regulated.

Robert Monks[b], founder of Institutional Shareholder Services and of "institutional activist" investment fund LENS described the problem:

> Despite attempts to provide balance and accountability, the corporation as an entity became so powerful that it quickly outstripped the limitations of accountability and became something of an externalizing machine, in the same that a shark is a killing machine – no malevolence, no intentional harm, just something designed with sublime efficiency for self-preservations, which it accomplishes without any capacity to factor in the consequences to others.[1]

---

[a] Attorney and author, *Folklore of Capitalism*, 1937, *Bottlenecks of Business*, 1940, *Future of Democratic Capitalism*, 1977; as Assistant Attorney General of the United States he was renown for having prosecuted 230 companies for monopolistic practices in violation of the Sherman Anti-Trust Act.

[b] Robert A.G. Monks is an "insider" activist for corporate reform, having served as a member of the board of directors of ten publicly held companies. Graduate of Harvard, Cambridge University and Harvard Law School, he co-authored with Nell Minow Power and Accountability, Corporate Governance and Watching the Watchers. Subject of a biography Traitor to His Class, by Hilary Rosenberg (Wiley, 1999), chronicling the corporate governance movement.

Rarely a day goes by that the business press does not report on a company charged with or convicted of scamming consumers, stockholders, taxpayers, or our government. "Business ethics is an oxymoron" has become a wry and well-deserved cliché from a public cynical over Big Business.

What the author hopes the preceding pages have illuminated is not that corporate officers are extraordinarily bad people, but that they are people driven to do bad things by the corporate culture. The demands of the financial markets and the expectations of those with whom they associate, deal and compete set their moral standards, not the Golden Rule. Moreover, there they are granted an open invitation to indulge themselves without penalty or restraint, a temptation few humans can resist.

Let me be very clear: we are not describing the hundreds of thousands of officers in the tens of thousands of small corporations that form the bulk of the corporate executive population. As previously described, those who deal face to face with customers, suppliers, stockholders, and employees are ethically "regulated" by these personal interactions.

Our problem as a nation and democracy resides in the giant firms — the Fortune 500 — whose enormous size and reach defines how business is conducted. Their enormous wealth gives them the power to buy government favors, determine public and foreign policy, even determine who may run for and win public office.

The ethical and moral standards of CEOs as a class are no better or no worse than those of any cross-section of humans. Their ethical elasticity is a result of the power granted them and the lack of effective oversight. The business culture in which they operate offers them strong incentives to skirt or break the ethical code. In addition, these wielders of great power are shielded from personal accountability and suffer no personal consequences for their actions. Thus, we can no more expect CEOs to refrain from questionable practices than we can expect a male dog to walk away from a female in heat. It's the nature of the beast.

The recent epidemic of scandal did not signal a sudden decline in business and executive class morality. It was simply a replay of a cycle of corporate dishonesty that has plagued the capitalist world since the mid-1800's. After each wave of dishonesty, Congress and regulatory agencies enact measures to reign in the malefactors. But reform measures might just as well be labeled "Full Employment Acts For Lobbyists." Armies of lobbyists and public relations specialists are marshaled to stop, weaken, or repeal corrective measures.

Business law enforcement is infrequent and inconsistent. It will always be so. People of high station, great wealth and great power can afford the highest quality legal representation available. Thus media exposure, arrest, incarceration, even the threat of "locking them up and throwing away the key" provides little more than temporary embarrassment for many corporate lawbreakers. Truth be known, laws and regulations offer a competitive edge to those willing to break them. When executive lawbreakers are caught and convicted, it's the stockholders, not the perpetrators, that pay the price.

Out of the hundreds of malefactors revealed in the scandal-fraught Enron era the first one actually brought to justice was a relatively small-time insider-trading cheater, Samuel D. Waksal of ImClone. [c] *New York Times* Money & Business section columnist Jeffrey L. Seglin noted that the sentence – the maximum recommended by federal guidelines – was intended to "send a strong message to corporate executives that those who are caught breaking the law will be dealt with harshly." But then he quotes Professor Daryl Koehn, director of the Center For Business Ethics at the University of St. Thomas in Houston, who doesn't believe prison sentences for corporate executives will act an effective deterrent to unethical behavior. "I don't think its really going to accomplish anything," she said. "It's merely a distraction." [2]

Corporate law attorney Jeffrey M. Kaplan, counsel to the Ethics Officer Association, told Seglin that "when chief executives are seen picking among rules to follow, stated ethical core values within corporations ring hollow." [3] Seglin's final source, Harvard Divinity School professor Ronald F. Theimann, concluded that if society really wants big business to start behaving ethically for the long term, then "some greater and more enduring resolve must enter the picture." [4]

The only conclusion a reasonable observer can make is that enforcement of the law is only a Band-Aid™ on the cuts and bruises society suffers from corporate crime. We simply cannot expect high ethical standards in the executive suites of our largest corporations. The result is a "kind of wild power," writes Willis Harman in his essay "Business and the Future Society":

> We have large corporations… girdling the globe – and
> with tremendous power – and that power is not under any
> control. It's kind of a wild power. It responds to various

---

[c] Samuel D. Waksal, founder and former CEO of ImClone Systems, was convicted of securities fraud, conspiracy, perjury, and obstruction of justice; he was sentenced to jail for 87 months.

financial signals, but it's not responsible to the people in the sense that a democratic government is responsible to the people. Yet in some ways it represents more power....

Now one temptation is to blame the people in business for their values, and that doesn't really make much sense, because if any of us were elevated to these positions, we would behave in the same way because we are part of a system, and it's the system values and the system logic that are being responded to." [5]

After 200 years of the growth of "wild" corporate power, one might hope that We the People and We the Investors might recognize reality: it is time to change the system.

Changing the system: revolution or evolution

In the inaugural years of this millennium, investor losses climbed beyond the $7 trillion mark. Tens of thousands of Americans saw their retirement nest-eggs shrink by one third or more because of corporate fraud. Hundreds of thousands, both blue and white collar, became unemployed through no fault of their own. Trust in the system has been severely eroded.

Trust is essential to capitalism. Without it no rational person will give a portion of his or her wealth to another to manage. But trust is fleeting, difficult to win, and easily lost. Capitalism demands a System of Corporate Governance that engenders trust; that trumps the human motivations and temptations of corporate managers with a system that encourages pursuit of industry while minimizing the damage overzealous pursuit may cause.

As they are now constituted, Corporate charters are a failure at almost every level. They fail in being responsive to the owners – the stockholders. They fail to provide a two-way working relationships with employees. They fail in providing a mechanism for communicating with and responding to community concerns. They fail in protecting "the public good."

If capitalism is to survive, we must rebuild investor confidence and that requires a realistic standard of business ethics. The business and corporate community must accept that of all games, the game of commerce requires an umpire – government – to keep the game honest. We must forget regulatory patchwork, and give up the naïve hope of a moral makeover of executive personas.

People do not change and "for profit" corporations have no reason to change so long as they can operate as they operate under today's corporate charters. Executives have no reason to give up their positions of absolute monarchy over their corporate kingdoms. Yet unless control over our largest corporations is put back into the hands of shareholders and the public, our largest corporations will cause increasing damage to both democracy and capitalism. Eventually as President John Fitzgerald Kennedy warned: "Those who make peaceful revolution impossible will make violent revolution inevitable."

As this is being written (September 2003), some 3.3 million workers have lost their jobs because of the economic downturn caused, in great part, by a stock market hammered by fraud and loss of trust. Some 9 million Americans walk the streets, hit the unemployment office, pour over the want ads and network with their friends who still have jobs. Another 5 million want full-time jobs but can find only part-time work. That's 14 million Americans un- and under-employed; the highest unemployment rate since 1995.

Because of the broad spectrum of people that have been and are being hurt, any "tipping point" will create enormous political energy for change. Fed up with executive excess, dishonesty, and fraud, the investor class will march arm in arm with a middle class angered by competition with third-world wages for meaningful jobs. Their combined rage may reject not only corpocracy but capitalism itself. The baby may be thrown out with the bath water.

The road to redemption

James McRitchie, Editor of *Corporate Governance* writes:

> The keys to creating wealth and maintaining a free society lie primarily in the same direction. Both require that broad based systems of accountability be built into the governance structures of corporations themselves. [6]

In other words, accountability must be written into the charters of incorporation granted by the states.

The roadmap to corporate accountability has already been drawn for us by our founders. The challenges of corporate governance today are exactly what our founders faced in their day: wealthy interests manipulating government and public resources for private advantage. It is a challenge our founders understood both philosophically and practically. They resolved the natural conflict between public good and private gain by permitting industrial, financial, and commercial growth within carefully considered boundaries. As long as those boundaries held firm corporations served their investors and our nation well.

The challenge is to look beyond short-term fixes and legal patchwork. In our government we expect the Separation of Powers to temper the exercise of executive authority. The same process must be applied to the corporation by adding effective stockholder, employee and public representation. Our objectives should be (a) to allow the entrepreneurial spirit to blossom, (b) to guarantee competition, (c) to lessen and limit control of the giants in every field, and (d) not to do damage to our democracy.

Rescuing the corporation may begin by legislatively and legally reaffirming and re-imposing the criteria applied by the thirteen colonies and early states to corporate personhood:

(1) Incorporation is a privilege, not a right.
(2) A corporation must serve a public need and serve the public good. (Criminal behavior obviously does not serve the public good.)
(3) A corporate charter will be for a fixed period of "life" and may not be renewed.
(4) A corporate charter will be revoked if the corporation fails to serve the public good or meet its financial and safety obligations to employees, venders, lenders, customers, and investors.
(5) An official of the charter-granting authority will serve as a voting member of the corporate board to assure investors that the company stays within allowable limits.

At this point defenders of the status quo can be expected to go ballistic. They will predict economic disaster for the nation and raise the specter of (gasp) Socialism or worse, Communism. Yet these were the very same criteria applied by our capitalist founders in our initial period of industrialization. Not one of the charter conditions they imposed, those listed above, limited entrepreneurial creativity, industrial productivity, efficiency, or economic vitality in our young country. Nor would they today.

What is the alternative? The alternative is to accept recurring feeding frenzies of corporate fraud, dishonest financial reporting and massive theft of our investments as inevitable. The alternative is passing more laws and regulations knowing they will be ineffectual and largely ignored. We can ask business schools to add additional courses in ethics, even require the Ten Commandments to be posted in every corporate board room and watch our free enterprise system strangle on its own excesses before our eyes.

The challenge

To begin our rescue of capitalism and concurrently our democracy, the ownership conundrum must be resolved.

As it now stands, we place our nation's wealth, natural resources, condition of our environment, our jobs and our childrens' futures into the hands of CEOs elected by no one, accountable to no one, and answerable to no one but themselves.

Stockholders must be given a real voice in electing the board of directors. The best method, "scaled" voting as described in Chapter 10, offers every stockholder an opportunity to influence the composition of the board.

The next step in importance is for some courageous state to revoke the charter of a corporate criminal. The penalty for corporation crime should be "one strike and you're out" — death of the corporation. Investors will be far more careful in selecting those they place in charge of the corporation when the penalty for wrongdoing is the total loss of their investment.

By far the most important cure for corporate excess is to revisit the 1827 decision of the Supreme Court – "The Dartmouth College Case" – by Chief Justice John Marshall, and overturn the fraudulent reading of the 1886 Supreme Court decision in *Santa Clara County v. Southern Pacific Railroad Co.* For a paper fiction, a corporation, to have the same rights of personhood as our creator gives to living, breathing human beings is ludicrous. We can only hope that one of the more powerful firms of attorneys of this nation will take up the cause of setting this nonsense right. It is time to put an end to this fraud upon our nation and our democracy.

Quo vadis – where do we want to go?

How do we achieve a balance between corporate power and people power? What should we as individuals want out of our time on this earth, and what should we expect from our government to assist us in pursuing our goals?

Given the opportunity, Americans would not choose as a national goal to make a few people rich as Croesus and let the rest fight for survival. Yet that is the case today. In the 18 years between 1979 and 1997, the average income of the bottom fifth of American families dropped by one percent, losing $100 in after-tax income, while the income of the top one percent of Americans increased 157 percent, by $414,200.

The income differential widened even more dramatically in the two years between 1995 and 1997, as the top one percent of Americans enjoyed a 40% increase – average income up by $194,000 – as well as a 4.6 percentage point drop in their federal income taxes. The lowest one-fifth of wage earners suffered a decrease in income and an increase in federal taxes.

To maintain the family's standard of living, or even survive, in the face of shrinking paychecks, a majority of wives now work outside the home, turning millions of children into "latchkey kids" whose primary education in reading and writing, good and bad, right and wrong, comes from hours of unsupervised TV viewing.

That there has not been a popular uprising against corporate power may be the result of the incessantly promoted illusion that anybody in America can become rich with hard work. "People vote their aspirations," says writer David Brooks, referring to a *Time Magazine* survey which noted, ironically, that 19% of Americans believe they are in the richest 1% income bracket. [7]

As previously noted, our founders permitted the chartering of corporations for the public good, not simply to make money.

> *"If the applicant's object [for incorporation] is merely private or selfish; if it is detrimental to, or not promotive of, the public good, they have no adequate claim upon the legislature for the privileges." U.S. Supreme Court, 1809* (Horowitz: 1977:112)

Human nature has not changed over the 300 years since the nation's founders permitted carefully proscribed charters of incorporation. Since that time government control has eroded to the benefit of the corporation and the detriment of the public. Decade by decade, congressional session by session, the corporate monsters we created have escaped our control and now control us.

> *Capitalism is not too strong; democracy is too weak. We have not grown too hubristic as producers and consumers; we have grown too timid as citizens, acquiescing to deregulation and privatization (airlines, accounting firms, banks, media, conglomerates, you name it) and a growing tyranny of money over politics.*
>
> [Benjamin R. Barber] [8]

This argument over corporate power is not about capitalism versus socialism or communism. It is a question as to about where the seat of power should be located: on our Main Streets or in executive suites. Unless substantive changes take place in the way corporations are structured, chartered and governed they will continue to prostitute and distort the American economic and political systems. If Americans see no hope for corrective action from a government controlled by corporations, they may be driven to take "corrective" action themselves. The danger is that frustrated people often seek an authoritarian replacement for the democratic government that failed them.

Return to the fundamental question: Is the goal of capitalism to equitably distribute scarce resources over an infinite need? Or is it to rob the many to enrich the few?

> What's the purpose of economic product? Fundamentally, the purpose is to add richness to the human life.
>
> We want a certain kind of a society for our grandchildren to live in. We want the environment preserved enough. We want them to have enough resources so that they are not wanting, so that they have the same kind of chances that we had."[9] [Dr. Willis Harman][d]

Finally, for anyone not convinced that something needs to be done, answer this question:

> *If stockholders own a corporation*
> *and CEOs are employed to manage it,*
> *why do the hired hands come out so far ahead*
> *and the owners so far behind?*

finis

---

[d] Dr. Harman (1917-1997), president of the Institute of Noretic Sciences, Sausalito, CA until 1996, was senior social scientist at SRI International (formerly known as Stanford Research Institute, Menlo Park, CA), founding member of the World Business Academy, emeritus professor of engineering economic systems at Stanford University, from 1980-1990 a member of the Board of Regents of the University of California, and co-author with John Horman of Creative Work, Global Mind Change, and co-author of Changes Images of Man and Higher Creativity.

[1] *Power and Accountability,* by Robert A.G. Monks and Nell Minow, Harper Collins, New York, 1991, pg. 24.

[2] "The Jail Threat Is Real. So, Will Executives Behave?," by Jeffrey L. Seglin, in The Right Thing, *The New York Times,* Money & Business, July 20, 2003.

[3] Ibid.

[4] Ibid.

[5] Interview of Willis Harmon by Michael Toms, in "Business and the Future Society," Chapter Seven, page 153, of *The Soul of Business,* New Dimensions Foundations, originally published in 1936 by Houghton Mifflin Company, reprinted 1999 by ISI Books, Wilmington, Delaware.

[6] "Enhancing the Return on Capital Through Increased Accountability," by James McRitchie, Editor, *Corporate Governance,* www.corpgov.net, revised December 23,2001.

[7] "The Triumph of Hope Over Self Interest," by David Brooks, *The New York Times* Op-Ed page, January 12, 2003.

[8] "A Failure of Democracy, Not Capitalism," by Benjamin R. Barber, *The New York Times,* "Op-Ed" page, July 29, 2002.

[9] Taken from *The Soul of Business,* Chapter Seven, "Business and the Future Society," an interview of Willis Harman by Michael Toms, published by New Dimensions Foundation, Hay House, Inc., Carlsbad, CA, 1997.

EPILOGUE
The road to Freedom is not paved.

Thirty years or so ago this then-young father was taking his three daughters, ages sixteen, eleven, and eight, on an "adventure" – an un-programmed driving trip from Salt Lake City, Utah, of unscheduled length or destination.

On our first afternoon we stopped in a small Idaho town to see the soda springs that gave the town its name. They were unimpressive, a small stream of gaseous water bubbling up through a lava stone foundation. "It tastes funny," was our reaction.

Leaving Soda Springs we were returning to the main highway when a side road and large warning sign caught our eye. It read: "The road to Freedom is not paved."

We looked in a Rand McNally road atlas (we were not totally unprepared) and decided that the little town of Freedom, Wyoming, was where we wanted to go.

And we did. And it was unpaved. And the 16-year-old got her first try at driving a car to the tune of a stream of advice from both parent and sisters in addition to squeals of mock fear.

That sign came to mind when I first considering the task of writing a book about a subject for which my academic credentials are minimal. The 10+ years of gathering materials, thoughts, and words have been filled with wonder at how research materials somehow appeared when needed, concern that I'd bitten off far more than I could chew, and despair over my ability to navigate this gravelly road to completion.

Yet the unpaved road has been traveled and, for good or ill, the book is completed.

Early-on I discovered that I'm not the only person awake to the dangers of uncontrolled corporatism. Far better scholars with far grander credentials than I have expressed its dangers and suggested corrections.

Can others be awakened to the problems and become motivated to correct them? Do we have the will to solve the riddle of corporate power before capitalism collapses in a paroxysm of over-indulgence and greed?

To do so we must gird our loins for a tough, long fight for, as the sign read: *The road to Freedom* is unpaved.

Thank you.

Hilton Head Island, South Carolina
October 16, 2003

ADDENDUM A
Corporate Power Activist
Organizations

- Alliance for Democracy, www.alliancefordemocracy.org
- AR – Alternative Radio, www.alernativeradio.org
- Baobab's Corporate Power Information Center now found at, www.timsbrain.com
- Center for the Study of Democratic Institutions, www.oac.cdlib.org/dynaweb/ead/ucsb
- Citiaction, www.citiaction.org
- Citizen Works: People Over Profit, www.citizenworks.org
- Common Dreams, www.commondreams.org
- Contentville www.contentvile.com
- Corporate Accountability Project, www.corporations.org
- Corporate Watch, www.corpwatch.org
- Dismal Scientist, www.dismal.com
- Ending Corporate Governance, www/ratical.com/corporations
- Essential Action, www.essentialac.org
- Focus on the Corporation, www.essential.org
- Fox Professing – Opposing Corporate Power, www.dennisfox.net
- Free The Planet, freethep@u.washington.edu
- FreeUS: Restoring American Democracy, www.prorev.com/freeus.htm
- Global Issues That Affect Everyone, www.globalissues.org
- Global Policy Forum, www.globalpolicy.org
- Globalise Resistance, www.resist.org.uk
- How the System Works (or doesn't), www.enviroweb.org/issues/system
- Jean Kilbourne Resources for Change, www.jeankilbourne.com/resources
- Newswise – Medical, Scientific, Business, www.newswise.org
- Olympia Earth First, www.earthfirst.org
- Organic Consumers Association, www.organicconsumers.org
- People For The American Way, www.pfaw.org
- Peoples Coalition for Justice, www.scn.org/peoplescoalitionforjustice

- POCLAD (Program on Corporations, Law and Democracy), www. poclad.org
- Policy.com, www.policy.com
- Public Information Network, www.endgame.org
- Reclaim Democracy, www.reclaimdemocracy.org
- Seattle Young Peoples Project, www.sypp.org
- Sky Hen, www.skyhen.org
- Social Justice, www.socialjustice.org
- SpeakOut, www.speakout.com
- The Center for Democracy and Technology, www.dct.org
- The Community Environmental Legal Defense Fund, www.celdf. org
- The Corporate Library, www.thecorporatelibrary.com
- The Experiment Network, www.theexperiment.org
- The New Rules Project, www.newrules.org
- The STARC Alliance – Students Transforming and Resisting Corporations, www.corpreform.org
- The White Rose, www.spiritone.com
- Truth Seeker Journal, www.truthseeker.com/truth-seeker
- Women's International League for Peace & Freedom
  1213 Race Street, Philadephia, PA 19107-1691, www.wilpf.org

ADDENDUM B:
Suggested Reading List

America, What Went Wrong, Barlett and Steele, Andrews and McMeel, 1992.

Bankrupting of America, David P. Calleo, AVON Business, 1992.

Big Money Crime: Fraud and Politics in the Savings and Loan Crisis, by Kitty Calavita, Kenry N. Pontell, and Robert H. Tillman, University of California Press, 1997.

Boiling Point: Republicans, Democrats and the Decline of Middle-Class Prosperity, Kevin Phillips, Random House, 1992.

Bottlenecks of Business (The), by Thurman W. Arnold, Beard Books, 1940.

Buying America Back: Economic Choices For The '90's, edited by Jonathan Greenberg and William Kistler, Council Oak Books, 1992.

Captive State: the Corporate Takeover of Britain, by George Monbiot, Macmillan, 2000.

Cheating of America (The); How Tax Avoidance and Evasion by the Super Rich are Costing the Country Billions – and What You Can Do About It, by Charles Lewis and Bill Allison and the Center for Public Integrity, William Morrow/Harper Collins, 2001.

Commonwealth: A Study of the Role of Government in the American Economy, Massachusetts, 1774-1861, Revised Edition, by Oscar Handlin and Mary Flug Handlin, The Belknap Press of Harvard University Press, 1969.

Corporate Crime – Contemporary Debates, Edited by Frank Pearce and Laureen Snider, University of Toronto Press, 1995.

Corporation Nation; How Corporations are Taking Over Our Lives and What We Can Do About It, by Charles Derber, St. Martin's Griffin, 2000.

Corporations Are Gonna Get Your Mama: Globalization and the Downsizing of the American Dream, by Kevin Danaher (editor), Common Courage Press, 1997.

Corporate Planet (The), by Joshua Karliner, Sierra Club Books, 1997.

Corporate Predators: The Hunt for Mega-Profits and the Attack On Democracy, by Russell Mokhiber and Robert Weissman, Common Courage Press, 1999.

Corporate Reapers: The Book of Agribusiness, by A.V. Krebs, Essential Information, 1992.

Corporate Violence, Injury and Death for Profit, edited by Stuart L. Hills, Rowman & Littlefield, 1987.

Divine Right of Capital: Dethroning the Corporate Aristocracy, by Marjorie Kelly, Berrett-Koehler, 2001.

Economic Policy and Democratic Thought, Pennsylvania 1776-1860, by Louis Hartz, Quadrangle Paperbacks, 1948.

Ethical Issues in Business: A Philosophical Approach, Seventh Edition, by Thomas Donaldson, Patricia H. Werhane, and Margaret Cording, Prentice Hall, 2002.

Ethics and the Conduct of Business, Third Edition, by John R. Boatright, Prentice Hall, 2000.

First Dissident (The): The Book of Job in Today's Politics, William Safire, Random House, 1992.

Folklore of Capitalism (The), by Thurman W. Arnold, Beard Books, 1937.

Globalization and Its Discontents, by Joseph E. Stiglitz, W.W. Norton & Company, 2002.

Government and the Economy (The): 1783-1861, edited by Carter Goodrich, The Bobbs-Merrill Company, Inc., 1967.

History of Business (A), Vlms I and II, by Mirriam Beard, Ann Arbor Paperbacks, 1963.

Imperial Middle (The) - Why American's Can't Think Straight About Class, Benjamin DeMott, Morrow, 1990.

Jefferson, Corporations, and the Constitution, by Dr. Charles A. Beard, National Home Library Foundation, 1936.

Making Capitalism Work, by Leonard Silk and Mark Silk, New York University Press, 1996.

Missing Middle (The): Working Families and the Future of American Social Policy, by Theda Skocpol, W.W. Norton & Company, 2000.

Modern Corporation and Private Property (The), by Adolf A. Berle, Jr, and Gardiner C. Means, The Macmillion Company, 1936.

Modern Times: The World from the Twenties to the Eighties, by Paul Johnson, Harper & Row, 1983.

Money Talks; Corporate PACS and Political Influence, Dan Clawson, Alan Neustadtl, Denise Scott, BasicBooks, 1992.

Mystery of Capital (The): Why Capitalism Triumphs in the West and Fails Everywhere Else, by Hernando de Soto, Basic Books, 2000.

Natural Capitalism: Creating the Next Industrial Revolution, by Paul Hawken, Back Bay Books, 2000.

Pawns or Potentates: The Reality of America's Corporate Boards, by Jay W. Lorsch with Elizabeth MacIver, Harvard Business School Press, 1989.

Pigs At The Trough: How Corporate Greed and Political Corruption Are Undermining America, by Arianna Huffington, Crown, 2000.

Progress and Poverty, by Henry George, Abridged Edition, The Robert Schalkenbach Foundation, 1998.

Reinventing Government, David Osborne and Ted Gaebler, Plume, 1992.

Selling Our Security: The Erosion of America's Assets, Martin and Susan J. Tolchin, Knopf, 1992.

Soul of Business (The), edited by Michael Toms, Hay House, Inc., 1997.

Stealing From America: A History of Corruption From Jamestown to Reagan, Nathan Miller, Paragon House, 1992.

Stupid White Men and Other Sorry Excuses for the State of the Nation, Michael Moore, Regan Books, 2001.

Suddenly: The American Idea Abroad and At Home, George F. Will, Free Press, 1992.

Tyranny Of The Bottom Line; Why Corporations Make Good People Do Bad Things, Ralph Estes, Berrett-Koehler, 1996.

Unequal Protection: The Rise of Corporate Dominance and the Theft of Human Rights, by Thom Hartmann, Rodale Press, 2002

Wealth of Nations (The), by Adam Smith, Modern Library Edition, 1994.

Who Owns America: A New Declaration of Independence, Edited by Herbert Agar and Allen Tate, ISI books, 1999.

Wealth and Democracy, by Kevin Phillips, Broadway Books, 2003

Who Will Tell The People - The Betrayal of American Democracy, William Greider, Touchstone/Simon-Shuster, 1992

Who's Running The Nation?, How Corporate Power Threatens Democracy, Kathlyn Gay, Franklin Watts Div. Of Grolier Publishing, 1999

Index

F

G

About the Author

John David Rose's weekly column *Think About It* has been the best read, most provocative and controversial feature of the *Carolina Morning News*' op-ed pages since he began submitting them in 1995. Over 50+ years experience in business, he has worked in politics, the media, directed marketing, advertising and public relations for companies large and small, and founded, operated and sold his own business. Born and raised in Idaho Falls, Idaho, he now lives in Hilton Head Island, South Carolina with his musician wife Penny.

Printed in the United States
128821LV00004B/10/A